Kitchen Upgrade
Manual

Author acknowledgements

A big thanks to my wife, Leanne, for helping with the photographs and for her infinite patience. Also, to my business partner Neil 'Sugs' Hayes and my mate Wade for all their help. Finally to my son, Marty (who managed to avoid some health and safety incidents with all the tools I left lying around the house whilst writing this book).

First published in July 2017

British Library Cataloguing in Publication Data
A catalogue record for this book is available from the British Library.

ISBN 978 1 78521 082 2

Library of Congress control no: 2016959369

Published by Haynes Publishing,
Sparkford, Yeovil, Somerset BA22 7JJ, UK
Tel: 01963 440635
Int. tel: +44 1963 440635
Website: www.haynes.com

Haynes North America Inc.
859 Lawrence Drive, Newbury Park,
California 91320, USA

Printed in Malaysia

Credits

Author:	Andy Blackwell
Project manager:	Louise McIntyre
Copy editor:	Beth Dymond
Page design:	James Robertson
Illustrator:	Ian Moores
Index:	Helen Snaith

Kitchen
Upgrade
Manual **A PRACTICAL STEP-BY-STEP GUIDE**

Andy Blackwell

Contents

Introduction

The kitchen is generally regarded as the most important room in the home. It's where we cook, it's often where we eat, and the entire family always seems to congregate there. It's where we entertain and, if you have a party, it's apparently where you'll find Jona Lewie (younger readers may have to ask an older relative about this one)!

Ask any estate agent or realtor and they'll tell you that the kitchen is the room that will most often make or break a house sale. It's usually the determining factor in either getting the price you asked for or missing it by a country mile.

Linked to all of this is the fact that the kitchen is also the room into which you're likely to pour the most money. This would be no bad thing if it wasn't for the fact that the line between a dream kitchen and a nightmare money pit can be depressingly thin, which is where this manual comes in.

If you want to do everything yourself – and about 10% of homeowners do – this manual will lead you around the pitfalls of kitchen planning, navigate you through the dos and don'ts of kitchen installation and give you detailed step-by-step instruction on every stage of your kitchen project. However, I have assumed that you will be fitting a kitchen you have bought, rather than building a kitchen from scratch. This is not a manual for advanced joinery or cabinet making.

For those people for whom the very thought of DIY brings on a cold sweat, fear not. Knowing how to plan your kitchen and at least understanding the basics of kitchen installation will allow you to control the project and ensure that what you end up with looks vaguely like what you'd dreamed about.

1 PLANNING YOUR KITCHEN

With any DIY project it is often very hard to resist the temptation to just don your old clothes, grab a hammer and 'get on with it'. Alas, this approach rarely, if ever, works out for the best and with kitchens it never works out at all. Regardless of how much money you are going to be spending, what you end up with is going to be determined by how well you planned things from the start.

Kitchen fitting terminology

One of the most intimidating aspects of any new venture is dealing with the jargon that comes with it. Below are the main things that you'll come across, and we'll be adding to this basic list as we go along.

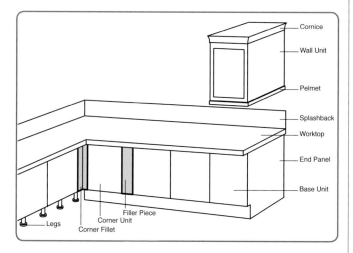

Cornice
Wall Unit
Pelmet
Splashback
Worktop
End Panel
Base Unit
Filler Piece
Corner Unit
Legs
Corner Fillet

APPLIANCES

Also called kitchen appliances or 'white goods', these are generic terms used to describe the main mechanical items that every kitchen should have. Examples include washing machines, refrigerators, freezers, ovens, dishwashers, etc. Appliances come in two distinct forms: freestanding and fitted:

FREESTANDING

As the name suggests, these are not designed to fit into any

specific kitchen or unit and, as such, you get the opportunity to shop around. The upside of freestanding is that they are easy to replace and often cheaper to buy. The downside is that dirt can accumulate in the small gaps around them and they are highly visible in the kitchen.

FITTED

These are appliances designed to fit within specific units or within a certain kitchen range. These can be hidden within the kitchen giving a cleaner and more uniform look, the

downside is that they are often more expensive and can be difficult to replace.

BASE UNITS

Also called base cabinets, these support the worktop and provide most of the storage space in the kitchen. If you're planning on a heavy, stone-type worktop, bear in mind that these units will be supporting all this weight – this may dictate the type of base unit you require. Base units come in a variety of sizes and functions and we'll discuss these in detail in the chapter 'Cabinets', but let's have a quick look at the two main types:

HIGHLINE UNIT

More commonly known as a cupboard unit, it's just a full height door and when you open it – voila! – nothing but space, with perhaps a shelf or two.

DRAWERLINE UNIT

When people talk about a drawerline unit, what they usually mean is that the main door to the unit is smaller because it has a single drawer above it. However, a drawerline unit can be a unit made up entirely of drawers.

Highline unit

Drawerline unit

COOKER HOOD

Also called an extractor hood or just an extractor. These are essential if you're contemplating an open-plan kitchen-dining room layout, as without one you'll have cooking smells permeating the whole area.

There are two basic designs of cooker hood: visor hood and chimney hood. There are also two basic principles; extraction, where the air above the cooker is sucked up and blown out of the house, and recirculation, where the air is drawn through a series of filters and blown back into the kitchen, hopefully minus the smell. Extraction tends to work much better, but can look unsightly as you'll need to run a conduit from the cooker position to the outside of the house. Recirculation doesn't tend to work as well and you'll have to replace and clean the filters regularly.

CORNER UNIT

I've mentioned this specialist unit here because it has such a bearing on the amount of storage space you'll have access to and the cost of the kitchen – corner units are often by far and away the most expensive base units you'll buy. There are a number of ways of dealing with corners:

BLIND BASE UNIT

These are units that have a section that goes into the corner, which connects to another unit to complete the corner. You can also get blind wall cabinets. As a general rule, these don't maximise all of the corner space – you will usually have a dead area that is not accessible.

DIAGONAL CORNER UNIT

Also called wall angle cabinets, these are usually wall units, but you can get base ones as well. These utilise all of the corner space but can protrude out into the kitchen area. If the cabinet is designed to fit on the end of a row of units it's called a wall angle end cabinet.

LAZY SUSAN

Basically, any cabinet that has rotating shelves of some form is called a Lazy Susan or 'revolving corner cabinet'. There has been a lot of innovation on this theme and some wondrous devices have emerged that can give you handy access to the very darkest recesses of your kitchen but, sadly, they invariably come at a price.

CORNICE

A cornice is the name given to any ornamental moulding that sits on top of something else. In kitchens it's usually a length of

decorative wood that is fixed to the top of the wall units, but it could also refer to any decorative effect you have going around the top of the kitchen walls or the kitchen door. Just to make things a little more confusing, coving at the top of your walls is often considered to be a type of simple cornice.

END PANEL

To keep costs down, most manufacturers deliver a single colour of wall and base unit – usually white. This works fine because, in most fitted kitchens, you only ever see the front of the units and this part of the unit is itself hidden behind the cabinet door. The exception to this is the cabinet or unit at the end of a row.

Where you'll be able to see the side of the wall or base

unit, you'll need to purchase an additional part called an 'end panel'. This is a decorative piece in the specific colour and style that you've picked for your kitchen, which is screwed or glued over the basic white side panel. End panels can either be the length of the unit or 'full height', reaching down past the end of the unit to the ground.

FILLER PIECE
In a fitted kitchen, the chance of finding a series of kitchen units that exactly fit is remote. With this in mind, you aim to get as close to the size of the kitchen space as you can and then add filler pieces to 'fill' any gaps.

ISLAND
This is a group of base units placed into the middle of the kitchen. You can get units designed specifically to be in an island but, more often than not, it's the location, rather than the units, that defines an island.

KITCHEN SINK
Most sinks are stainless steel, as it is a cheap material to use and results in a long-lasting product. More expensive materials include enamelled cast iron, clay and composite, where granite, quartz, or some other decorative stone is ground up and mixed with a resin to create a decorative and hardwearing finish.

Most sinks these days tend to be single-holed and can only be used by monobloc or

Right: Monobloc/mono mixer tap
Below: Deck mixer tap

mono mixer taps, but you can still get two holed sinks to fit either separate hot and cold taps or a deck mixer tap.

There are a number of different sink layouts:

SINGLE BOWL INSET SINK
Also called top-mounted or 'drop-in' sinks, these are usually made from stainless steel and they fit into a hole cut into the worktop. They will often come with a drainer attached to them in a left-hand or right-hand variant.

1½ BOWL OR DOUBLE BOWL INSET SINK
These have one full-sized bowl with a smaller bowl next to it. Again, they can be bought with a drainer attached.

SIT-ON SINK
Rather than being set within a worktop, these replace the worktop section altogether. They are still popular in commercial kitchens, but are much less common in the home.

UNDERMOUNT SINK
Rather than fit the sink onto the worktop, you can hang the sink from underneath instead. These can look very nice, but you need either a preformed worktop with the hole for the sink already

made and prepared, or a solid stone or wooden worktop. In other words, an undermount sink is a far more expensive option. The taps for an undermount sink are usually set into the worktop itself.

BELFAST, BUTLER, FARMHOUSE OR APRON SINK

There are lots of names for these sinks because they all have small variations in design. For example, a Belfast sink has a built-in overflow and a Butler sink does not. The Farmhouse sink is sometimes called a French Farmhouse sink, despite not necessarily being located in France, and is deemed to be more elegant than its Belfast and Butler counterparts. In truth, the names tend to be interchangeable, so just use the one you feel most comfortable with and, if in doubt, just call it an Apron or Apron-front sink, since that's the most generic term.

Regardless of the name, these are like undermount sinks, but rather than being set into the worktop, they are set into the front of the worktop and replace a section of the kitchen unit underneath. In some cases, the sink actually replaces a section of the worktop altogether. As a result, you will usually have to buy a base unit to specifically hold this type of sink. Like undermount sinks, the taps are usually, but not exclusively, set into the worktop or into the wall behind the sink.

PELMET

Pelmet and cornice can be interchangeable, but when talking about kitchens the pelmet is the decorative edge – often identical in form to the cornice above it – that is fitted to the base of the wall unit. While the cornice is entirely decorative, the pelmet is often used to hide lighting attached to the base of the wall units. Be aware that the board above a curtain that hides the curtain rail is also called a pelmet.

PLINTH/KICKBOARD

One of the best places in a kitchen for dirt to build up is under the kitchen units themselves and the easiest way to get around this is to

fit a plinth under all of the base cabinets. The plinth, also known as a kickboard, is usually just a decorative piece of wood that's clipped to the legs of the base units and makes a nice seal with the floor.

If you don't fit a plinth you will be able to see the legs of the base unit. The legs that usually come with basic units are horrible old plastic things that are expecting to be hidden, so if there's no plinth you'll almost certainly need to purchase more decorative legs.

SPLASHBACK/UPSTAND

This is the decorative and protective surface behind the worktop that prevents dirt and oil staining the wall. Often this term is used to describe only that area of the wall behind the cooker hob, but it can be used to describe the wall behind the worktop in general. This is usually a tiled area, but there are many other options (see Chapter 9).

An upstand is usually a section of the worktop material, about 100mm (4in) high, that you fit to the back of the worktop. If you are a very tidy cook it can replace the splashback altogether.

Granite upstand and tiled splashback

WALL UNIT/CABINET

Kitchen units – also called cabinets – come in two forms; wall units and base units (see above for more details).

WORKTOP/COUNTERTOP

This is the work surface of the kitchen, and in terms of looks and function, is usually the centrepiece of the entire kitchen. More often than not the worktop has to be cut out to accommodate a sink and/or a cooker hob. With this in mind, choose your material carefully if you are planning on installing the kitchen yourself; cutting out a laminate worktop is a piece of cake; cutting out a solid granite worktop is not.

Kitchen design terminology

There is, by definition, going to be a lot of crossover between fitting and design jargon, but I've tried to separate it out based on where you're most likely to hear it. The following terms are those you'll most likely come across during the planning stage and mainly refer to particular styles of kitchens or design features.

ACCENT LIGHTING

If you want to light up something in particular you'll use an accent light. In a kitchen, the term is usually used to describe the lights that fit under the wall cabinets and are used to light up a section of the worktop underneath.

ALCOVE

This is any recess in a wall, but in the kitchen it's usually the recess beneath an old chimney. Rather than keep the kitchen chimney as it is, you knock it out to enlarge it and then place your new cooker underneath. You can use the old chimney as part of an extractor, but more often than not it just remains as a decorative feature.

AMBIENT LIGHTING

In contrast to an accent light, this is the general lighting used in the kitchen as a whole. When it comes to design, ambient and ambience

are closely linked and the ambient lighting you use can have a big effect on how warm and welcoming a kitchen can feel, often not by where it's placed but by what sort of light bulbs are used.

BREAKFRONT

While there are advantages to having all the units in a kitchen projecting into the room by the same amount, it can look a little

dull, especially in larger kitchens. To break up the line, you can bring forward a unit or an appliance. This effect is most commonly used with the cooker or, in more traditional kitchens, with a feature unit along the lines of a Welsh dresser.

CHAIR, DADO AND PICTURE RAIL

This is a moulding, usually made of plaster or wood, that runs

horizontally around a wall, separating it into two sections. It was originally used to prevent chairs, etc. from damaging the wall and to hide rising damp – underneath the dado rail the wall was often covered by wooden panelling. Today it's just a decorative feature, and if it's set higher up the wall it's often called a picture rail.

CLEARANCE SPACE

A critical part of the planning process is making sure you have enough clearance space in your kitchen. This is an essential part of the planning and design stage, so we'll look at it in more detail later on.

CORBEL

This is just the name for a decorative shelf support. If you're going to have a snack bar style area in your kitchen, you may unwittingly find yourself the owner of a few corbels.

Below: Now that's what I call a corbel

ELEVATION PLAN/ DRAWING

An 'elevation plan' is where you show a single wall of your room on a plan or layout as if you were standing in front of it.

FITTED KITCHEN

In a fitted kitchen the units are secured to the wall and, usually, to each other, i.e. they are fixed in place. The advantage of this is that everything is secure, there's less space for dust and dirt to collect and the cost of the individual units can be reduced because the back and sides of most units are hidden from view.

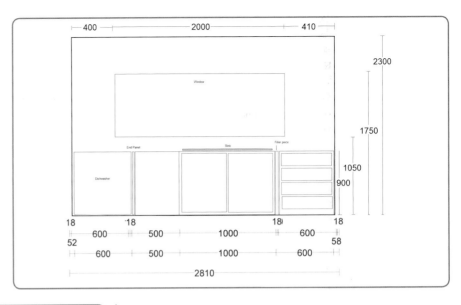

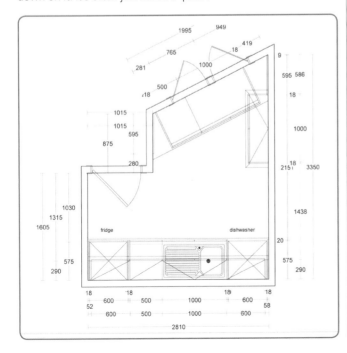

FLOOR PLAN/DRAWING

The floor plan is a plan of the floor, as seen as if you were looking down on it. It's often just called a 'plan'.

FOOTPRINT

This is a term used to describe the layout of the base units of your kitchen and the area of floor they cover. If you're going to renew your kitchen you can save money and time by reusing the existing footprint: you save money because you're unlikely to need much in the way of new flooring or electrical and plumbing work, and time because you can use the existing kitchen as a base plan for the new one, keeping what you like and only changing the design in areas where it currently lets you down.

FREESTANDING KITCHEN

In days of yore most kitchens were freestanding, then they almost vanished completely for a few decades and are now making something of a comeback.

In a freestanding kitchen most, if not all, the units are just placed into position and that's it! As a result they're a piece of cake to fit and if you get bored with your layout there's not much stopping you from changing it around. On the downside each

individual kitchen unit tends to be more expensive, but then that's because they are invariably of a far higher quality. Sadly, you'll also have to learn to enjoy dusting and cleaning behind them.

Freestanding kitchens tend to be designed for and to work best in a more traditional setting. This is fine if you have an old ramshackle, rose-covered cottage but they look a bit out of place in a modern home. However, more and more contemporary freestanding designs are now available and no doubt this trend will continue.

MANTLE

In kitchens, mantle or mantle shelf is the name given to an ornamental surround and shelf, usually over the kitchen cooker, which is either part of the chimney or alcove, or designed to look as if it is.

Below: Mantle over a cooker supported by corbels

OBLIQUE PROJECTION/PERSPECTIVE DRAWING/3D ELEVATION

These are all attempts to give your kitchen drawings a more 3D look. In kitchen planning you might also hear the term 'cabinet projection', as this was a common way of drawing items for sale in the furniture catalogues of days gone by. These days you are more than likely to be given a plan of your kitchen that can be loaded onto a computer to give you a genuine 3D feel for how it'll eventually look.

PENINSULA

This is the name given to a section of base units and worktop that juts out into the kitchen. It can be used as an alternative to an island, as they offer a similar function but result in more usable space – you don't need the 900mm (36in) walkway all the way around a peninsula. They're also a nice way to separate the kitchen and dining room areas, while still giving an 'open plan' feel to the room.

PILASTER

A decorative column feature, popular in more traditional kitchens. The contemporary versions are subtler and can be used as ornamental filler pieces.

POCKET DOOR

A more obscure term for a sliding door, although in a true pocket door the door slides back into the wall, or in the case of a kitchen, into the unit. A variation on the theme is where the door swings open as normal but, once it's open, it can then be pushed back into the unit.

RADIUS FEATURE END

Rather than just fit a standard end panel to the end of a run of units, you might want to make the end a little more stylish and give it a more forgiving rounded finish, for example if it's in an area near a door where it might be bumped up against.

SCONCE

A sconce is a light fitting fixed to a wall.

SHAKER STYLE

A very popular kitchen style named after a religious sect famed for their love of simplicity, utility and honesty. I guess the shaker style door, where a plain door is edged all around by a wooden strip, epitomises these principles.

SHELF/DRAW FRONTAGE

This is a way of calculating how much storage space your kitchen design has, and is something we'll look into in more detail later.

SNACK/BREAKFAST BAR

This is often a part of an island or peninsula, offering high-level seating.

TOE KICK

When you're standing close up to a work unit you need somewhere for your feet to go that won't damage either the cabinet or your feet. To accommodate this anatomical need, most base cabinets will have an indented area at the bottom. The back of this area is where you'll find the plinth or kickboard.

TRAFFIC PATTERNS

A basic tenant of kitchen design is the work triangle (see below) and an extension of this is the kitchen traffic pattern, i.e. working out how most people will move around the kitchen on most occasions.

UNIT/CABINET CONSTRUCTION

The unit construction and worktop material you opt for will generally have the biggest impact on the overall cost of your kitchen. We'll cover this in greater detail later, but for now just be aware of the two basic types: solid wood (expensive) and laminated chipboard or particle board (much cheaper). In a fitted kitchen the only part of a cabinet that people will see is the door, so it makes sense to save a bit of money by buying units with nice doors but with the rest of the unit made from laminated particleboard. That said, solid wood cabinets will usually last longer, can cope with being dowsed in water much better and are close to essential if you opt for a freestanding kitchen.

UNIT/CABINET REFACING AND REFINISHING

This is one of the cheapest ways of making it look as if you've bought a new kitchen, without actually going to the expense of buying a new kitchen. In refacing you renew the surface of the existing doors or add ornate bits to them; in resurfacing you sand down, or chemically remove, all the old varnish, etc. and reapply a new finish. Both are time-consuming, but – if you're the one doing it – cheap.

WORK AISLE

Another term for the clearance space in front of the main kitchen work areas; see 'Clearance space' on page 13.

THE WORK TRIANGLE

Most cooks will spend most of their time moving between the sink, the cooker and the fridge. This is called the work triangle and working out how you're going to implement this in your kitchen is an important aspect of the design.

Working out your budget

I vividly recall the first time I ever went into a kitchen showroom. My wife and I had just bought our first house and were naively looking at what we might do to bring the kitchen into the 21st century. We wandered into a very nice-looking showroom, I saw the prices and I had to have a sit down, a long sit down. I cannot emphasise enough just how expensive kitchens can be if you let your dreams control the process and not your bank account. Below are some of the steps you need to go through to work out not only your budget, but also what you can realistically achieve.

HOW MUCH DO I HAVE?

Only you know how much money you can throw at your kitchen, but be realistic. This kitchen is going to last for at least ten years, probably far longer, and if you ever decide to sell your home, it's one of the first things a potential buyer is going to look at. As such, it makes sense to spend as much money on it as you can realistically afford without going too mad. Remember that over a fifth of all kitchens installed in any one year will go over budget, so you should always keep aside a reserve to cover yourself for unforeseeable circumstances – although the better you plan, the more foreseeable most things become.

NEW KITCHEN, OR REFURBISH THE OLD?

There are a number of online budget calculators that can work out a rough cost for an average kitchen; just type 'working out budget for kitchen', or something along those lines, into any search engine to find them. Try a few and use the average price as a rough budget.

A more low-tech approach is to just count the number of wall and base units in your existing kitchen, add a sink, a cooker hob, an oven and a fridge and hand the list to a few of your local kitchen retailers. This process will at least give you an idea of what prices to expect and that in turn will allow you to decide if you can afford a completely new kitchen or if you'd be better off focusing on refurbishing what you already have.

SECOND-HAND KITCHENS

There is a surprisingly large market in second-hand kitchens. If you think a brand new kitchen might be beyond your budget or if you need to raise a bit more money then have a good look at this area. Nearly all of this trade takes place on the internet, so actually seeing the kitchen for real can be a problem, but this is usually more than offset by the bargains on offer. Of course, you don't have to buy an entire kitchen; you could just buy a few units or maybe indulge yourself in a granite worktop.

HOW MUCH ARE YOU GOING TO CHANGE?

If you're happy with your current layout this is going to help bring the cost down, as there is a very good chance that you'll need very little plumbing or electrical work. If you're planning on moving things around then you'll need to get some quotes to cover moving water and gas pipework, and electrical cables and sockets. Even if you're planning on doing most of this work yourself, it's still worthwhile getting some prices, and for some of this work you'll need a qualified professional.

If you're changing the floor plan, bear in mind that any floor covering that you have probably ends the moment it disappears under the current base cabinets. As a result, you may need to renew the floor altogether.

WHAT ARE YOU GOING TO DO FOR YOURSELF?

Installation usually accounts for about 20% of the cost of a kitchen so the more you can do for yourself the better. But again, be realistic. Yes, plastering is doable by the DIY enthusiast, but it requires a lot of practise to get good at it and your kitchen will look a right mess if you get it wrong. You can bring down costs by boarding the walls yourself and bringing in a plasterer to just apply the final skim. For electrical work you could channel out the walls, fit the sockets and run the cables into position but employ an electrician to make all the final connections and test everything. These are all feasible ways of saving money, but they rely on finding a plasterer or electrician happy to work for you under these circumstances. Also, bear in mind that this might not save you much money. Some professionals may assume that they'll spend so much time changing things you've done wrong that they'll knock little or nothing off the bill.

The following list covers all the basic work that you'll need to budget for. Get at least three quotes for each area and then decide if you're going to do it yourself, partially do it yourself or leave it completely to a professional. This decision isn't necessarily a reflection on your abilities; in many cases, by the time you've bought the appropriate tools and materials, it would have been cheaper to just let a professional do it for you.

BUILDING WORK

Are you planning on knocking down walls, putting up new walls or moving and removing windows? If so, work out the costs now.

ELECTRICAL WORK

If you're moving or installing an electric cooker you'll need new cables directly back to your consumer unit. A cooker draws a lot of power, so this area needs to be at least checked for safety by a professional.

What are your plans for ambient and accent lighting? Are you having lighting under the new wall cabinets? Are you planning on moving any electric sockets? Do you need USB connectors to supply power for laptops, phones, etc.?

PLUMBING WORK

Are you moving the sink, the washing machine or the dishwasher? Are you planning on installing a fridge with an icemaking/cold drinking water facility? All of these will require at least some plumbing work.

GAS WORK

Are you moving a gas oven or hob, or are you planning on replacing a small cooker with a bigger range-style cooker? Also, will you need to move or replace your existing gas boiler? If so, you'll need to get quotes in from a professional. Bear in mind that even if you're just removing and refitting your existing cooker you'll still need a professional to come in and do the removing and refitting – they must undertake a gas tightness test to check that all is safe and completely leak-free afterwards.

DECORATING

Are you planning changes to your ceiling, walls or floors? If so, decide what materials you are planning on using and get some quotes. If you plan on doing this work yourself, now would be the time to work out your material costs.

TIP  *If you have an Artex ceiling, the cheapest and quickest way of dealing with it is to 'over board' the ceiling – fit new plasterboard sheets over the top of the existing ceiling. This will lower the ceiling by 12–15mm (approx. ½in) but this is rarely an issue. Always remember that the old Artex might contain asbestos. This approach also works well if the existing ceiling is old and badly damaged.*

TILING

The price of tiles can vary enormously and this is usually a reflection on their quality. An exception to this are 'end of range' tiles, where the design is not being produced any more and the manufacturer is just happy to get rid of the remaining tiles at the best price they can muster, which drops as the amount of remaining tiles falls. These can be great value for money, but you aren't going to be able to get replacements so make sure you buy enough to cover

future damage. It usually pays to work out the square metreage you'll need and then add 20%.

Wall tiles in a kitchen are really just decorative, but if you are using tiles on the floor they will need to be hard enough to withstand dropped pans and have a surface that won't become too slippery when the tiles get wet.

If you buy porcelain tiles, bear in mind that they're very hard and, as a result, need to be cut with tile cutters using diamond-cutting wheels. If you opt for large tiles, which are very popular these days, you'll need tile cutters capable of taking these larger tiles.

Good quality floor tile adhesive usually needs mixing on site so you'll need a mixing bucket, drill and a tile adhesive (paddle) mixer.

If you're planning on doing the tiling yourself you'll need to include the cost of all this equipment, plus the cost of tile adhesive, grout and tile trims.

TIP *You can reuse your old tiles, but bear in mind that you're unlikely to get them all off the wall without breaking them. Once you've taken them down, put them in a large bucket of warm soapy water and leave them for a few days. You can now scrape off the old adhesive with relative ease.*

If you don't get all the tiles off intact, it's worth considering using what you have and adding a contrasting tile as a horizontal or vertical border tile.

HEATING

Traditional radiators can take up valuable wall space in a kitchen so it's worth looking at what alternatives are available and allocating a cost for these. You can get away without any heating in a kitchen if it's only used for cooking – the cooker provides all the heat the room needs – but if it is going to be a general meeting area you will need some heating to keep it comfortable in winter. See 'Heating your kitchen' on the opposite page.

FURNISHINGS

Many of your current appliances can be used again in your new kitchen, but some will need replacing, so work this out at this stage and add a cost for the replacements.

Bright colours in a kitchen can make it look beautiful, but the effect can be ruined if your kitchen appliances don't match the colour scheme. Bear this in mind at this stage and add a cost for things like blenders, kettles, slow cookers, microwaves and all the other smaller appliances that will make or break your 'vision'.

HEATING YOUR KITCHEN

In yesteryear many kitchens had no heating apart from the kitchen stove. This was fine, as the kitchens themselves were fairly small and the act of cooking was usually more than enough to heat the room up. As kitchens have grown larger and their functionality has expanded, the need to heat them has grown.

RADIATORS

The cheapest, and therefore the most common way of heating a kitchen is with wall-hung radiators. To save valuable wall space, you might want to consider vertical radiators, which take up less base cabinet room and are usually much kinder on the eye. When picking a radiator you need to ensure it's going to be powerful enough to heat your room. Fortunately, there are umpteen free calculators online. Just type in something along the lines of 'Radiator sizing calculator software', enter your kitchen dimensions and jot down the BTU, wattage or Therm value.

TIP *BTU is the British Thermal Unit, and as such doesn't travel far from the UK. Wattage is a more universal unit, but in the US they use the Therm. There are roughly 100,000 Therms to the BTU and 1 BTU is equal to 0.29 watts. The values we are trying to find don't need to be exact, just ensure you pick a radiator slightly more powerful than the value you've calculated.*

In a large kitchen, it is better to opt for a number of small radiators rather than one huge one, as this will ensure the heat is more evenly spread. Fitting radiators is outside of the scope of this book, although Haynes do a very good *Home Plumbing Manual* that does cover this area and that I can heartily recommend.

UNDERFLOOR CENTRAL HEATING

This works very well in kitchens, but can be an expensive option. It works best with a tiled floor, but you can get systems that work with wooden and laminated floors. The main advantage of UFCH

Below: Wet UFCH

Above: Electric UFCH

is that it uses no wall space at all and spreads the heat around the kitchen perfectly.

There are two basic variants: electric UFCH and wet UFCH. The former uses an electric cable that heats up when the power is turned on. It usually comes as a mat that you lay on the floor and tile over. The advantage of this is that it can be laid over an existing floor and doesn't raise the floor height to any great extent. It's fairly inexpensive to buy and can generally be fitted by anyone willing to read the installation manual. On the downside, it's more expensive to run than a wet UFCH system.

Wet UFCH is linked to your main central heating system. It can be very expensive to retro fit, as it often requires you to dig out the existing floor in order to fit the insulation and pipework. However, there are more and more 'low-level' options coming onto the market each year, so it's still well worth looking at.

The cost of all UFCH is based on the area of floor being heated. You only want to heat that floor area that is not going to have base cabinets on top of it so, with that in mind, you need to decide your basic kitchen layout before getting in quotes for UFCH.

KICKBOARD HEATERS

This is a nice compromise that works very well in kitchens. In essence these are radiators that fit under your base cabinets. Like UFCH you can get 'wet' or electric kickboard heaters and both types usually come with a fan that blows the heat around the kitchen. They are more expensive than traditional radiators but far less expensive than UFCH. Bearing in mind that their pipework is hidden under the kitchen cabinets, they can be fitted using plastic push-fit pipework and fittings, making the job quick and easy enough for the home owner to have a go at – although you'll possibly need to read that wonderful *Home Plumbing Manual* first and get an electrician to wire them up afterwards.

Basic design concepts

Different countries have different rules and regulations that will impact on your kitchen and it makes sense to double-check that you're not breaking any local by-laws. The act of collecting quotes from the various trades will often bring some enlightenment in this regard, but if you're still in doubt, join a few internet forums or try your Citizens Advice Bureau.

DRAWING UP A PLAN OF YOUR KITCHEN

Get a piece of paper and a tape measure and start measuring up the kitchen and drawing a plan. You can do this on a computer, but it's usually much easier and quicker to at least start the process off with a hand-drawn plan on paper and then transfer this to a computer once you're sure of your measurements.

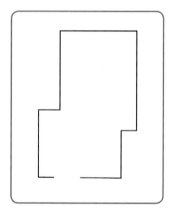

1 Draw up the rough shape of the room as a floor plan. It doesn't need to be overly accurate; at this stage just get the basic shape right – it's usually easier to do this on graph paper.

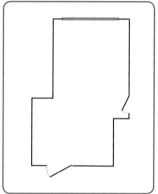

2 Add any doors and windows. You can use the standard symbols for these, but don't get hung up about it. You need to be able to understand and explain this drawing, that's all.

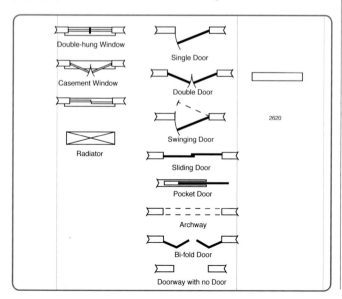

Double-hung Window

Casement Window

Radiator

Single Door

Double Door

2620

Swinging Door

Sliding Door

Pocket Door

Archway

Bi-fold Door

Doorway with no Door

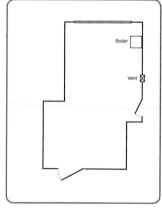

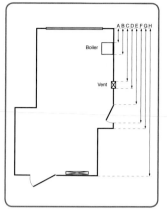

3 Now add any other fixed items that are going to remain in the room, such as boilers, air vents, radiators, pipes, drains, light switches and electric sockets.

4 Now you can start measuring everything. Make sure you use the same unit of measurement throughout the project, ideally either millimetres (mm) or inches (in).

If you've indulged yourself in a laser measure, feel free to measure away on your own, but if you have a tape measure you're best off getting someone in to hold the other end for you. If you do have a partner don't swap roles; one person should hold one end in place and the other should take all the measurements. To keep errors to a minimum it's always best to measure everything on one wall from a single point. Yes, it's more awkward, but it's more accurate and easier to check and test afterwards.

Always measure doorways from the edge of the casing trim. You need to know how much usable wall you have for your units. That said, if you're thinking of buying a nice big range cooker, it's probably worth checking at this stage if you can actually get it into the kitchen, so jot down the actual size of the door openings.

The same applies to the windows; we're not particularly interested in the size of the window but in how much usable wall space it leaves us. Measure from the edge of the window casing, if there is any, and from the edge of the window opening in the wall itself if there isn't.

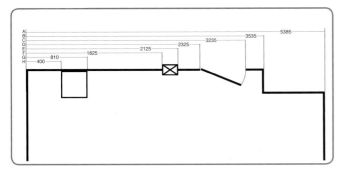

5 Once you have all the measurements for a single wall jotted down, you can work out the width of the fixtures and sections of the wall and then test your measurements by re-measuring each section directly. For example, in the above diagram you can see that the boiler width is G–H, which is 810mm minus 400mm, so it's 410mm wide. The distance between the boiler and the vent should be 1015mm, the vent should be 300mm wide, the edge of the vent should be 200mm from the door and the door should be 910mm wide.

Test all of these by measuring these distances directly. If there is a big difference, re-measure everything, and never forget that the most useful adage in all DIY projects is 'measure twice, cut once'.

6 Your diagram will be easier to read if you write down the measurements for each section.

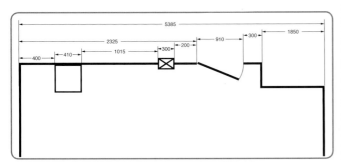

7 You can never have enough measurements of your kitchen, but it pays to produce a number of relatively simple plans rather than trying to pack every measurement into a single diagram.

If you look at the diagram to the right you'll notice that the opposite walls aren't exactly the same length, which in turn would suggest that the angles between the walls are not perfect right angles (90°). This is not at all unusual and is why you need to also measure the walls about 600mm (24in) – the depth of a standard cabinet

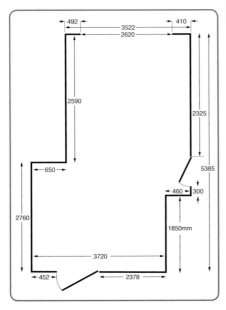

and worktop – into the room if you're planning on having units going from wall to wall.

In our example, we can see that wall A is slightly narrower when we measure it from 600mm (24in) into the room. On this wall it is critical that we know this, because it is this smaller measurement that will dictate which base units we can fit against this wall, while the longer measurement is needed to work out how long our worktop needs to be. In our example we can see that this measurement 600mm (24in) into the room is only really needed for wall A; on wall B it will only affect the width of the passageway to the door and a few millimetres difference here isn't going to be a tragedy.

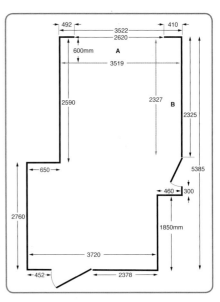

8 You now need to measure the height of everything in the room. This would be straightforward if your kitchen floor was perfectly flat and level, but it almost certainly isn't.

If you are replacing an existing kitchen you should already have a perfectly horizontal reference point – the kitchen worktop – that you can use. If the room is empty at the moment just draw a level mark across the wall and use that as your reference point. The height of this line isn't critical but, since you're planning on putting a kitchen in, you might as well draw it at the height of your base units – about 900mm (36in) from the floor.

Ideally, you want to draw this horizontal base line around the whole kitchen and to do this a good laser level really does come into its own. If you don't fancy buying one, it might be a good idea to hire one just for the day.

Below: Marking off our laser level.

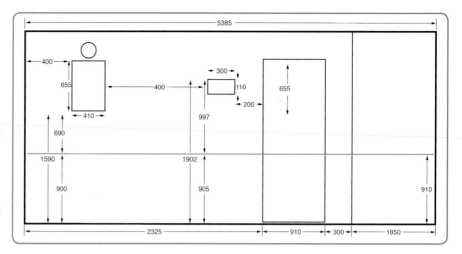

Right: Elevation plans aren't common in kitchen design but they are very handy to have.

9 Now you have a base line, you can measure up and down from this to get the heights of all the fixed items in the room, including windows, boilers, pipes, vents, etc. You can now add these to the measurements you took earlier to draw up an elevation plan for each wall. You can measure everything if you like, but as a general rule we're not that interested in the height of the doorways and, while you need the breakdown of the heights – above and below your base line – it also makes sense to jot down the full height.

10 You should now have a floor plan and four elevation plans of your room and a base line you can use later. You also know how flat the floor is and, if it has a slope, which way it's sloping. This will come in handy later on.

This is a good time to convert your sketches to a scale drawing. The easiest way to do this is to measure the workable length of a sheet of A4 paper (about 260mm) and then divide your longest length, (5385mm) in our example, by this amount: 5385 / 260 = 20.711. To make the subsequent maths easier, and in doing so reduce potential errors, let's go for a scale of 1:20 – each 1mm in your drawing will equate to 20mm in your actual kitchen.

So, to draw a wall of 5385mm we will divide by 20, which gives us a line on our drawing of 269.25mm. If you feel this makes your drawing a bit too big for your sheet of paper, then change the scale to 1:25, i.e. divide 5385mm by 25, giving a line of 215.4mm. What we're trying to do is get a usable scale that avoids any fiddly maths – 1:21 is a scale that might work better for your sheet of paper, but is difficult to work out in your head.

This final process is also a good way of rechecking measurements – the most common error here is having the decimal point in the wrong place – 600mm becomes 60mm, for example. Always mark the scale on your drawing, so for our example add 'scale 1:20' in the bottom right-hand corner.

You might want to make a drawing on something bigger – a sheet of A3, for example – that you can then use to help design your kitchen layout. This is also a good stage to load everything onto your computer program of choice – see 'Using kitchen planners' on page 31.

DESIGN ERGONOMICS

While it's great to have a good-looking kitchen, it must be functional. It needs to have enough cupboard space for all your pots and pans but not so many that you don't have enough drawers. You also don't want to spread your essential appliances all over the place and then find yourself dropping to the floor with exhaustion every time you attempt a dish more complicated than cheese-on-toast.

THE KITCHEN WORK TRIANGLE

The work triangle is a 1940s idea, based around the notion that a kitchen can be separated into three functions: cooking, food preparation/cleaning and food storage, and that each of these functions can be focused around a single appliance; we cook using our oven, we prepare food around the sink and we store it in the fridge.

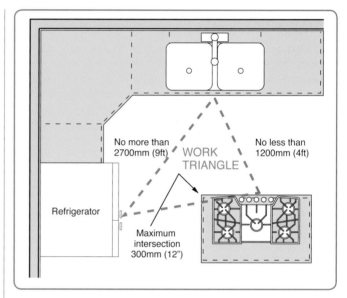

If we draw a line between each appliance we end up with a triangle and this triangle should have certain properties:

- No side of the triangle should be shorter than 1.2m (4ft) or longer than 2.7m (9ft) and when we add the three sides together they should total less than 7.9m (26ft).
- There should be no regularly used walkway passing through this work triangle.
- If there are any obstructions, they shouldn't push more than 300mm (12in) into the triangle.
- You should avoid placing any full height units between any of the appliances.
- The triangle approach generally works best in small kitchens where only one person is doing the cooking and kitchen appliances and gadgets have been kept to a minimum.

WORK ZONES, WORK CENTRES AND MULTIPLE RECTANGLES

There have been big changes in kitchens since the 1940s. Most of us now have far more kitchen appliances to think about; the kitchen is no longer just a place to make a meal and, as a consequence, they now tend to be much larger. Another big change is that there is often more than one person in the kitchen at the same time.

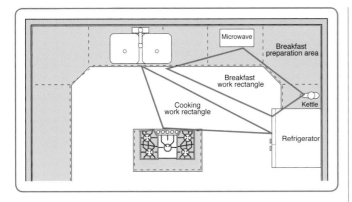

A quite popular approach to design for this modern kitchen was the idea of multiple triangles that didn't overlap, so two people could function in the same kitchen without bumping into each other all the time. To cater for all the new appliances, this idea was expanded with the notion of multiple rectangles, into which you added the microwave oven, the dishwasher and cookers now separated out into multiple ovens and separate cooker tops (hobs).

Work zones and work centres are a more flexible and, possibly, a more rational approach to kitchen design. The idea is simple enough; you go through all the things you want to do in your kitchen, you allocate an area of the kitchen to it and you group everything you need in that area. For example, we can create a zone called 'baking'. Inside this zone you'd need a slightly lower worktop, you'd need storage for your bowls and utensils, plug sockets, a work area for your baking appliances, access to a sink for water and an area to store your main baking ingredients.

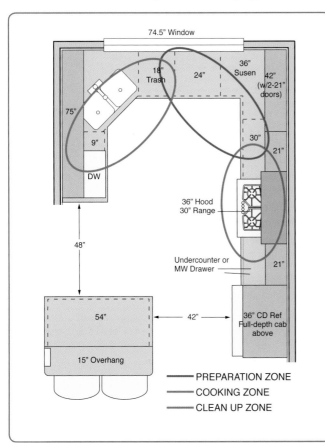

We then might have a zone called 'cleaning up', where we have the sink and the dishwasher, a cupboard for all our cleaning chemicals and cloths, and area of worktop set aside for holding the dirty dishes and another for draining and holding the clean stuff.

The main advantage of this approach is that you can create zones that work for you. If you're going to use the workzone approach it makes sense to get everyone in the house to contribute his or her thoughts and to then prioritise the list.

COMMON LAYOUTS

Most kitchens come in the following basic shapes, and we can use these with the work triangle and work zone concepts to create a basic layout.

ONE-WALL KITCHEN

This is for small kitchens, often bedsits. Here the kitchen is all against one wall with the sink in the middle and the cooker and fridge at each end. An advantage of this layout in bedsits is that the entire kitchen can be hidden behind sliding doors when not in use.

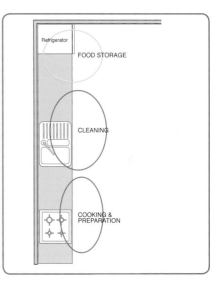

GALLEY KITCHEN

Once the most popular kitchen layout, it's faded away as kitchens themselves have become bigger. The optimal width between worktops for a galley kitchen is 1200–1500mm (48–60in). If that's not possible, the absolute bare minimum is 900mm (36in) for one cook, 1200mm (48in) for two.

This layout is pretty much ideal for the work triangle concept. The basic principle is that one of the main appliances is on the opposite wall, roughly in between the other two. If you have a full-height fridge, it's best to put this on the wall opposite the sink and cooker. If you have an under-counter fridge, then place the sink on the opposite wall.

The biggest problem is that you block the work aisle when you open the fridge, dishwasher and oven doors. As such, place the dishwasher on the far side of the sink so it's out of the way

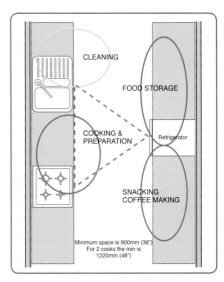

and make sure the oven and fridge doors don't hit each other. Also, if you fill both walls with wall units it makes the kitchen look very small so, if at all possible, put the wall units on one wall only.

U-SHAPED KITCHEN

This design only really works if you have enough space for the sink at the foot of a galley kitchen and works best if there is enough space for the sink and the dishwasher at this base – the optimal width is roughly 3000mm (120in) –

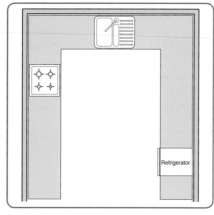

below this width you might be better off with a galley kitchen layout.

Again, the work triangle works well for this layout with the fridge positioned close to the kitchen entrance. In terms of looks, put any full-height units at the end of the legs close to the entrance – a full-height fridge works well with a high-level oven or pantry opposite.

L-SHAPED KITCHEN

In larger kitchens, an L-shape offers an open-plan kitchen, which can interact nicely with a dining area and lets multiple cooks whip up culinary delights simultaneously. This shape works well with a traditional dining table, but you can add an island or

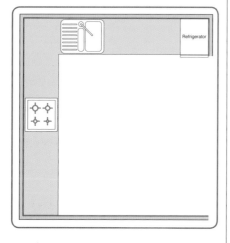

peninsula and go for a breakfast bar instead.

If you make the two sides of the 'L' too long you could end up trekking a fair bit every time you cook, so you'd need to work out your work zones. Ideally, you should keep the legs less than 4500m (180in) long. If you do exceed 4500mm only do it on one leg.

ISLANDS AND PENINSULAS

If you have a large kitchen, the above layouts are going to result in a lot of walking for the cook. If your kitchen is more than 5500mm (220in) wide, then the odds are that at least one leg of the work triangle is going to be longer than 2700mm (108in). It's not essential, but at this point you should start thinking about islands and peninsulas to maximise the useful area of your kitchen. Islands are a popular design concept at the moment, but they really can be more of a hindrance than a help in a smaller kitchen, acting as an obstacle and making it look too cramped.

The minimum size of an island should be 1000 x 1000mm (40 x 40in) and the absolute minimum space between the island and

the main worktop should be 800mm (32in). In a U-shaped kitchen, this gives us a minimum width for the room of 3800mm (112in).

To avoid a kitchen that looks and feels cramped you should go for an island more like 1000 x 2000mm (40 x 80in) with a

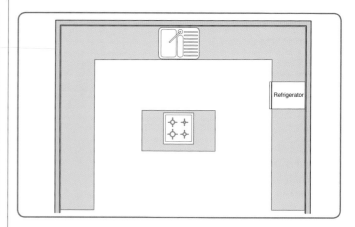

space around of 1000mm (40in). The work aisle, where you'll be spending most of your time preparing and cooking, should be at least 1050mm (42in) wide, while a walkthrough should be at least 900mm (36in).

Islands and peninsulas come in really handy when you have a walkway through the kitchen. In the example shown here we are creating a galley-style kitchen to give us a disturbance-free work area, while still letting people walk through the kitchen.

As a general rule, you ought to place one of your main appliances on the island or peninsula. On an island this can create problems; cables, gas, water and waste pipework all have to be run

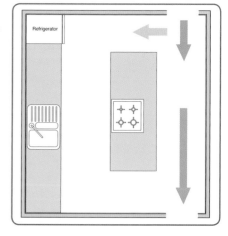

under the floor, which can add quite a bit to the cost of your kitchen. You can avoid this by using it as a preparation area or breakfast bar, or opting for a peninsula instead.

A cooker on the island allows you to look out of the kitchen at your guests while you're cooking. On the downside, you'll need to consider how you'll extract the cooking smells – it might be

easier to have a general kitchen extraction fan system rather than a cooker hood. You'll also need to leave at least 225mm (9in) behind the cooker and the edge of your island.

If you're thinking of combining a seating area with a cooker on a single island then you need to consider the fact that cooking can result in oil spitting and water splashing. As such, it's best to leave a gap of at least 600mm (24in) or have the seating area worktop set higher than that of the cooker hob – 150mm (6in) difference works well.

CLEARANCES AND DESIGN DISTANCES

One of the best ways of ruining a perfectly good kitchen is trying to fit too much into it – usually a dining area or island. With that in mind, let's have a look at the basic clearances you need.

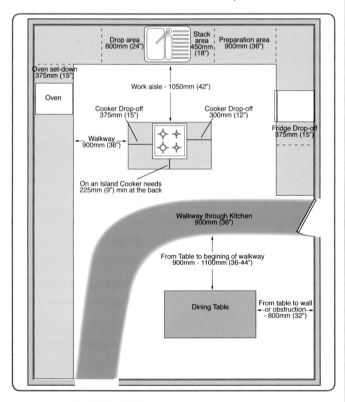

AISLES AND WALKWAYS

There are two basic aisles in any kitchen: ones where you'll stop, stand and work (work aisles) and those you just pass through (walkways). Work aisles should be least 1050mm (42in) wide for one cook and 1200mm (48in) for multiple cooks. The walkways should be at least 900mm (36in) wide.

DINING AREAS

If you want a dining area in your kitchen then you'll need 800mm (32in) between the counter/table edge and any wall or other obstruction – assuming you're planning on having people sitting on that side of the table. If there's a walkway behind the seated diners, allow at least 900mm (36in) to edge past or at least 1100mm (44in) to walk past. The distance you choose should be based on how often this walkway is used; a regularly used walkway needs 1100mm (44in) but if it's rarely used, especially during meal times, then 900mm (36in) should be fine; any less than this and you'll be blocking the walkway during meals.

Use the following table to work out table sizes:

CIRCULAR TABLE		
Seats	Diameter (mm)	Diameter (in)
2-3	900	36
4-6	1200	48
7-8	1500	60
8-9	1800	72
9-11	2100	84
10-12	2400	96

SQUARE TABLE		
Seats	Side length (mm)	Side length (in)
2	750	30
4	900	36
4-5	1200	48
5-6	1500	60
8-10	1800	72
10-12	2400	96

RECTANGULAR TABLE				
Seats	Width (mm)	Length (mm)	Width (in)	Length (in)
2	750	1050	30	42
4-6	750	1500	30	60
6-8	900	1800	36	72
8-10	1050	2400	42	96
10-12	1350	3000	54	120

For countertops, you need a width for each diner of 600mm (24in). The minimum depth of the countertop is determined by its height – the higher the top, the less knee room you need underneath. The table below shows the knee spaces required.

Countertop height (mm)	Countertop height (in)	Knee space required (mm)
750	30	450
900	36	375
1050	42	300

Bear in mind that these knee distances are based on an average height of about 1.78m (5ft 10in). If your family are much taller than this then you might want to just sit them at a few tables to figure out how much knee room they need.

The countertop itself needs a minimum depth of 380mm (15in) available in front of each diner.

SINK AREA

You'll need to be able to drop off all your dirty dishes on one side of the sink and stack up all the clean dishes on the other side. So set aside 600mm (24in) on one side and 450mm (18in) on the other – you can include the draining area on your sink, if it has one, in this 450mm (18in).

PREPARATION/WORK AREA

I'm of the opinion that the preparation area should be as big as you can possibly make it. However, where space is short you should always have a continuous work area of at least 900mm (36in) and it should, ideally, have a sink at one end. In our example diagram, you'll note that we've already allocated a space to the sink and it is possible to overlap these two distances, but this rather depends on how quickly you wash-up and put everything back into their cupboards.

TIP *As a general rule, where two areas overlap, take the longest distance and add 300mm (12in). In our example diagram, we have a sink 'stack-area' of 450mm (18in) up against a food preparation area of 900mm (36in). This gives us a combined area of 900 + 300 = 1200mm (36 + 12 = 48in).*

REFRIGERATOR LANDING AREA

Most of us will generally drop off our shopping and put much of it straight into the fridge. We also tend to browse the fridge, taking out a few things at a time. To make these actions easier you should have a worktop area of at least 375mm (15in) on the handle side of the fridge. If this isn't possible, aim to place this drop-off area as close to the fridge as you can. For under-the-counter fridges, the most obvious drop-off area is the worktop directly over the fridge.

AROUND THE COOKER

You'll need to be able to place your ingredients to one side of the cooker ready to throw them into the pan and you'll need an area to set pans down once you've finished. As a general rule, set aside at least 300mm (12in) on one side of the cooker and 375mm (15in) on the other. Again, these can overlap with food preparation areas if they have to. In an island or peninsula, the worktop should extend a minimum of 225mm (9in) behind the cooking surface.

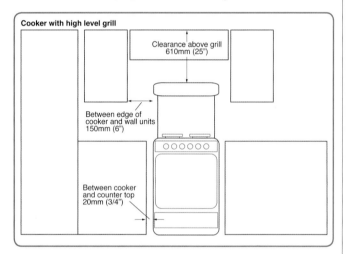

In addition to these ergonomical clearances, you need to consider the safety aspects of the cooker. The cooker hood (extractor) should have minimum distances above the cooker clearly stated by the manufacturer, but if in doubt, 600mm (24in) is a good minimum. The cooker itself will come with a set of minimum distances from combustible materials, i.e. wall units and worktops. It's possible to make these materials non-combustible by putting decorative metal covers between them and the cooker. For example, metal worktop end-strips allow you to place the

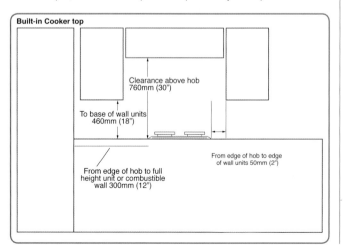

cooker closer to the edge of the worktops without risking a fire.

AROUND THE OVEN

You'll need to put food down that has just come out of the oven or is just about to go in, so set aside at least 375mm (15in) next to or above the oven. If that's not possible, ensure it's within 1200mm (48in) of the oven door. You don't want to be taking hot food across a walkway if at all possible, so plan the drop-down area to avoid this situation.

TOTAL WORKTOP AREA

Obviously, the size of your kitchen is going to be the limiting factor here but, where at all possible, you should aim for a total worktop area of at least 3950mm (158in) long. In addition, the worktop should be about 600mm (24in) deep and have a clearance above it of at least 375mm (15in). Less than this and you'll struggle for room in your kitchen.

CALCULATING KITCHEN STORAGE

There are umpteen ways of calculating the amount of storage you should have in a kitchen and in truth the answer is always 'as much as you can fit in it'. As a general rule, aim to have about a quarter of your storage in wall cabinets, a third of your storage as drawer space and the rest as base unit cupboards.

TIP *Remember that too many wall cabinets can make the kitchen look very small and cramped and they're going to create problems if the main cook is too short to easily reach them.*

The basic way of calculating storage is by 'shelf/drawer frontage'. Personally I'd take these calculations with more than a pinch of salt, but the table below shows an example of the frontage for three different-sized kitchens.

To convert this 'frontage' to actual units you need to calculate the width of the unit by the number of shelves it contains, so a 600mm (24in) wide unit with four shelves in it would have a frontage of 600 x 4 = 2400mm (24 x 4 = 96in).

The easiest way to work with these calculations is to design your kitchen and then check the storage you have against these tables. The end value doesn't have to be exact but it helps if they're within 10% of each other and that the ratio between base, wall and drawer units is about right.

	Wall units	Base units	Drawers	Pantry space	Other	Total
Small kitchen – 14sq m (150sq ft)						
Total frontage (in)	294	441	363	150	42	1290
Total frontage (mm)	7350	11025	9075	3750	1050	32250
Medium kitchen – 14–32sq m (151–350sq ft)						
Total frontage (in)	360	618	399	231	96	1704
Total frontage (mm)	9000	15450	9975	5775	2400	42600
Large kitchen – 33+sq m (351+sq ft)						
Total frontage (in)	345	654	519	294	143	1955
Total frontage (mm)	8625	16350	12975	7350	3575	48875

ADDING TO THE BASIC DESIGN PRINCIPLES

These are the basic principles of kitchen design, but we can use a bit of common sense to fill them out a bit more:

- Often a column attached to the island but coming down from the ceiling can help deliver pipes and cables to the area without having to rip your floor up.
- You can fit a sink into an island, but this requires that the sink waste pipework runs under the floor to the main drain. This can be a very expensive business and can cause all sorts of problems if the waste pipe gets blocked a few years later. It's always better to run all underground pipework in 110mm (4in) pipework, as this will reduce the chances of a blockage. An alternative would be to fit a peninsula or place the food preparation area on the island and place the sink opposite.
- The sink is best placed against an external wall to simplify the waste pipework – the pipe taking away the waste water from the sink is the most likely pipe in your home to get blocked. You don't want to have to dismantle the entire kitchen just to unblock it, so try to keep the distances to the main drain short and easy to get at. People also like to look outside when washing the dishes, so the sink is usually under a window.
- The dishwasher should be situated within 900mm (36in) of the sink and the door should not interfere with any other appliance or cabinet.
- To keep smells and smoke down to a minimum you ought to consider an extraction hood over the cooker. As we've already mentioned, extraction works better than filtering, but an extractor has to terminate outside. With this in mind, a cooker works best up against, or at least close to, an external wall. If this isn't possible, work out how you'd get an extractor to work and, if the answer is 'you can't', then plan for a filter hood from the outset or an extractor fan that will work for the whole kitchen.

TIP *Bear in mind the location of any boiler flue when considering where to terminate your extractor fan.*

Even though it's usually blowing air out of the kitchen, it should still be placed far enough away from the flue to avoid the danger of it allowing boiler fumes back into the house. The boiler flue also takes in fresh air for the boiler here, so fumes from an extractor fan are likely to interfere with the purity of this air.

The manual that came with your boiler should show the minimum distances required based on the type of boiler you have and if the extractor fan terminates alongside, above or below the boiler flue. If you can't find your service manual, many are available online free of charge.

- The refrigerator is the appliance most likely to be used by other people whilst you are cooking. To prevent these people interfering with the cook it's best to place the fridge close to the main entrance to the kitchen, but not so close that the fridge door blocks access to the kitchen when it's open.
- The reason most people head to the fridge is to grab a bottle of milk so they can make themselves a cup of tea or coffee, or to get a snack. Think about these subsidiary activities from the start and make sure the area you set aside for them is close to the entrance to the kitchen, if possible.
- The food preparation area is best placed away from the main kitchen entrance and any walkways. Ideally, it should be between the sink and the cooker and should be equipped with enough plug sockets for all your food preparation gadgets.
- Creating a meal is easier if you can keep an eye on the cooker hob from the preparation area.
- In a galley kitchen, or one in which you're planning an island or peninsula, you need to consider where your appliance and cupboard doors are going to be. Try to avoid siting appliances opposite each other because in a narrow work aisle the odds are you won't be able to have both doors open at the same time. With this in mind, it might be worth paying a little more for sliding doors, bi-fold doors or pocket doors.

 WARNING

Bear in mind that to fit a gas cooker, your kitchen must have a door or openable window direct to the outside for ventilation. This is a regulation in the UK but, since the gas hob is only safe while it can get constant access to fresh air, it makes sense wherever you live. You can get around this by fitting a ventilation system into your kitchen, but you need to check that the system adheres to the gas safety regulations in your area. Avoid placing the cooker under an openable window, as this will affect the heating process and, with gas cookers, can result in the flame being blown out and gas building up in the room.

- It's best to place a microwave fairly close to the main cooker/oven – directly above it works well. The ideal height for a microwave base is 75mm (3in) below the shoulder height of the principle user. As with the main oven and cooker you'll need an area of at least 375mm (15in) next to the microwave for putting things down.
- If there will be multiple cooks, think about separate non-overlapping work zones and wider work aisles.
- Allocate a space for storing cookbooks. Many people now download recipes from the internet, so think about a section in the food preparation area for a laptop or tablet with WiFi access and a charging point.
- If you're incorporating a dining area, think about where you'll place a TV and sound system.
- If you have a pet, think about where you'll store their food, where you'll feed them and, if they are going to be sleeping in the kitchen allocate a space for this.
- Think about the other activities you want to do in the kitchen and if you'll need any storage for non-kitchen-related items.

Creating your design

Are you now starting to feel a little daunted? Well I really can't blame you, so let's have a look at how we can make this easier.

1 If you have an existing kitchen, think about what works and what doesn't and jot these down. The easiest way to get this list together is to add to it as you go about your everyday kitchen routine.

2 Write down all the activities you want your kitchen to cater for and what you'll need to hand to accomplish them. Here are some examples of typical kitchen activities:

- Cooking and preparation
- Baking
- Cleaning up
- Food storage
- Making coffee/tea
- Setting the table
- Entertaining
- Homework
- Breakfast
- Snacks
- Sleeping quarters for the dog.

It helps to place these activities into three groups, something along the lines of: essential, useful, nice-if-we-can. This way, you can make sure the most important activities are best catered for and can make compromises with the less important activities.

For each one of these, put together a list of what each activity will need. For example:

Cooking and preparation
- Preparation area – the bigger the better, and amply equipped with plug sockets
- Sink
- Cooker hob
- Oven
- Microwave
- Kitchen knives
- Chopping boards
- Pots and pans
- Utensils – whisk, fish slice, potato peeler, weighing scales, measuring jugs
- Access to food storage area
- Recipe books – area for laptop/tablet and recharging/USB ports might be handy.

Making coffee/tea
- Water – sink or some other water dispenser
- Cups
- Teaspoons
- Coffee, tea, sugar
- Milk from fridge
- Tray.

The more exhaustive this list is, the better. It's also good to get the entire household involved.

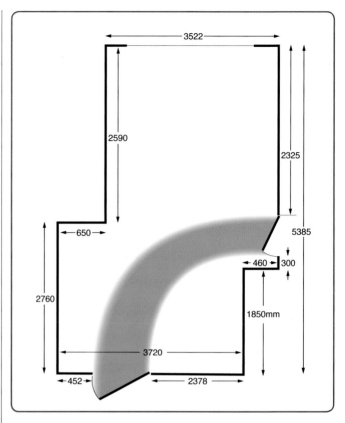

If you write down each activity and its requirements on a separate sheet of paper, you can then arrange them in order of priority and go through them one by one.

3 Now grab the scale plan drawing we made earlier. The first thing to do is mark in any walkways dictated by the doors into and out of the kitchen. These need to be at least 900mm (36in) wide – wider if they're frequently used.

In our earlier example we used a scale of 1:20, which would mean a 900mm (36in) wide walkway would be drawn in as 45mm (1¾in) wide (900 / 20 = 45mm) – if you're using A3, the odds are your scale will be more like 1:15.

TIP *It's possible to do all of this on a computer or online, but it is often far easier to visualise these things when you use an actual piece of paper and bits of drawn-to-scale cardboard. It's also easier for everyone involved to gather around, give their own input and to chop and change things.*

4 We've already gone over the basics of positioning the sink and cooker, namely that they're expensive to move. So the best starting point with a new kitchen is to place the sink and the oven roughly where they currently are – unless you already know why that doesn't really work and are happy to budget in the cost of moving them.

Many kitchen designers start off by placing the sink into position, so let's grab some cardboard and make a rough sink shape. In our example I know I want a twin bowl sink with a built-in draining board, which is usually about 1200mm (48in) wide x 500mm (20in) deep. In our scale drawing (1:20) this would make my cardboard 60 x 25mm (2⅜ x 1in). It pays to be able to see which way around the draining area is going to be in relation to the sink itself.

In our example I have placed the sink against an external wall, away from the walkway and as far away from the main entrance to the kitchen. This is pretty much the optimum place. You might want to add the worktop 'drop-areas' to your sink cut-out.

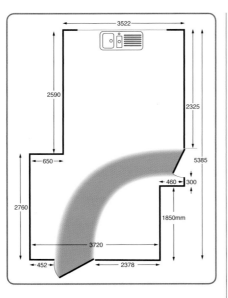

around. Now I have more space between the sink and the cooker and my cooker is against an external wall, so I can have an extractor that is easy to install, but not too close to the door or the boiler flue.

6 Although the kitchen triangle is regarded as out of date, it still makes sense to put the

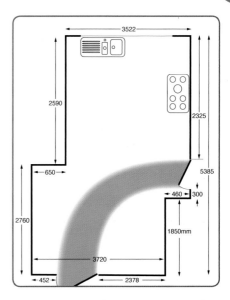

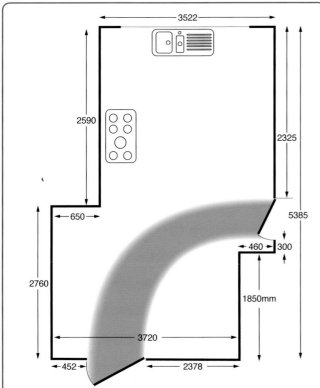

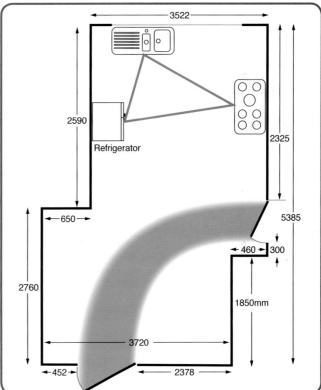

5 Now let's place the cooker. At this stage you're just trying to get a feel for our kitchen work areas, so it's not essential to get sizes exact. That said, if you know what you'd like just find the dimensions and put them in. In my example, I'd ideally want a 1000 x 600mm (40 x 24in) range cooker. So I just cut out a 50 x 30mm (2 x 1¼in) shape and stick it in my plan, where it currently is in my old kitchen.

Putting the cooker and sink back where they were in my old kitchen will save me a fair bit of money and both items are on the same side of my walkway, which is pretty essential. Sadly, what I don't like about my old kitchen is that I don't have much continuous worktop for all my preparations and the cooker is against an internal wall, which makes extraction a bit of a problem. So I could move them

fridge into your plan in this position at this stage. It should also be closer to the door, but not on the other side of the walkway from the sink and cooker. For now, let's put it almost opposite the cooker.

7 At this stage, we could really do with finding out if certain ideas are feasible. The main ones to consider at this stage are:

- Can we fit an island?
- Can we have a dining table?
- What about a breakfast bar?

Have a look at the tables on page 25 and use them to make a scale model of your table or breakfast bar based on the number

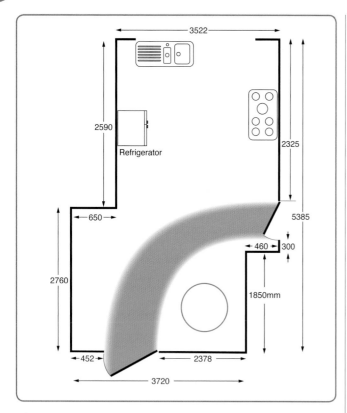

and different shapes, but it's unlikely that this kitchen will be able to accommodate any dining table that will seat more than two people. This might be a shame, but it's a godsend that we've worked it out this early in the project.

8 Add the rest of your large fixed appliances. The dishwasher needs to be near to the sink for convenience and ease of fitting. The microwave oven is often best near the main cooker.

9 You should now have a basic layout that you think will work. Dispense with bits of cardboard and actually draw the main appliances and any islands or dining areas onto your plan, together with the general worktop area you envisage.

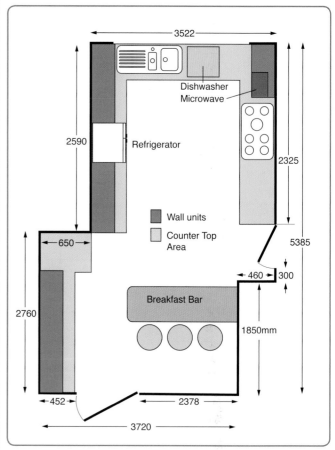

of people you envisage using them at any one time and see if you have the necessary clearances.

In our example, we can fit a round table with a diameter of 1000mm (40in) in our kitchen, but the moment we apply an 800mm (32in) clearance around it we can see that we haven't got nearly enough room. We could play around with smaller tables

10 You now have all the basics in place, so at this stage it makes sense to take your design to a kitchen showroom. They can use this to draw up a 3D image of this layout and fill it with the wall and base units that they supply. This will usually result in them moving your appliances a little to accommodate their standard-sized base cabinets.

11 If you discuss your main work zones with the designer at this stage, you should be able to work out between you a rough idea of the number of base cupboards and drawers and the number of wall cabinets you'll want.

Once you have these, you can think about how to accommodate all your work zones and allocate a function to the cabinets and make sure you have the right type in place – cupboard or drawer space, or a combination of the two. For

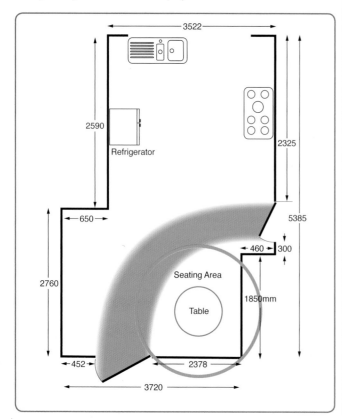

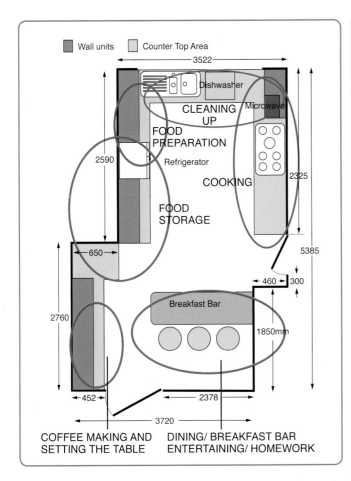

■ Wall units	□ Counter Top Area

3522

Dishwasher
Microwave

CLEANING
UP

FOOD
PREPARATION

2590

Refrigerator

COOKING

2325

FOOD
STORAGE

650

5385

460   300

Breakfast Bar

2760

1850mm

452   2378

3720

COFFEE MAKING AND   DINING/ BREAKFAST BAR
SETTING THE TABLE   ENTERTAINING/ HOMEWORK

example, near the kitchen door I want a worktop area upon which I'll put my kettle, tea, coffee and sugar pots; a cupboard with shelves for cups; and a drawer for cutlery. I also want my 'setting the table' zone here so I'll need more shelves and cupboards for my plates and cutlery. We can use our plan view to get a general feel for the entire kitchen work zones, but an elevation plan, which the retailers ought to have supplied by now, will allow us to check the cabinet layout for our work activities.

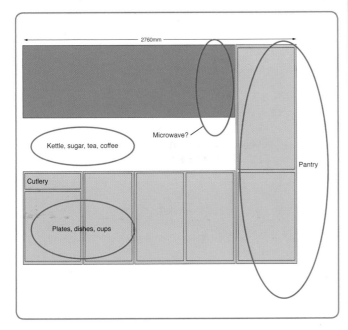

2760mm

Microwave?

Kettle, sugar, tea, coffee

Cutlery

Pantry

Plates, dishes, cups

This is the stage when ideals start to leave the room and we come down to compromise. For example, can you actually buy base units that will fit inside your 'coffee making' area, bearing in mind it's a maximum of 450mm deep? I'd love a second small sink or water fountain near the coffee area so people don't have to wander right into the kitchen to fill the kettle, but I might have to settle for a fridge that delivers water or a longer walk to the main sink. The staging area to the right of my cooker is too small, but is that better than none at all, or should I move the cooker to maximise the space to the left of it?

The kitchen retailer should be able to help you out with these final details and the end result should be a plan that accommodates most of what you wanted at a fixed price.

USING KITCHEN PLANNERS

To find an online kitchen planner, just type 'kitchen planner' into your search engine of choice. Most of these planners fall into two brackets: those that actually let you design a kitchen based on your room size and the units you want, and those that just give you an idea as to how a particular range will look in combination with different wall/floor styles and colours. The latter have the advantage of being easy to use and give you a real feel for what colour combinations are going to work. However, to actually plan a kitchen you'll need something that will allow you to enter the exact size and shape of your room and place the units and appliances of your choice into that room. There's no shortage of these planners available online, but as a general rule, the more functionality and flexibility they offer, the longer they'll take to learn.

Most of the big kitchen retailers have planners with enough functionality for most people, but they often only let you plan a kitchen based on the appliances and units they supply. The upside of this is that you often get to see what your finished kitchen will look like and exactly how much it will cost. The downside is that it's difficult to just create a generic design and then take that around to all high-street retailers. There are a few generic planners that aren't linked to specific manufacturers and a good example is http://www.easyplanner3d.com.

⚠ WARNING

Don't just rush off and buy a new kitchen at this point! There are a number of things you need to be sure about before you part with your money, so read the rest of the manual, make notes, go and see the kitchens you like and make sure there are no installation surprises lying in wait for you.

2 GETTING STARTED

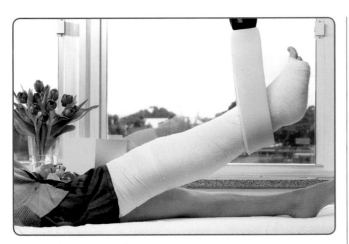

Safety first

COMMON INJURIES

Installing a new kitchen or renovating an old one isn't that physically taxing. Possibly because of this, people tend to just rush in and somtimes injure themselves as a result. The most common injuries are tennis elbow, a slipped disc or a nasty cut. Fortunately, it is quite simple to avoid all of these; all that is needed is a modicum of common sense, some relatively cheap safety equipment and some decent power tools.

TENNIS ELBOW

Tennis elbow (*lateral epicondylitis*) is an intense pain in the outside of your elbow that is caused by repetitive flexing of the wrist. Tennis will do this quite nicely, but you can develop it more quickly and cheaply by simply using a screwdriver all day, especially if it's the first screwdriver you have picked up for many a year! In the old days there wasn't much you could do about this, other than just staying aware and not overdoing things, but with the advent of the electric screwdriver (see 'The basic tools you'll need' on page38), all excuses for developing this condition – other than playing a lot of tennis – evaporated.

It's not just the immediate pain that ought to be enough to put any sane person off the condition for life; it's the frequency with which it returns once it's got a hold on you that can be the most frustrating. Once you've got it almost any activity can bring back the pain and, while anti-inflammatory drugs can help, the only genuine cure is a good long rest.

SLIPPED DISC

There are a number of heavy and awkward things to lift and move when putting together a kitchen and most of them are that most dangerous weight; not too heavy to put you off the idea of lifting them, but too heavy to

guarantee that you won't dearly regret it afterwards.

The most useful tool in your armoury when it comes to avoiding a back problem is your brain, so use it; if it looks and feels a little too heavy, it really is. Get a friend to help, or use a hand or dolly trolley to move it.

If you are going to be lifting, do it properly:

1 Set your feet about a shoulder width apart, with one foot slightly ahead of the other. The idea here is to just make sure you're stable before you attempt to lift anything; slipping or falling while carrying a heavy load is pretty much guaranteed to result in injury.
2 Squat down, keeping your back straight. You might find it more comfortable to put one knee on the floor, while the other knee is in front of you, bent at a right angle.
3 Try to lift the load without using your back. You need to keep your back straight; it's best to puff your chest out, bring your shoulders back and look straight ahead.

4 Get as close as you can to the object you're going to lift, and start the lift by straightening your hips and legs. Keep the object close to you, roughly at stomach level.
5 Whatever you do, don't twist your back. If you need to turn do so by taking small steps, while keeping your back straight.
6 To lower the load keep your back straight and bend your knees and hips.

NOTE *It's not always possible to lift a load like this – there might not be enough room, the load might be awkward or you might need to lean over it to get a good grip. If this is the case, stop what you're doing, make room and ask a friend to help. Now make the lift with both of you adhering to the steps shown above.*

CUTS

Aside from being careful, not rushing things and stopping when you feel tired, there's not much you can do about cuts. Fitting a kitchen involves jigsaws, saws, routers and many other sharp instruments. As a general rule, people recognise these for the obvious dangers they pose, and then go on to badly cut themselves handling steel sinks or sweeping up broken tiles – both of which can have razor-sharp edges.

You can minimise the chance of getting cuts by wearing gloves, but they make handling things far more awkward. My compromise is to use fingerless or partially fingerless gloves.

SAFETY EQUIPMENT

If you're going to undertake any DIY projects, you are best off purchasing all the items listed below. Most of them are cheap and readily available in DIY stores.

KNEE PROTECTION

The most comfortable way to keep your knees in good shape is to wear work trousers that have little pockets over the knees, into which you can insert foam kneepads. The trousers themselves are useful because they normally come with a wide variety of pockets and

straps for your tools and they're robust enough to survive the day-to-day rigours of DIY.

There are two basic types of work trousers: ones where the kneepads are pushed up into the pockets, and ones where the pads are pushed down into the knee pockets. I prefer the latter because the pads tend to stay in place better.

The downside of work trousers with kneepad pockets is that

they can be quite pricey. A cheaper alternative is strap-on kneepads, which will work with any trousers, including shorts. The downside to these is that the straps tend to dig into the back of your knees and they can get quite uncomfortable after a while.

A more comfortable alternative is the knee cushion, but these come with an obvious disadvantage; namely that you have to lug them around with you and, inevitably, they will not always be where your knees are.

EYE PROTECTION

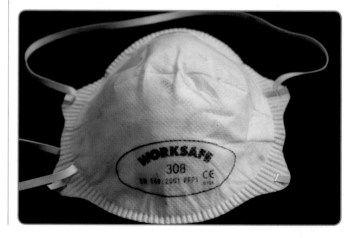

Getting sawdust into your eyes is very painful and can occasionally involve a trip to A&E. Most DIY stores sell PPE (Personal Protective Equipment) packs, which consist of a set of goggles, a dust mask and a pair of ear defenders.

Goggles are the best protection as they enclose the eye completely. Ordinary safety glasses are less prone to fogging but aren't as good at keeping dust out of your eyes. The downside of goggles is that they are very prone to fogging up; seemingly regardless of how many air vents they come with! To reduce the chances of your goggles fogging up:

■ Rub a bit of saliva around the inside of your goggles.
■ Smear baby shampoo or liquid detergent over the inside and outside of your goggles. Leave for a few minutes to dry and then polish them up.
■ Pop over to a motorcycle shop and buy a visor demister product.

DUST PROTECTION

Simple disposable dust masks are all that you generally require for keeping the dust from kitchen fitting at bay. You can buy slightly more expensive versions with disposable cartridges in them but you shouldn't need anything too fancy.

NOTE: *Ordinary dust masks will not protect you from asbestos, so have a read of the section opposite just to make sure you recognise asbestos if you come across it.*

Be aware that some wood dusts – oak and beech, for example – are very nasty. If you are using these woods, it's essential that you wear a good dust mask.

EAR PROTECTION

Aside from hammer drills and mechanical saws, there isn't a lot of noise associated with working on a kitchen. That said, tinnitus is a very annoying condition, so it makes sense to wear ear defenders.

GLOVES

Gloves are always a good idea, but it can be difficult to work with them on your hands. A compromise is fingerless gloves – yes, your fingertips might still get cut, but you can work much easier with them on and they will protect the rest of your hand.

WORKBENCHES

From a safety point of view workbenches keep things nice and secure, reducing the risk of injuring yourself. They also provide a nice workspace at a good height for your back.

ASBESTOS

Depending on the age of your home there is a risk that you might come up against asbestos. In its day, this was regarded as a wonder material; it was a good heat and sound insulator, and it was fireproof. As a result it was used a lot, right up to the point they discovered that it was also deadly, which rather dampened everyone's enthusiasm.

In the home you're most likely to come across crocidolite, more commonly known as white asbestos. This is the least dangerous form of asbestos, but should still be treated with the utmost caution. Asbestos concrete was used to make corrugated roofing tiles, guttering, downpipes, water tanks, toilet cisterns, windowsills and boiler flues; sheets of asbestos concrete were often used to line boiler rooms and gas meter housings. You can have asbestos ceiling tiles and asbestos in vinyl floor tiles. Even old paint can contain asbestos, especially some decorative textured ceiling finishes – Artex, for example.

Because asbestos was so pervasive for so many years, it makes sense to familiarise yourself with asbestos products before you undertake any DIY in the home. The UK HSE (Health & Safety Executive) has a gallery of asbestos products and their website is well worth a read: http://www.hse.gov.uk/asbestos/gallery.htm

By now, you may be wondering how anyone born in the 1960s and 1970s made it out of the house alive. Well, fortunately most white asbestos products are relatively safe, as long as they remain in good condition. An exception to this rule is asbestos lagging. If you discover any pipework covered in a fairly hard, white fibrous-looking material do not touch it and get it looked at by an expert as soon as possible.

For the rest, the best advice – if it's in good condition – is to just leave it well alone. If it can't be left alone or if it looks like it's deteriorating get an expert in to test it and remove it if necessary. Whatever you do, don't try and remove asbestos yourself. Always remember that ordinary dust masks will provide little or no protection and that mesothelioma is a particularly unpleasant way to depart from this world.

Courtesy of the Asbestos WatchDog

What can we do for ourselves?

By 'cannot undertake for yourself' what I really mean is that there are either laws where you live stating that you must hold particular qualifications and licences to undertake certain work; or that this work is so complex and the potential for making a mess is so large that, if you aren't qualified, you'd be a fool to give it a go. As you might imagine, there is a huge overlap between these two distinctions.

FITTING KITCHEN UNITS

This is an area that is eminently 'doable' by the average vaguely fit, vaguely sensible homeowner. That isn't to say that is doesn't require some skill but, for the most part, they are skills readily acquired.

There are of course caveats to the above statement. For example, if you spend £20,000 on new kitchen units and then decide to fit them yourself I'd have to admire your bravado. If you've fitted a number of kitchens before that's OK, but if you haven't, you might be about to make some very expensive mistakes. Yes, this book should help you to avoid most – if not all – of these, but it only takes one slip.

Another reason to stop and question if you really ought to be doing this for yourself are the materials you have opted for – laminate worktops are fairly easy to work with and relatively cheap to replace if you make a mistake; granite worktops require specialised tools and can cost a fortune.

TILING AND OTHER WALL AND FLOOR COVERINGS

These areas really are the icing on the proverbial cake: get it right and your kitchen will look wonderful; get it wrong and they're the only thing that anyone will notice. So, having put you off the idea, let's try to summon up some enthusiasm! Firstly, tiling is quite easy to learn and not that difficult to get right – we will be going through the art of tiling later. Secondly, you don't have to tile at all – there are all sorts of alternatives that look great and are often much easier to undertake for yourself.

PLASTERING

I've tried my hand at plastering and, if the area is small enough and not somewhere where it's always going to be seen, I have no problem with giving it a go. However, even if you complete a course you'll still need to practise a lot to get good at it and I'm still of the opinion that good plastering is more art than labour – in other words you either have it in you or you don't. So personally, I'd shy away from doing the actual plastering.

That said, you could still save money by doing all the preparation work yourself, such as fitting and taping new plasterboard ready for plastering, which we'll be covering later.

PLUMBING

The sort of general plumbing work you come up against in the kitchen is relatively straightforward and well within the capabilities of the

average DIY enthusiast. Plastic pipework and fittings make things even easier, but they do come with one problem; rodents tend to view plastic fittings in much the same way as I view cookie dough ice cream. So, if you think you

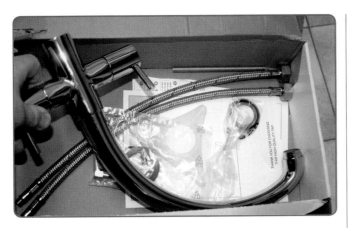

might have a rodent problem, you either need to eradicate the problem and ensure they can't get back in again, or you need to opt for copper pipework and fittings. If the idea of soldering fills you with fear, go for compression fittings or metal push-fit, such as Tectite.

ELECTRICS AND LIGHTING

Now we move away from the world of DIY and into those areas where you really ought to think about bringing in a professional. It's not that electrical work is particularly difficult, but you need knowledge to do it right and it has to be tested properly in order for it to be safe.

On a brighter note, it's possible to 'first fix' the electrical work yourself, which involves fitting the back boxes for the electric sockets into place, making all the holes in the ceiling for the lights, channelling out the walls and running all the cabling into position. The advantage of this is that you get to save a bit of money, you put everything exactly where you want it and you're not waiting for an electrician to turn up before you can carry on with your kitchen fitting. However, I wouldn't do this until you have an agreement in place for an electrician to finish off the job, test it all and issue whatever certificates are required.

If you're thinking about doing the electrical work yourself then I'd advise the following:

- Find out what, if any, regulations apply where you live.
  - In England and Wales, look here: http://www.planningportal. gov.uk/permission/commonprojects/electrics/.
  - In Scotland, try here: http://www.electricalsafetyfirst.org.uk/ guides-and-advice/building-regulations/scotland/.

- In Northern Ireland there are currently no statutory regulations, but this may change. Try here for the latest information: http://www.electricalsafetyfirst.org.uk/guides-and-advice/building-regulations/northern-ireland/.
- Some work may need to be checked by your local building controller. If you're in doubt, assume building control needs to be informed. Notify them before you start work, even if it's only to find out how much an inspection costs – it may work out cheaper to get a qualified electrician in instead.
- Steer clear of working on the electrics for an electric cooker for two reasons. Firstly, they draw an awful lot of electricity so they must be wired back directly to the main consumer unit. Secondly, because of the first point, they are a serious fire hazard if not wired and tested correctly.
- Most kitchen appliances draw a lot of electricity, so avoid having 'spurs' and run all your electric sockets directly off the ring main.
- Most regions will have some regulation or guideline with regards to how close an electrical socket can be to a kitchen sink – in the UK the guideline is 300mm (12in) from the socket to the edge of the sink. Find out what this is where you live. If you can't find anything, work on the idea that getting an electric socket wet is never a good idea and an electric appliance falling into the sink is even worse, so go for 300mm (12in) or more.
- Downlights can be a fire hazard if they are covered in insulation or anything else that is either combustible or restricts the movement of air around the light fitting. LED lights get around most of this danger by not generating much heat, but if you use halogen lighting make sure you are not fitting the light too close to anything combustible and/or use fire-rated lights.
- When it comes to selling your home many countries require a whole host of certificates to show that work has been carried out properly and that the property is safe. Electrical work is invariably included, so check if you'll need to get these.

GAS

Some countries don't have any regulations with regards to gas work. However, not having a law doesn't make natural gas or LPG any safer to deal with and it is safety, not difficulty that we're talking about here. For the most part, the gas work required in a kitchen is minimal and the cost of getting it done properly is far, far less than the cost of doing it yourself and making just one tiny error.

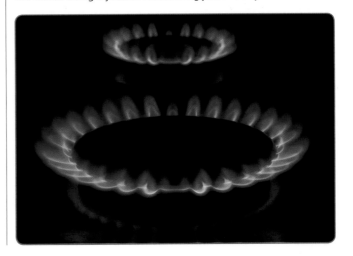

The basic tools you'll need

The great thing about taking on a kitchen project yourself is that the tools you need are pretty much the basic tools you need to hand for all DIY work. OK, there are a few oddities that are specific to kitchens, but very few. To keep them in good condition, always check that the tool comes in a good carry case that has enough room for the add-ons – drills, bits, jigsaw blades, etc.

LEVEL

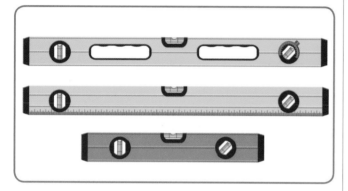

Laser levels are relatively cheap and are available in most DIY stores. They're brilliant for the initial surveying of a room and getting perfectly level marks along the entire length of a wall, but less effective when it comes to actually checking the level of kitchen units. If you're going to buy one, aim for something that is self-levelling and that throws a laser light both horizontally and vertically.

If you really want to push the boat out, you can get laser levels that can be set up on a tripod in the middle of the room and that throw a laser beam right around the room. This is handy for very large kitchens, but they can be expensive and unless you are going to take up surveying or tiling, the price might be difficult to justify – although you can usually hire them.

Even if you do buy a laser level you're also going to need at least one traditional level, ideally two; a good long one – at least a metre in length – for checking your units are level, and a short one – a 'boat level' – for the more fiddly areas where a laser is useless and a long level is just too long. With this in mind, you can buy level packs with all the different lengths you'll need. Bear in mind that levels are more accurate the longer they are so, where you can, always use the longer level.

TAPE MEASURE

If you get someone to pop over to measure up your kitchen there is a good chance they will arrive bearing a laser measure in their hand. These used to be very expensive but are far more affordable these days. Like laser levels, they are great for measuring long distances when initially surveying a room, for example, but the traditional tape measure is still easier to use for the day-to-day stuff.

CRAFT/UTILITY KNIFE

Another stalwart of basic DIY. You might not need to use one of these for the actual fitting of a kitchen but they are pretty indispensible for opening up all the packaging and for sharpening your pencils in a manly fashion!

BRADAWL/CARPENTER'S AWL

This is basically a spike with a handle. They are very handy in general woodwork, but particularly useful when dealing with laminated products.

You just push the spike through the laminate, give it a little twist and – hey presto! – you can screw into the laminate with ease. They are also handy for marking your drill holes.

2B PENCIL OR MARKER PEN

Another DIY essential that costs little or nothing. A standard HB pencil will work, but the lead is a little too hard so it's worth going to a DIY store or

craft shop and getting a softer pencil. Marker pens leave a more visible line, but you need to make sure they are not permanent markers. It's best to test whiteboard markers before using them, as some can leave a stain on many surfaces that is difficult to remove afterwards.

SCREWDRIVERS

As we've already mentioned, you can't fit a kitchen without screwing things together and you can't use a screwdriver all day without running the very real risk of developing tennis elbow. With this in mind I'd strongly recommend you buy an electric screwdriver.

ELECTRIC SCREWDRIVER

With a kitchen you will be spending most of your time driving in fairly small screws, so you're usually best off going for something

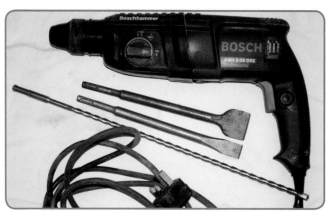

fairly small and cordless that you can get into awkward places with. Ideally, get one that has variable speed and torque control and just feels comfortable in your hand.

IMPACT DRIVER

When you're putting kitchen units together, a small and controllable screwdriver is best. However, when you're hanging wall units or fixing batons you might find yourself needing something with a bit more 'oomph'. An impact driver is ideal for this kind of work, firing a large screw into hard wood with few, if any, problems. They are also very handy for taking out large or damaged screws. The downside is that they're generally too powerful for everything else and I wouldn't really recommend them for general kitchen fitting.

> # TIP
> *Manufacturers are delighted when you buy their entire range of tools. When it comes to cordless tools they encourage this loyalty by making the batteries interchangeable across their range and allowing you to buy the tools without any batteries. If you're going to buy a number of cordless tools this can save you a lot of money, so it's always worth making a list of all the tools you need and seeing what deal is available if you buy them from a single manufacturer.*

HAND SCREWDRIVER

There are always going to be times when you need an ordinary, old-fashioned screwdriver. It's generally cheaper to just buy a set of them, or at least go for those manual screwdrivers that can reach the places your electric one can't; namely a few 'stubby' screwdrivers – ones with very short shafts – and a few extra-long screwdrivers.

DRILLS

Again, it's difficult to take on any DIY project without having a drill to hand, so it makes sense to buy a good one. Personally, I always have a powerful corded hammer drill available, as well as a smaller cordless drill. The cordless drills are easier to use, but it always pays to have something more powerful in reserve.

CORDED SDS HAMMER DRILLS

Drills that come with an electric cord and have to be plugged in are usually cheaper and more powerful than cordless drills. If you're buying a corded drill, I'd advise the following spec:

- Get an SDS (Special Direct System) drill. Not only are the drills themselves more powerful, but the drill bits are usually far more heavy duty.
- Make sure it has hammer action – also called 'rotary hammer action'.
- Most good drills with hammer action will also have 'no rotation mode' (also called 'chisel action'). This is useful for channelling out walls to accept pipework and cables.
- If you already have a cordless drill then you'll only really need this one for the heavy-duty stuff. With this in mind go for something about 800W that is rated in the 2kg hammer class.

CORDLESS HAMMER DRILL

If you have a good, powerful, corded SDS drill then you don't need to go over the top with your cordless drill, which is just as well as powerful cordless drills can cost a small fortune! That said, the more powerful the cordless drill the less often you'll have to drag a big, awkward corded drill around.

The following spec should ensure that your cordless hammer drill can cope:

■ The voltage rating of the drill is effectively a measure of how powerful it is. An 18v drill is ideal for general DIY, but you could get away with 12v for kitchen fitting.
■ Smaller drills will have smaller chucks. For general DIY this only becomes an issue when you want to use the drill with a holesaw (see the section on 'Holesaws and augers' on page 50) as most of these require a chuck that can accommodate a 13mm (½in) bit. If you want to fit a kitchen, the odds are you will need to use a holesaw, so make sure your cordless drill chuck capacity goes up to at least 13mm.
■ Torque control allows you to, in effect, adjust the power of the drill. Kitchen fitting often requires a fair bit of delicacy so torque control is handy. Most drills with torque control also have a screwdriver mode, which can be useful as a backup if nothing else. The more torque your drill has, the more jobs it can cope with. A maximum torque of 55Nm should be more than adequate, but you will get away with far less than this for kitchen fitting.
■ Speed control also allows for a more delicate approach. Some drills come with only one speed, others have a high and low, while the better drills let you control the speed with the trigger. The more control you have the better.
■ Hammer action is essential if you don't want to have to drag your corded drill out of its box every five minutes.
■ The type and power of the batteries determines how long you'll be able to work before changing them. They also tend to be the most expensive part of the drill, so you can save a fortune by just downgrading your battery requirements. The two most common types of battery are Li-ion (lithium ion) and Ni-Cad (nickel cadmium). If you are a professional kitchen fitter then you'll want a Li-ion battery as they last longer, weigh less and charge faster. Alas, you'll pay a lot for this. For most DIY work you should be fine with a Ni-Cad battery – just make sure your drill comes with two of them so one can be on charge while you use the other.

TIP *If you are using a Ni-Cad battery you'll notice the battery running down because the drill, or whatever you're using, will get slower and slower and then, after a few minutes, stop altogether. With a Li-Ion battery you don't really get this notice; one second they are running at full power, you get a second or two when it seems a little slower, and then… nothing! No power whatsoever! This can leave your drill firmly stuck in the wall you're drilling into until you've changed the batteries.*

JIGSAW

Again, this is a tool that is used a lot in general DIY and as such it makes sense to buy as good a quality jigsaw as you can afford. That said, there's no need to go over the top if you're only going to be using it a few times a year.

■ In terms of power, 550W should be more than enough for what we're going to need.
■ Go for something fairly small; you're better off sacrificing power for manoeuvrability.

■ The price difference between corded and cordless jigsaws is big – really big. For occasional DIY use I'd opt for corded and make sure that it has all the other features listed below, rather than blowing all your money just on the fact that it's cordless. Cordless jigsaws can be quite bulky, which can be a problem, but on the other hand you're far less likely to saw your way through the electric cord.
■ Variable speed allows you more control of the saw, especially if it's part of the trigger – the more you pull back on the trigger the faster the blade will go.
■ The accuracy with which you can use a jigsaw is helped if it comes with a laser light or at least some sort of illumination on the cutting line.
■ Jigsaw blades come in two types: T-blades (also known as Bayonet) and U-blades. Bosch originally designed T-blades and as such they are popular in Europe. The U-blade was originally used with Black & Decker jigsaws and is far more popular in the USA. Which one you opt for should be based on how readily you can get your hands on the blades, but bear in mind that the T shape is more universal and that most jigsaws can accept a T-blade.
■ Replacing blades can be a tedious process on some jigsaws, requiring a screwdriver. I'd always advise buying a jigsaw with a quick-release mechanism, which invariably means opting for a T-blade jigsaw.
■ The foot, or base plate, of the jigsaw should allow an angle change, but since you'll rarely need this it doesn't really matter how this is achieved.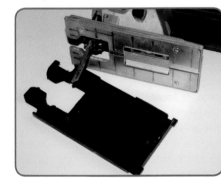

- When fitting kitchens you'll often be using the jigsaw on the top of finished wood surfaces. The last thing you want to do is to scratch or otherwise mark these surfaces, so it pays to have a jigsaw with a smooth, plastic overshoe. If you can't get one of these, remember to either apply masking tape to the base of your jigsaw before use, or ensure that the area you'll be cutting on is protected with masking tape.
- Jigsaws kick up a lot of dust and since you'll be using it indoors it makes sense to buy one with a dust extraction system.

TIP *In Europe, the power of a tool is generally denoted in watts, but you may still come across 'horsepower' – car engines, for example, still stubbornly refuse to be measured in watts. If you do come across horsepower just bear in mind that 1 horsepower (hp) = 746 watts (W) and that 1000 watts is 1 kilowatt (kW).*

JIGSAW BLADES

It's usually cheaper to buy a variety pack of blades and these will cover most of your needs. Be aware, though, that cheap blades are far more likely to bend and flex, which can cause real problems, so don't go too cheap. The following 'specialist' blades are useful when working on kitchens:

Down-stroke laminate blade
These come with lots of relatively small teeth but, most importantly, the teeth are designed to cut on the down-stroke – most jigsaw

blades will cut on the up-stroke. This is important when working with laminates as the normal 'up-stroke' blades will lift, and therefore splinter the laminate surface. The danger of down-stroke blades is that they cause the jigsaw to 'bounce' up, so you need to make sure you are pressing down firmly on your jigsaw when you are using them.

Scroll/tight curve blades
General jigsaw blades are wide enough to make cutting a straight line relatively easy. However, there are times when you need to make a tight curve and for these you'll need these thinner

blades. Note that they, like most blades, are upward cutting, so if you have to use them on laminate make sure that the surface you don't mind splintering is at the top and the finished surface is underneath.

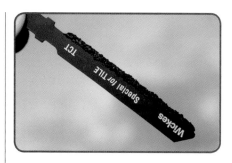

Tile blades
These are ideal for cutting out square holes to fit around plug sockets. They work fine with softer, thinner wall tiles, but don't even think about using these on floor tiles or anything made from porcelain. See the section on page 162 for alternatives.

SAW
Yet another mainstay of general DIY, it's hard to imagine any work involving wood for which a saw isn't going to become essential at some point.

RIP SAW
The classic rip saw (often just called a hand saw) is cheap and – when you're mainly working with soft woods, which we usually are – isn't overly taxing to use. I'd advise buying mid-range.

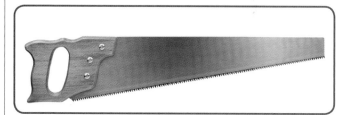

RECIPROCATING SAW
These have two advantages: firstly, they take little energy to use; and secondly, you can buy just one saw and purchase a variety of specialist blades for each specific task. They can be bought cordless and, as usual, it's weighing up the cost of cordless versus the convenience.

The downside of these saws is the cost of the blades and the speed at which you go through them. They also seem to be priced the same as laser printers, namely, the cheaper the saw, the more expensive the blades.

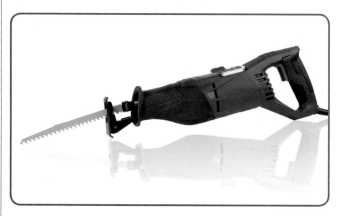

With kitchens, you're rarely going to be cutting through anything particularly thick or hard so a smaller saw that can get into tighter spaces is probably more valuable than a great big powerful thing.

Other things to look out for are quick blade change options; variable speed, which always results in more control, and stroke length – the longer the stroke length, the longer the blades will last.

TENON SAW

These have finer teeth and a strengthened blade that doesn't flex. As a result they're much better for fine work. Reciprocating saws are great for the tougher jobs, but for finer work I find it easier to do things by hand.

As with rip saws, the price reflects the quality of the handle and how long the teeth with remain sharp, so try to avoid the really cheap ones.

MITRE SAW

Hand mitre saws are cheap and easy to use for the kind of work you're most likely to come across in the kitchen. Powered mitre saws are better for bigger work, far less physically taxing and often offer a lot more flexibility. If you go for a powered mitre saw, keep an eye out for the following:

■ Check the size of the blades the saw will accept – 254mm (10in) is average – and the price and availability of replacement blades. The bigger the blade diameter, the thicker the wood it will cope with and the more versatile it will be as a result.
■ Test the ease of use and the accuracy of the mitre angle and check that the blade can move both left and right.
■ Saws that allow the blade to also slide forward and back cost a bit more, but make the tool so much more flexible that it's well worth the extra cost.
■ Check that the blade can also be set at an angle (bevel) and how easy and accurate the angle setting is.
■ A laser light on the cut line is really handy, as is dust extraction.

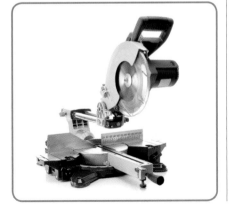

MULTITOOL (FEIN SAW)

As the name would suggest, you can buy a range of blades for the multitool (also called a Fein saw, a multi-cutter or an oscillating multitool) that allow you to cut, grind, sand, scrape and much more. While they aren't much good if you have a lot of cutting, sanding, etc., they are very good for detail work and are excellent for getting into places that most tools just can't get to.

Remember that their versatility is determined by what blades are available, so either buy a well-known brand or buy something that can use the tools from a well-known brand. As with pretty much every tool these days, there is the option of corded or cordless and the main issue is cost versus convenience.

The multitool is most useful in hard-to-get-to places, so avoid anything too big and bulky. On the other hand, you need something fairly powerful just to ensure that it survives the rigours of general DIY.

ROUTER AND TEMPLATE

Routers are used to create fine, intricate edges on wood, to cut out shapes, to create decorative grooves, for wondrous wood engraving and all sorts of other spectacular things. From a kitchen perspective, they are used to create almost invisible joints in worktops and to make decorative finishes to cabinet doors.

■ There are two main types of router: plunge and fixed. In a plunge router the main motor and bit can be moved up and down quickly and easily, allowing you to change the cut depth and create a neat hole or design in the middle of a piece of wood. In a fixed router the depth of the bit is set at the beginning and that is it until you stop what you're doing and change it again.

A plunge router is only essential if you are going to be making holes in the middle of a piece of wood. If you're planning on making nice edges or cutouts from an edge, then you don't really need the plunge feature. That said, you get a neater, cleaner cut if you go through wood in stages, and to quickly and easily adjust your cutting depth you'll want a plunge router. In general kitchen fitting, the only time that you'll use a router is for making mitred corners in worktops and it's easier to do this with a plunge router. On the other hand, a fixed router (also called a hand router or trimmer) is far less bulky, easier to handle and often cheaper.

■ If you do opt for a plunge router, check how deep the plunge is – go for at least 55mm (2¼in). Also, check how smoothly the mechanism works and make sure you can operate the mechanism when you're holding the router handles.

Bear in mind that some manufacturers make routers where the plunge mechanism is a separate part and can be quickly removed, turning your plunge router into a fixed router within minutes.

■ The whole point of using a router is to get a very neat, clean and precise cut, but you only get this if the bit is spinning very quickly and steadily throughout the cut. As a result, the power of the router is important and often dictates the price. For most kitchen work you'll be routing soft woods and laminated chipboard and these will usually be less than 50mm (2in) thick. As a result it's not essential that you get a 2.5kW beast, but you really shouldn't go below 1500W.

■ Linked to power is the rpm (rotations per minute). It's good to have variable speed and it's especially good if the router slowly comes up to max speed. On the more expensive routers the motor will vary its output so as to maintain the rpm.

■ The bits fit into the router via the 'collet'. There are two main sizes: ¼in (6.35mm) and ½in (12.7mm), and you really ought to go for the ½in (12.7mm) version. You can put smaller bits into the larger collet, but not the other way around.

■ Routers can quickly generate a spectacular amount of dust, so it pays to buy one with a good dust extraction system.

■ If you're going to cut your own kitchen worktops, you'll need a kitchen worktop router template to go with your router.

TIP *It often makes sense to hire a high-quality tool just for the few days you'll need it. Not only do you get cheaper access to a tool that really is up to the job, but you also get a chance to 'test drive' a tool before deciding what to buy. Make sure you hire it for long enough to spend some time getting used to it.*

CLAMPS

Many clamps come with soft rubber grips. These help prevent

damage but also allow a little movement, which can be a problem. Metal clamps need a bit of wood between themselves and the finished surface to prevent damage, but tend to create a much firmer, immobile grip.

CLAW HAMMER/RUBBER MALLET

Few projects are completed without reaching for a claw hammer at some point. In kitchen fitting, a rubber mallet also comes in handy.

STUD DETECTOR

Most stud detectors will find any hidden studs, cables or pipes, which means that they are detecting electrical current, wood and metal – magnetic and non-magnetic. The price of these detectors varies enormously – they tend to detect more things with greater accuracy as the price rises.

Realistically, you shouldn't screw a screw or hammer a nail without first checking for pipework and cables in your target area, and as such it makes sense to buy a decent detector. If you really want to push the boat out you could purchase a scanner, which shows the location of all the cables, etc. on a little screen, allowing you to quickly mark up the location of all danger points before you start hammering in nails.

Bear in mind that these detectors aren't 100% accurate, so you should still use care and common sense even if your detector has said that there is nothing to worry about.

TIP *If you haven't got a detector, you can just use a good old-fashioned magnet to detect the metal studs used to build stud walls.*

CARTRIDGE GUN

Most glues, sealants and caulks now come in plastic cartridges, so at some point the DIY enthusiast is going to need a cartridge gun. Because they are so useful you ought to avoid buying the cheapest you can find. The very cheap ones also have a nasty habit of discharging sealant, etc. even when the trigger has been released, which is both annoying and potentially damaging to your home.

A brief guide to walls and wall plugs

To put a kitchen together you're going to have to drill holes and use screws. How you go about this is going to be determined by the materials you're up against. Most of the time this is quite obvious, but when it comes to walls things can get a little trickier.

KNOW YOUR WALLS

How the walls in your kitchen have been constructed will have a huge impact on how you'll go about securing things to them.

SOLID BRICK WALLS

You can make a fairly accurate guess as to how your home has been constructed by its age and location; if it was built in the UK before the 1960s, the odds are all the walls are going to be built from bricks or stone that have had a thick layer of plaster spread over them (usually called 'rendering') and then a final, thin layer of finishing plaster applied to create a smooth surface. You can easily identify these walls by giving them a hard tap; no matter where you tap they will always sound solid. Solid walls are perfect for hanging heavy wall units from. All you need is the right wall plug and screw and away you go.

However, brick walls are expensive and time-consuming to construct, so more recent homes will often have 'stud' and 'drylined' walls, which can be a problem for the kitchen fitter.

STUD WALLS

Internal walls that aren't actually keeping anything up (non-supporting walls) are usually called 'stud' walls. These are made by creating a wooden frame and then screwing plasterboard over the frame.

If you're screwing into stud walls you will, ideally, find the wooden batons behind the board and drill into these (see 'Stud detector' on page 43). Sadly, this isn't always possible, so you will almost certainly have to secure directly to plasterboard at some point, which will require the use of one or other of the fixings described later.

When stud walls were first used you could guarantee a clear space behind the plasterboard, but these days that once hollow area between the studs is filled with insulation in order to make the wall more soundproof and heatproof. Two types of insulation tend to be used: 'rockwool', which is a

fairly soft, fleecy material; or insulation board, which is a fairly hard foam, usually covered with a silver-foil-like coating. Both come in a variety of names, but they all look pretty similar. This insulation does create problems with certain plasterboard fixings.

DRYLINED WALLS

These days, most walls will be drylined, which involves sticking plasterboard directly over brickwork using a method called 'dot and dab'. A drylined wall sounds hollow, but just behind the plasterboard is the brick, or block, wall. While you can't tell the difference between a stud wall and a drylined wall by tapping it, you can tell the difference by where the wall is –

if it's a hollow-sounding external wall it's most likely 'drylined'.

Sadly, none of this is certain; older houses are often renovated using drylining techniques and the insulation properties of very old solid brick walls are often improved by building a heavily insulated stud wall over the top. So why do you need to be able to tell the difference between a stud wall and a drylined wall? Because they require two very different approaches when it comes to hanging things on them.

OTHER WALL TYPES

Just to make matters more complicated, there are other ways of building houses. Compressed straw was used in the UK to make non-load-bearing walls for a time and when they gave up on that idea, they started using honeycomb cardboard. If you're lucky, these materials have been used within a traditional stud wall so you can just cut away the wall surface and fit a wooden baton between the studs that you can then screw into. If you're unlucky you might have to do something along the lines of fitting sheets of 19mm (¾in) plywood over the face of the wall to create a secure surface. If this is the case, you really ought to have a chat to a professional before going much further.

WALL PLUGS

If you're going to hang kitchen units on plasterboard, bricks, mortar or concrete walls, you'll need to fit some sort of fixing system for the screw. Depending on where you live and the mood of the retailer

these are called wall plugs, screw anchors, expansion anchors, dowels or Rawlplugs, after their inventor John Rawlings.

For brickwork, mortar and concrete, the gauge of screw you're planning to use determines the size of the hole and wall plug. 'Gauge' is the pre-metric measure of the diameter of a screw and these days you'll see screws often sold using the modern metric equivalent.

In those wondrous days of old they also used a colour coding system for the wall plugs themselves, so that a gauge 4 screw, for example, went with a bright yellow wall plug. Alas, this was considered far too straightforward, so not only do you now have to contend with two measuring systems, but you also have wall plugs in any and all colours. That said, you can still buy the original coloured plugs and the table below shows how gauge, metric and plug size all fit together.

Screw Gauge	Metric equiv.	Drill Size	Masonry plug size
3	2.5mm	5mm	Yellow (5mm hole)
4	3.0mm	5mm	Yellow (5mm hole)
6	3.5mm	6.0mm	Red (6mm hole)
8	4.0mm	6-7mm	Red (6mm hole) or Brown (7mm hole)
10	5.0mm	7-8mm	Brown (7mm hole)
12	5.5mm	8mm	Brown (7mm hole)
14	6.5mm	10mm	Blue (10mm hole)

With bricks and mortar you can get away with using a screw that's a little too big for the hole and wall plug. For tiles it's far more important that the screw, hole and wall plug are sized properly; put too large a screw into too small a hole and you risk cracking the tile.

1 Drill your hole using the appropriate drill bit (see page 49 for more information on drill bits). For example, if you have a 1in, size 6 screw you'll need a 6mm drill bit and a red wall plug.

2 Push the wall plug into the hole. You might need to use a hammer to 'persuade' the wall plug to go right into the wall until it's flush with the surface, but do this gently – especially if it's a tiled surface.

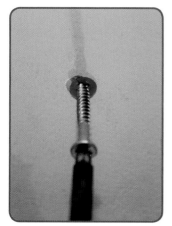

3 Now insert the screw into the wall plug and screw away. If you've got the hole size wrong or are using very large screws, you might find that the wall plug just starts to go around and around in the hole or disappears into the hole altogether. If this happens try the following:

Remove the plug and fit it to the end of the screw. Hold the plug in a set of pump pliers

and gently turn the screw a turn or two into the wall plug. You should see that this has caused the wall plug to expand a little.

Now push the wall plug and screw into the hole – tap with a hammer if needed – and when the plug is flush with the wall surface, start screwing the screw in. The expanded plug should now hold in place.

TIP *If your wall is crumbling away you might have a problem drilling a clean hole. There are a number of products available for just these situations, some using a quick-drying, plaster-impregnated material. You wrap the material around the wall plug, dampen the lot, push it into the hole and then leave to harden. Other products use resins or quick-drying putties to fill the crumbling hole and give the wall plug something to push against. If you can't find any of these, try cleaning out the hole with a vacuum cleaner and then filling it with a grab-adhesive. Push the wall plug into the hole while the adhesive is still wet and once the adhesive is dry (read the instructions as this varies), screw in your screw.*

FIXINGS FOR STUD WALLS

Stud walls are easy to put up, but not so easy to fix things to. The different approaches available will usually have a section on the packaging letting you know how much weight they're designed to bear, and it doesn't pay to ignore these limits.

SELF-DRILL PLASTERBOARD FIXING

These look like large, broad metal screws with a very wide thread, and are called all sorts of different names – you can get plastic versions but I personally steer clear of these. These are great for more lightweight items and will work with both stud and drylined walls, providing you aren't using them directly over a stud or a 'dot' of the cement used to stick the drylined wall to the brickwork. That said, there are better fixings for drylined walls: see below.

1 Screw the fixing into the plasterboard. It's best to do this by hand, but if you have an electric screwdriver with an adjustable torque setting you can carefully use this at a low level.

If the fixing gets so far and then stops it's probably hit either a wooden stud or the adhesive used in drylining. Don't keep on going, as you'll just rip out a useless hole in the plasterboard; instead stop, remove the fixing and shine a light into the hole to try to see what you've hit. If it's a wooden baton, then discard the fixing and just screw directly into the baton. If it's a dot of mortar or adhesive then consider using a drylining fixing discussed below. If it looks like plastic or copper, you might be about to drill into a pipe or an electric cable – abandon this hole and see if there's somewhere else you can put the screw.

2 Once the fixing head is flush with the plasterboard you insert the screw it came with into the hole in the middle.

These fixings are surprisingly strong but I like to also use a bit of grab adhesive on whatever you're fixing to the wall, as this helps to spread the load across the whole surface of the plasterboard.

The downside of this approach is that you'll ruin the wall if you ever have to take whatever you're fixing to the wall off again, so you'll need to weigh up the potential wall damage against the desire to have said item hanging securely.

SPRING TOGGLES
I avoid these like the plague because they are such a hassle to use. However, they do tend to be able to hold heavier items onto plasterboard walls – see the packaging they come in for the weight

limit, which varies from toggle to toggle.

These don't work if the stud wall has been insulated with insulating board or if you have a drylined wall, as

the void behind the plasterboard is too small for the toggles to open up. This can also apply if the builder who put the wall up was overly generous with rockwool insulation. If you have a void behind your plasterboard, follow these steps:

1 Drill the hole into the plasterboard. The hole size needed should be stipulated on the packaging that the toggle came with, but 10–14mm (approx. ½in) is usual.

2 Taking note of which way round the toggle is fitted to the screw, unscrew the toggle.

3 Put the screw through whatever it is you're trying to secure to the wall.

4 Now put the toggle back on to the screw again, making sure it's the right way round.

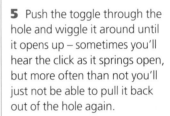

5 Push the toggle through the hole and wiggle it around until it opens up – sometimes you'll hear the click as it springs open, but more often than not you'll just not be able to pull it back out of the hole again.

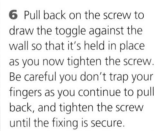

6 Pull back on the screw to draw the toggle against the wall so that it's held in place as you now tighten the screw. Be careful you don't trap your fingers as you continue to pull back, and tighten the screw until the fixing is secure.

Bear in mind that if you need to undo the fixing again you'll lose the toggle inside the wall, as it falls off into the cavity the moment you withdraw the screw.

There are a host of variations to the spring toggle, all working on the idea that you push the fixing through the plasterboard and it then opens up and grips the plasterboard from behind. They all assume some sort of a void behind the plasterboard, but how much of a void varies between the different fixings. For example, the traditional spring toggle needs at least 30mm (1¼in) of void, whereas the GripIt fixing needs virtually no void at all and so will work with insulated board and drylined walls. They also allow you to hang enormous weights off plasterboard walls.

GripIt fixings.

DRYLINE WALL PLUGS

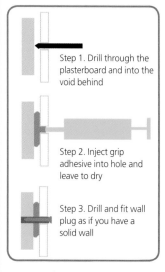

With drylined walls we need to make sure we're securing the screw into the solid brickwork behind the plasterboard. The simplest way to do this is to use much longer wall plugs that bridge the gap between the plasterboard and the block or brickwork behind. Two fairly similar products do this and are known as 'dryline plugs' and 'frame-fixing screws'.

TIP *Most modern homes are built using traditional bricks on the outside and grey blocks on the inside. These go by many names; breeze blocks, aerated blocks, Aircrete blocks, thermal blocks, lightweight blocks, concrete blocks, Thermalite, Durox or Celcon blocks.*

Most modern homes will contain a range of these blocks depending on what the wall is supporting and whereabouts in the wall the block is situated. While they might look very similar, these blocks vary enormously in strength and density; some take an age to drill into with a good masonry drill bit on hammer action, while others have the consistency of mature cheddar and are best drilled into using an HSS drill bit with no hammer action. In short, as a homeowner, you're not going to discover which type you have until you attempt to drill into it.

The first thing you need to do is to drill a deep hole for long screws, measuring about 75–100mm (3–4in).

1 Start off drilling using an appropriately sized masonry drill bit, but don't use hammer action.

If the drill goes through easily then you have a lightweight 'Thermalite' block and you might have to try the method below to hang anything of any weight on the wall.

If you are struggling to drill the hole, now would be the time to switch to hammer action, as you have either brickwork, concrete or high-density Thermalite.

2 If you're using a dryline plug you can now insert this in the hole and screw it into position. If you're using a frame fixing screw just push the wall plug and screw into your hole until the end of the wall plug is flush with the plasterboard.

3 Now screw into the wall. The idea behind both of

these approaches is that you're screwing into the wall not the plasterboard. You're also bridging the gap between the wall and plasterboard with something fairly strong so the plasterboard doesn't just crack and collapse when you tighten your screw. With this in mind, there are alternative approaches that might work out a bit cheaper if you're drilling a lot of holes.

The easiest one is to drill a hole through the plasterboard. Inject some grip adhesive into this hole so that the void is filled and, once the adhesive is dry, drill the hole and use an ordinary wall plug.

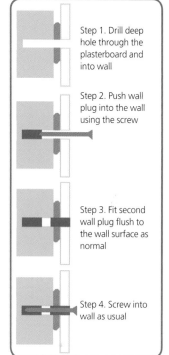

Step 1. Drill through the plasterboard and into the void behind

Step 2. Inject grip adhesive into hole and leave to dry

Step 3. Drill and fit wall plug as if you have a solid wall

Step 1. Drill deep hole through the plasterboard and into wall

Step 2. Push wall plug into the wall using the screw

Step 3. Fit second wall plug flush to the wall surface as normal

Step 4. Screw into wall as usual

To make it more secure you can drill a deeper hole and push the whole of the first wall plug right into the brick wall, using a screw to push it in, then fit a second plug as normal. The downside of this 'do-it-yourself' fixing approach is that, as you have no guarantee quite how strong the finished screw fixing is, you might find yourself spending a small fortune in grip adhesive and you have to wait until the adhesive is dry, which often means leaving it overnight to be sure.

SECURING TO LOW-DENSITY THERMALITE

If you discovered that it was ridiculously easy to drill into the Thermalite blocks behind your drylined wall then you might have a bit of a problem. The really low density blocks are so soft that they can just crack if you use ordinary wall plugs in them. Fortunately, there are still some options.

THERMAL BLOCK FIXINGS

These are really just longer versions of the 'self-drill plasterboard fixings' we talked about earlier. You just need to make a pilot hole first – the size will be stated on the packaging – and then screw them into place. Because they use a screw thread rather than compression, the block is less likely to crack when screwed into.

RESIN-BASED FIXING KITS

There are a number of proprietary kits based around the idea that you create a large hole in the Thermalite block, fill it with a liquid resin, put a bolt into the resin and then wait for the resin to dry and go hard. Each approach varies slightly, so it's best to check what weight they are guaranteed for and then follow the manufacturer's steps.

REGIONAL TERMINOLOGY

Regardless of where you live, a kitchen is a kitchen – unless, of course, it's a cookhouse, a galley or a scullery. With this in mind, anyone who can read English should be able to follow this manual and find it useful and appropriate for his or her region of the world.

That said, technical terms and tool names can be regionally specific so, where possible, I've given a range of common names for most items. Where this isn't possible I've stuck to those terms most commonly used here in the UK. For example, I have used the word 'tap' rather than 'faucet' because it's easier to spell, uses less space in the book and I like the word 'tap'.

For most sections of the manual I've used metric measurements and given the non-metric equivalent alongside. However, for the fitting instructions I've just stuck to metric for the simple reason that the millimetre is a far more appropriate measurement for kitchen fitting than tiny, obscure fractions of an inch.

Rather than list screw sizes in both metric and imperial all the time I've generally stuck to the UK convention, which despite decades of metric still stubbornly uses an imperial 'gauge' to define the diameter of the screw and inch fractions for the length. You can ask for a 50mm by 4mm screw in the UK but it will usually just result in a blank face whilst they wait for you to ask for a '2in, size 8 screw'. Most screws are, however, sold with both the metric and imperial sizes on the box.

For drill bits, metric tends to have been embraced with a little more enthusiasm in the UK, so asking for a 6mm drill bit will normally get you a 6mm bit, although it might actually be quarter-inch and therefore 6.35mm in diameter. However, unless you are intending to perform keyhole surgery with your drill, this small disparity is unlikely to be an issue for you.

By the way, the conversions used between inches and metric tend to be based on tradition rather than accuracy. 12mm is not exactly half an inch, but it makes life simpler if we say it is, and the errors involved are too small to be of consequence. The only area where this isn't the case is with routers, where exact conversions are the norm – a ½in router bit is not referred to as a 12mm bit, it is a 12.7mm bit.

SCREW GAUGES

Screw gauge (size)	Diameter in mm	Equivalent in inches
4	3	⅛
6	3.5	⁹⁄₆₄
8	4	⁵⁄₃₂
10	5	³⁄₁₆
12	6	⁷⁄₃₂
14	6.35	¼

SCREW LENGTHS

Screw length in mm	Equivalent in inches
12	½
20	¾
25	1
30	1¼
40	1½
45	1¾
50	2
60	2⅜ (usually sold as 2½)
70	2¾
75	3
80	3¼
90	3½
100	4
150	6

DRILL BIT DIAMETERS

Drill bit diameter in mm	Equivalent in inches
3	⅛
6	¼
8	⁵⁄₁₆
10	²⁵⁄₆₄
12	½
14	⁹⁄₁₆

The wondrous world of bits and screws

SCREW BITS

It pays to get a good quality set of screw bits to go with your electric screwdriver. You should always get the following types of bit in any set:

SLOTTED

Avoid buying slotted screws, as they really don't work with electric screwdrivers, as the bit slips off the screw with annoying regularity. However, in the old days these were the

only ones you could buy, so you will have to remove a lot of them. If you do use an electric screwdriver, keep the speed down and expect it to slip from time to time.

PHILLIPS

Phillips screws are much easier to use and are readily available. The most common size you'll use in kitchen fitting is Phillips size 2 (PH2) so it makes sense to buy a few PH2 bits, as they will break.

POZIDRIV

Pozidriv screws look, at first glance, like a Phillips, but you'll notice that the cross has what looks like a thin 'X' under it. If you need to use a large, long screw then a Pozidriv is the

better option, as you can apply more torque without increasing the risk of the screw head becoming mangled.

HEXALOBULAR

Hexalobular screws and bits are usually referred to as 'Torx' or 'Star Drives'. These seem to be very popular in Europe, especially in Germany. You

won't come up against them very often when assembling kitchen units, but you are likely to find them on appliances.

HEX

Hex screws and bits are commonly used in 'grub screws', which in turn are often used with kitchen taps. Like Torx, you're unlikely to come across them outside of taps and

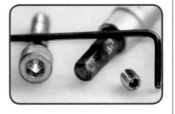

kitchen appliances. While it is an idea to have hex bits in any set you will usually tackle hex screws by using a set of Allen keys. Note that there are metric and imperial versions of hex screws and keys.

DRILL BITS

The most common drill bit sizes you'll need are 6mm, 8mm and occasionally 10mm, although you will need smaller ones for drilling pilot holes.

SDS

SDS drill bits are ideal for drilling into masonry and concrete, the only proviso being that you have an SDS drill that can use them. You can also buy a variety of SDS chisels for masonry work.

WOOD BITS

Ideal for wood; rubbish for anything else. To avoid splitting wood when screwing into it you need to drill pilot holes, which need to be a little

narrower than the screws being used, so if you are buying a set of these make sure some small (2–3mm) ones are included.

MASONRY BITS

If you want to drill into brick walls or concrete floors you'll need these. For harder materials and holes bigger than 10mm you might want to use an SDS masonry drill bit.

METAL DRILL BITS (HSS)

HSS stands for 'high speed steel', and these bits last much longer than carbon steel bits. You might also see drill bits advertised as 'cobalt steel'; these are harder still and

handy for bigger holes in harder metals, however they are far more brittle than ordinary HSS and as a result, the smaller bits tend to break all the time.

TILE BITS

Most kitchens have tiled splashbacks and tiled floors, so you'll almost certainly have to drill a few holes into tiles at some point.

Most wall tiles can be drilled into using a good quality masonry bit, but you'll shorten the life of the bit doing this. For harder tiles, especially porcelain tiles, you'll need a special tile bit.

For smaller holes, go for the pointy tile and glass drill bit that looks a bit like an arrowhead. These are usually tungsten tipped, but they still don't last that long. It's usually best to use these at a fairly low speed to keep the temperature down, and it's often easier to drill a small hole first and then work your way up to the hole size you require. Whatever you do, make sure your drill is not set to hammer action.

For bigger holes use diamond-tipped core drills. These don't come with a centrepoint, so getting started can be awkward. Fortunately, we cover this in chapter 9 – 'Tiled Splashbacks'.

COUNTERSINK BITS

Most screws that you buy have countersunk heads. With kitchens, it's often a good idea to use a countersink drill bit just to ensure that the screw heads are below the finished wood surface, allowing you to hide them completely with caulk or wood filler if needs be. To use:

 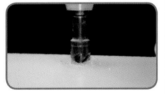

1 Drill your pilot hole.

2 Use the countersink bit to make a slight depression at the top of this hole that will just accept the screw head.

3 Screw in the screw until the head is nicely nestled in your countersunk hole. It's worth remembering that if you use a countersink bit your screw can now go deeper into the wood, so check the screw isn't going to be too long.

HOLESAWS AND AUGERS

If you fit a kitchen yourself, you're definitely going to have to make holes in wood and sometimes they are going to be fairly large holes. There are a few ways of going about this:

You can buy the holesaws shown to the right as kits, which are fairly compact, easy to use and come in the range of sizes you'll need. If you damage one you can buy each size separately. For kitchen fitting, these are probably your best way of making larger holes in wood.

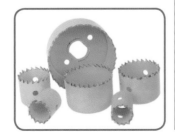

This is also a holesaw kit, but here the different sizes all fit onto one connector. The holesaws themselves are much more flimsy and I'd recommend spending a little more money and buying the first kit we discussed.

If you need to go through thicker wood you'll need an auger. The downside of these is that, because they are long they're often too bulky for the majority of kitchen fitting and, because the screw thread at the tip of the drill draws it through the wood the larger sizes usually require more torque than a cordless drill can provide.

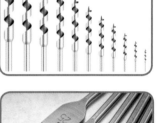

Spade drill bits are an alternative to the wood auger. They work better with cordless drills because they don't require as much power from the drill but, to make up for this, they require a lot more power from the person holding the drill. They can also make a mess of the hole. In short, if you have to go through thicker wood opt for an auger, even if it does mean digging out your corded drill first.

SDS CHISELS

No one likes to see pipes and cables and, while you can usually hide these behind or under the kitchen units, the odds are you are going to have to hide some by channelling out a bit of wall. You can do this with a large hammer, a bolster and a cold chisel, but it can be tiring work. A much easier approach is to fit an SDS chisel to your SDS drill and set your drill to chisel mode, so that it hammers away but doesn't rotate. If you go for this option, remember to wear ear defenders, a dust mask and safety glasses.

Using silicone sealant

If you're going to work in a bathroom or a kitchen you're going to have to work with silicone sealant. In truth, it's very easy to work with, but this doesn't stop people making a right mess of things, so to avoid these mistakes I decided to set aside a short section on how to do it right.

BUYING THE RIGHT SEALANT

While how you apply the sealant will have a huge impact on the final look of your kitchen, which sealant you use is also going to have a large role to play. You can buy sealant in a variety of colours, but white and clear are by far the most popular. You need to be careful with some of the more exotic colours, as they can be more difficult to work with.

The other thing to think about is mould. One of the properties of sealant is that it remains nice and warm most of the time. Add to this a touch of moisture and a bit of heat and you have the ideal habitat for mould fungi. The most common effect is an unsightly black stain spreading across your sealant and the only way to get rid of it is to remove the sealant and start again. To postpone this wearisome day, buy sealant that has anti-fungal properties. To delay the spread of mould still further you should keep the sealant dry and clean it regularly with a neutral or alkaline disinfectant – mould loves acids.

REMOVING OLD SEALANT

The easiest way to remove sealant is with a utility knife, either by using the blade on its own or with a scraper.

1 Run the scraper along the top line of the sealant, then along the bottom line, being careful not to damage the worktop.

2 Peel away the old sealant.

3 Use the scraper, or just the blade, to remove as much of the sealant residue as you can, before using a sealant-removing product to remove the rest – heavy-duty hand wipes work really well for this.

4 Use an anti-fungal/mould spray over the area to kill off any mould that is still present and let it dry before applying the new sealant.

APPLYING SILICONE SEALANT

There are two approaches to using sealant. You can apply masking tape all around the area – this is known as the very long way to apply sealant – or you can use a good sealant spreader, which is the much better option.

If you do want to use the masking tape approach, then you need to apply nice straight lines of tape on either side of the proposed sealant line.

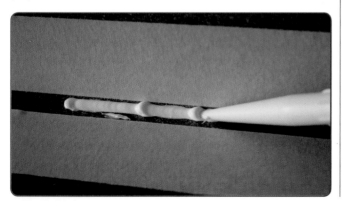

To use the much quicker approach, you need to buy a good sealant spreader and by far the best – in my humble opinion – is the 'Plasplugs Silicone Sealant Finisher'.

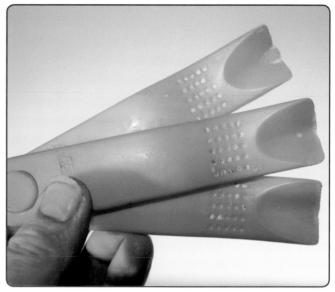

1 First off, avoid using an old tube of sealant if at all possible. It tends to go lumpy over time, especially if it's been stored somewhere where it can get very cold.

Use a knife to cut off the top of a new tube and screw the applicator nozzle into place.

2 Use your knife to cut the end of the nozzle at a slight angle. Aim for the hole to be about 5mm wide.

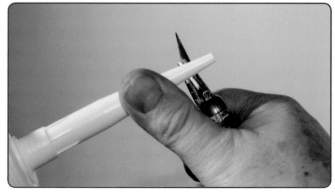

3 Put the tube of sealant into your sealant gun and squeeze the trigger a few times until you can see the sealant just starting to emerge.

4 Apply the nozzle to the edge you wish to seal so the cut edge of the applicator is flush with the wall. Now squeeze the trigger so that a nice steady stream of silicone emerges and move the applicator back to leave a neat line of silicone lining the edge.

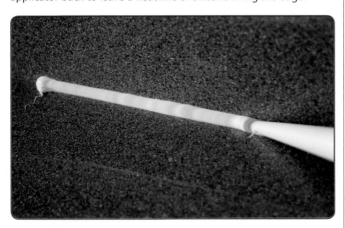

5 If you've bought a set of the 'Plasplugs' finishers, decide which size applicator you wish to use. A thick line of sealant is less likely to peel away and will form a better watertight seal; the thinnest lines look neater, but tend not to last as long.

Having made your selection, push the 'finisher' onto your sealant line and push it forward to scrape up the excess.

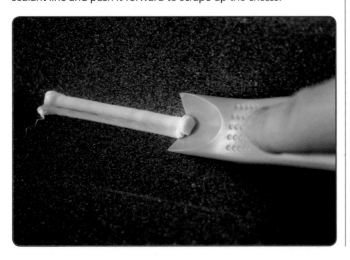

NOTE: *Many spreaders ask you to draw the spreader back along the line of sealant – which is also what you do if you are using your finger to spread the sealant. The Plasplug one is the opposite; you push it along the line.*

6 The silicone will build up on the finisher as you push it along. Don't let it build up too much before stopping and cleaning the excess silicone off with kitchen roll. Continue to push the finisher along, stopping along the way to clean off the excess silicone.

If you opted to use masking tape you could just use your index finger or thumb to spread the sealant. You just need to make sure your finger is clean and damp. Apparently, you should avoid just licking your finger as the bacteria in your mouth encourage fungal growth in the sealant, so have a finger bowl of water close to hand. Once your finger is damp draw it back along the sealant line. Don't press too hard and don't let too much sealant build up in front of your finger. When it does, stop, remove the sealant, dampen your finger again and continue along the sealant line.

7 Getting corners smooth can be an issue. The main thing is to try to remove as much excess as possible first and then use either your fingers or a spreader to smooth it down. You can buy sealant spreaders/smoothers that just look like a finger and these can be very useful for getting into tight corners – remember to keep them damp.

8 You should now have a nice clean line of silicone sealant. If there are sections where there wasn't enough sealant in the first place you might need to add a bit more and then run over the area again with your sealant finisher.

Avoid the temptation to overwork the sealant, especially as it starts to dry, as it will just go lumpy and horrible. If you think you've made a bit of a mess of things, just leave it to dry and then either apply fresh sealant over the dry stuff or peel the old sealant away and start again.

9 If you used masking tape, carefully remove it. You now need to leave the sealant for 24 hours to dry.

3 RENOVATING AN EXISTING KITCHEN

Changing the doors and drawers

FRAMED AND FRAMELESS CABINETS

There are two basic types of kitchen cabinet: framed (also called 'face-framed') and frameless. Most modern kitchens are supplied with frameless cabinets because they're cheaper to make and allow for more versatile door arrangements. The reason you need to know what type you have is that the door hinges differ and the different door types reveal more or less of the cabinet itself.

Below: Frameless cabinet with side hinges

On frameless cabinets, the door hinges are always set into the sides of the cabinets. These hinges are invisible when the door is closed and the doors themselves cover virtually the entire face of the cabinet. In other words, we only need to change or renovate the doors for a completely new look.

On framed cabinets, the doors can be 'overlay' doors that fit over the frame or 'inset' doors that fit into the frame. The

doors on framed cabinets are often attached to the frame front or to the frame edge. In both cases any renovation work to the doors has to include the cabinet frame and the visible hinges as well.

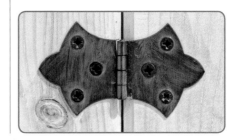

MEASURING THE EXISTING DOORS AND DRAWERS

If you're planning on replacing your existing doors and drawers then you're going to need to measure the old ones in order to purchase their exact replacements. It's generally easier to do this while the doors/drawers are in place.

1 Draw up an elevation plan for each wall of the kitchen. It doesn't need to be exact, but you do need to be able to see each door and drawer clearly. Ideally it should be large enough

to write your measurements in clearly; if not, then give each door a number and write up a separate list or spreadsheet showing the details against each door/drawer number. Record any special features, i.e. if a door contains a glass panel.

Count the total number of base unit doors, base unit drawers and wall unit doors you have and check this number against your plans once you've finished.

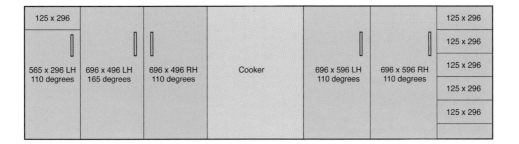

2 Open the door and measure its height and width using a tape measure. Measure the back of the door; the front often has a bevelled edge, which will make measurements inaccurate.

To measure drawers, open them and measure across the top for the width and the back edge for the height.

TIP *The end hook on a tape measure is designed to move slightly in order to give accurate inside and outside measurements. Sadly, this movement often increases over*

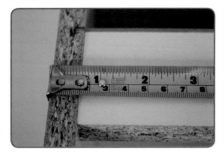

time, so measurements look longer than they actually are. Usually this isn't an issue, but with kitchens accuracy is important, so it pays to test your tape measure at the start of your measuring. To do this, measure a door using the end hook and then measure it again using the 10cm (4in) mark as the base. Take 10cm (4in) off this final measurement and compare the two.

For example, using the end hook I got a measurement of 312mm (12¼in), but using the 10cm (4in) mark as a base I got

310mm (12in). So, when I use the end hook I need to take 2mm off my measurements before I write them down. Repeat this exercise at the end of your measuring to make sure the error hasn't changed at all.

3 Write this measurement down as height x width and mark down if the door is left hand (LH) or right hand (RH). A left-hand door, for example, has the hinges on the left side, the door handle on the right side, opens towards the left and is easier to open with your left hand.

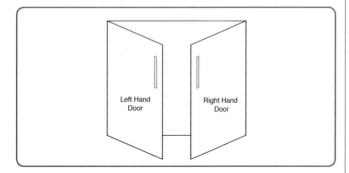

Left Hand Door   Right Hand Door

4 While the actual doors in your kitchen may look the same, the odds are their hinges will vary. For example, the hinges on corner units will often swing the door out as it opens and are specific for corner doors. Some hinges will only allow the door to open

to about 110° to stop them banging into walls, etc., while others allow the door to open almost fully – more like 165°.

You need to record this information on your plan and, if you currently have a door that smashes against a wall every time it's opened, you might want to buy new hinges to prevent this in future. The amount a hinge will allow a door to open is marked on the hinge package when you buy it.

This is also the stage to decide if you're going to reuse the original hinges or buy replacements. To keep costs down, decide on a door-by-door basis and just record your decision against each door. If you're reusing the old hinges, store them in such a way that you can find the right hinge for the right door. An easy way to do this is to use sticky labels to number the inside of each door and then use the same number on a plastic bag to store the hinge.

5 It's usually easier to measure the hinge positions once the door is off the wall – see 'Removing frameless doors with quick-release hinges' on page 89.

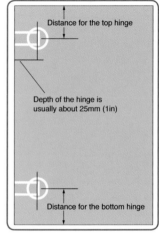

Distance for the top hinge

Depth of the hinge is usually about 25mm (1in)

Distance for the bottom hinge

If you're planning on buying new replacement doors, life is going to be so much simpler if the new door hinges are set at the same height as the old ones. With this in mind, measure the hinge positions at this stage and record their height. Measure the top hinge as the distance from the top of the door to the centre of the hinge and the bottom hinge as the distance from the bottom of the door to the centre of the hinge – always measure the back of the door and not the door front.

The depth of the hinge is the distance from the inside edge of the door to the centre of the hinge – for modern hinges this is usually a constant of about 25mm (1in).

6 Although you're eventually going to sell or throw away the old doors, it pays to keep them until you've completed your renovation. Give them a number and store their hinges, etc. with them so that you can double-check the new against the old.

7 You should now have a diagram and a list something like this. You should also have a neatly stacked pile of old doors stored with their hinges and handles and a large number attached to them to refer to if you have any difficulties.

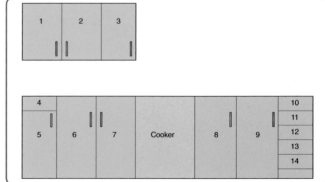

FITTING NEW DOORS AND DRAWERS

There are a host of companies offering replacement doors and drawer fronts. For the drawer fronts you just need to retain the drawer mechanism from the old drawers and fit these to the new ones in the exact same place. How you go about removing the drawers and their fronts can vary enormously – some are obvious, some take an age to figure out. For some clues on the process, have a read of 'Removing old doors and drawers' on page 90.

Many companies will offer to place the holes for the door hinges exactly where you want them. If you can't find such a company or would rather do it yourself then it's just a matter of ordering the right-sized doors and drawers and making a template for the hinge positions. You don't have to make up a template but they help to ensure consistency when marking the holes for hinges and the screw holes for drawer mechanisms and door handles.

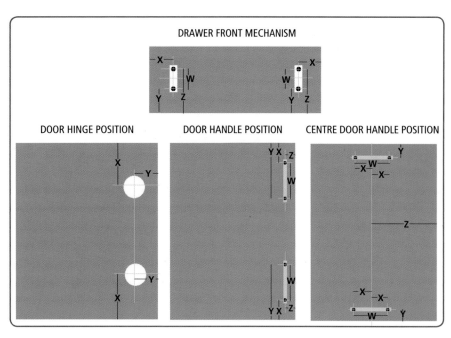

MAKING A TEMPLATE

1 The important distances for your templates are shown in the above diagram. Although your doors and drawers may vary in size, the position of the hinges, drawer mechanisms and handles remain constant in relation to their distance from the top or bottom edge of the door and – for the drawer fronts – in terms of how far the screw holes are from the left or right side of the drawer itself.

If you're drilling your own hinge holes you'll need to mark the centre position of the hinge for the main hole and the two screw hole positions above and below this main hole. This information can be found on the hinge packaging. If you're reusing old hinges, you can get these measurements from the old doors.

For drawer mechanisms, mark the positions of the screw holes – usually two each side. For door handles, it's easier to measure the distance between the screw holes using a ruler. If you use a tape measure, take the measurement from the 10cm (4in) mark and deduct 10cm (4in) from your reading.

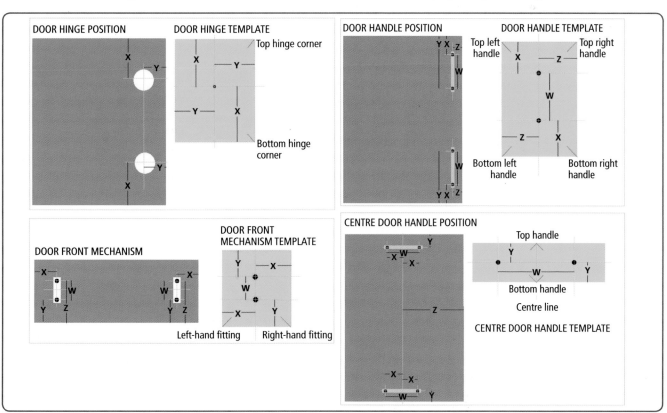

TIP *If you have an ornate door front you might want to use a distinct decorative feature as the start point for your templates, rather than the door edge itself. If the door is overly ornate it's usually best to mark everything on the plain, undecorated back of the door.*

2 Transfer your measurements onto card or a thin sheet of plywood – thin ply tends to last longer, which is handy if you've got a fairly large kitchen to do. If you use plywood, a bench/table saw is the easiest way to ensure your template has straight, clean edges.

The aim of a template is to be as simple as possible. If you can make them perfectly symmetrical (so that the holes are in the right place even if you use the wrong edge or have the template upside down) then so much the better, but always mark the edge of the template you're going to use to position the template and aim to always use that edge.

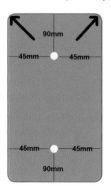

Left: My handle template will work for left- and right-hand doors and be accurate even if used upside down, although I've marked the preferred set-up edges.

3 Drill out the screw hole positions by placing your card or ply on a spare block of wood and carefully drilling through it using a 3mm wood drill bit.

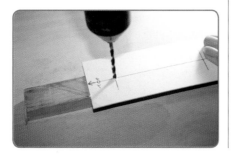

MARKING HINGE AND HANDLE POSITIONS

1 Check the back of the new doors for little punch hole marks, as manufacturers often mark the standard positions for hinge screws and door handles here.

If they haven't, or if you want to use your own marks, then cover the rough area of the door where you think the holes are going to be with masking tape, as it's much easier to see a pencil mark on tape than on the wooden veneer of the doors themselves.

On very ornate doors it's easier to mark everything on the back of the doors/drawers, but if you do this, always remember to protect the front of the door from damage. Laying it on an old, clean, blanket is usually sufficient.

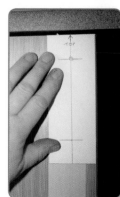

2 Set your template in position at the edge of the door/drawer and mark the hole with either a pencil, a centre-punch or a non-permanent marker pen.

If you're not using a template, be consistent in your measuring – use the same tape measure or ruler throughout and double-check your start position for the measuring each time. You're far less likely to make a mistake if you mark all your doors and drawers in one go and then return to drill your holes later.

If you're using a marker pen, check the mark wipes away cleanly by testing it on the back of a door or drawer first. Bear in mind that these marks will often wipe away cleanly after a minute but become pretty stubborn after 5–10 minutes.

TIP *For door handles, it's easier to mark and drill the holes once the doors have been hung in place. Always open the door first to double-check that you're putting the handles on the opposite side from the hinges.*

3 Sadly, pencil marks can be rubbed off and masking tape can unpeel and slip at the most annoying of moments. With this in mind, once you've double-checked the positions of your marks, replace them with a small hole from a centre punch, a bradawl or a small nail. This mark is also easier to use as a start position for drilling.

You can leave the masking tape in place, as it helps prevent any veneer splitting when you drill. You can also mark your new centre punch holes with a pencil mark, just to ensure that they're clearly visible.

For drilling and fitting the door handles, see 'Fitting door and drawer handles' on page 124.

FITTING OVERLAY DOORS ONTO FRAMELESS CABINETS

I'm going to assume from the start that you are using modern hinges with your doors – these are usually referred to as 'Euro Hinges' outside of Europe. These might look horribly complicated, but they are easy to use and even easier to adjust. If your old doors didn't come with these hinges, it pays to upgrade to them at this stage.

If you've bought new doors with the hinge positions in the right place, jump straight to step 7.

1 There are three standard hinge hole sizes: 26mm, 35mm and 40mm. The vast majority of kitchen hinges are 35mm, but check this before you go any further. Most hinges also require a screw position above and below the main hole to hold the hinge in place.

2 Having marked the position of the hole and the two holding screws using your template (See 'Making a template' on page 57), you now need to drill the main 35mm hole.

To make this hole you'll need a 35mm Forstner bit (often called a 'hinge cutter') and ideally, a drill press, as it's critical that you get the depth of the cut just right – too deep and you risk going straight through the door; too shallow and your hinge won't fit flush with the door.

If you have a drill press then just secure your door in position and set the depth of the hole on your drill press. Most hinges need a 12mm deep hole, but double-check this by measuring the depth of the hinge or reading the paperwork that came with the hinges.

TIP *Use an old door as a test door. Drill a few hinge holes until you're happy with the depth. You might even want to use your template to cut holes in the right place – just turn the door upside down and use the old handle side as your new hinge side. Fit the hinges and hang the old door to make sure your measurements are right, your template works and you're confident using the hinge cutter.*

---

3 If you don't have a drill press, you can cut hinge holes by hand with a standard hand drill. Just measure the depth of the hole you need – 12mm in this example – against the Forstner bit and mark the side of the bit. Most of the time the head of the bit is the depth you need the hole to be, so you just drill until it's flush with

the surface of the door. If this isn't the case, carefully wrap some masking tape or insulation tape around the bit head to mark the required depth.

4 If you have a workbench, you can secure the door by laying it face down on the bench with some clean, dry cloth underneath so

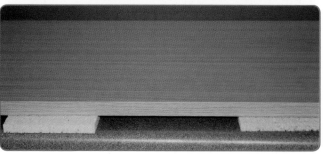

the door face doesn't get damaged, and then use the clamps that come with the bench to secure the door in place. If you don't have a workbench use any flat surface set high enough to make the job comfortable, use cloth or an old blanket to protect the face of the door and use standard clamps to hold the door in place, with wooden offcuts inbetween to stop the clamps damaging the door. Old kitchen sponges – ideally slightly damp ones – make a good surface for this kind of work, as they both cushion the door and hold it in place.

5 The drill bit comes with a small central spike that you can set on your mark – using a centre punch to make this mark comes in very handy at this point as you can feel when the central spike slips into the mark.

6 Having made sure your drill is not in hammer mode, keep the drill as straight and vertical as you can manage and start drilling the hole. When you are about halfway, stop, take the drill out and clean the hole. Now carry on until the hole is the right depth – usually 12mm.

Left: Most hinge cutters are at the right depth when the head of the cutter is flush with the top of the door surface.

7 Fit the hinge into the hole and check that it's flush with the door surface. Now screw the hinge into position using the screw hole marks you've made. If the door came with the

hinge hole already cut, you'll usually find they have also made two little dints in the door surface above and below this hole to mark the position of the hinge screws.

8 If you're fitting the door using the old hinges then the mounting plate for the hinge will already be in place, in which case jump to step 16.

The mounting plates vary from hinge to hinge, but most

modern ones are a cruciform shape and you fit them with the screw holes top and bottom and the longer arm of the cross pointing into the cupboard.

Your cupboard will often already have the holes pre-cut to accept the screws for the mounting plates. If this is the case, jump to step 15.

9 If the mounting plate hole positions haven't been pre-drilled you'll need to dig out the technical leaflet that came with the

hinge. This will show you the distance into the cupboard, the distance apart and the size of the holes you'll need to drill.

If you can't find this information, attach the mounting plate to the door hinge (see step 16)

and open the hinge. Now measure the distance from the inside edge of the door to the centre of the mounting plate screw holes.

10 Directly measure the distance between the mounting plate screw holes.

11 To work out the height of the mounting plates from the

top and bottom of the unit, use a tape measure to accurately measure the height of your door and then measure the height of the cupboard opening. The door on a frameless cabinet will be a little taller than the cabinet opening. You need to take this difference and divide it by two. For example, if your door is 693mm and the cabinet opening is 663mm, the difference is 30mm, so the door overhangs the opening by 15mm top and bottom.

We know the distance the centre of our hinge is from the top and bottom of the door because we worked this out earlier. In this example, let's say this distance is 100mm. This means that the centre of our mounting plate needs to be 100 – 15 = 85mm from the top and bottom of the cabinet opening.

12 We're now ready to mark the positions of the mounting plates. If you're doing a lot of doors with the same hinges, make up a template in card or thin plywood and mark the hole positions using a marker pen. However, it's best to fit this door first and only use the hinge measurements in a template once you know for sure that it works.

In our example, the centre position of the mounting plate is 85mm from the top/bottom of the cabinet, the screw holes are 37mm into the cabinet and are 32mm apart, so we've made up the template as shown.

Double-check your measurements by measuring the distance between the centre line on the top and bottom mounting plates and comparing this to the distance between the hinge centres on the door – they should be identical.

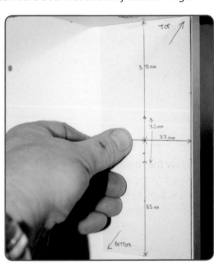

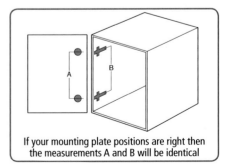

If your mounting plate positions are right then the measurements A and B will be identical

13 The information that came with the hinge and mounting plate will show what diameter hole you need to drill and the thickness of the cabinet side panel will dictate the maximum depth your hole can be.

If you haven't got the technical information for your hinge, measure the diameter of the screws supplied and then drill a hole a little smaller in diameter – as a general rule a 5mm hole will usually work. It's worth bearing in mind that if you drill a hole that's too small it will be difficult to get the screw in, but if you make it too large you're going to be in trouble – you can fill the hole with a mix of wood glue and wood shavings and push the screw in, but it's not ideal.

For the depth of the hole, put the screw into the mounting plate and then measure the length of screw coming out the other side. Check that this is less than the depth of your cabinet panels.

14 Mark this depth by wrapping some tape around the drill bit and then drill to this mark.

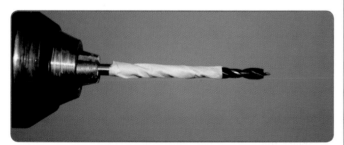

15 Screw the mounting plate onto the cabinet side panel. If you've had to measure and drill the mounting plate positions yourself you might want to fit the door hinges onto the mounting plates and check that the door is hanging properly before marking and drilling the holes for all the other doors.

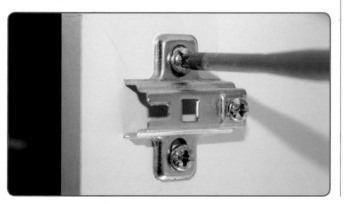

16 Again, all hinges tend to vary slightly but, as a general rule, to get the hinge onto the mounting plate, first open up both hinges on the door. If your hinges have the spring-loaded bar at the end

of the hinge arm that we discussed earlier then go to step 17. If the hinge arm just finishes in a cup shape then it uses a 'slide-on arm' mechanism, in which case jump to step 20.

17 Start with the top hinge. On the door side of the hinge base you'll see a metal bar. Place this bar in the little groove on the mounting plate.

This bar connects with the hinge plate

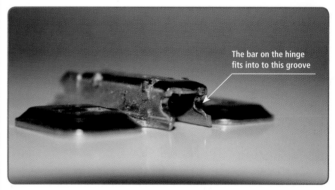

The bar on the hinge fits into to this groove

18 Now push the other end of the hinge base forward over the mounting plate. You'll hear a click as it connects with the plate.

Below: As you push, the clip slips into the end groove with an audible click

FITTING SOFT-CLOSE DOORS AND DRAWERS

If you buy a new kitchen, the chances are it will already come with soft-close hinges for the doors and soft-close runners for the drawers. If they don't come with these by default, you can usually upgrade to them.

For existing kitchens, you have the choice of replacing all the hinges and runners with their soft-close counterparts or leaving everything in place and just fitting a soft-close mechanism to the doors and drawers. If you want to replace the hinges altogether, see page 89, 'Removing old doors and drawers' and page 121, 'Fitting the doors'.

It's obviously easier if you just leave everything else as it is and fit a soft-close 'buffer' to each door and drawer. There are many to choose from and they're all fairly simple to fit, although each manufacturer has a slightly different approach, so follow the instructions provided if they differ from the ones below.

1 As a general rule, you fit them to the cabinet on the hinge side. It's usually easier to fit these to the top of your cabinets, and if you place them just under the hinges, they'll be hidden and out of view.

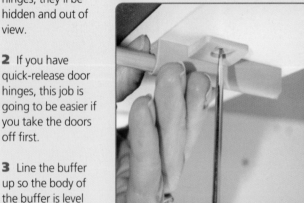

2 If you have quick-release door hinges, this job is going to be easier if you take the doors off first.

3 Line the buffer up so the body of the buffer is level with the edge of the cabinet and mark the screw holes with a bradawl, a pencil or a non-permanent marker pen.

4 After making sure the screws are not so long that they'll go right through the cabinet panels, screw the buffers into place. Refit the doors and relax in a wondrously quiet kitchen.

The buffers for drawers vary enormously and will only work if you have a drawer that opens and closes on some sort of rail. You can use door buffers, but these tend to get in the way when you're using the drawer. You're better off looking for buffers that either fit at the back or the side of the drawer; side ones are the most popular and versatile.

19 Repeat this with the lower hinge and close the door.

TIP *With overlay doors you can usually open the door without the handle. However, it can be a bit awkward to do and, with inset doors, it can be nigh on impossible. To make life a bit easier, just stick a bit of masking tape to the edge of the door and use this as a temporary handle.*

20 If you don't have the latest hinges with the 'quick fit' mechanism discussed in steps 17–19 then you probably have the 'slide-on arm' mechanism.

As the name suggests, you attach the hinge to the mounting plate by sliding it on until the C-shaped cup at the end of the hinge arm slides under the screw and the adjusting screw on the hinge slides into place on the mounting plate.

Now tighten this screw to hold the door in place.

21 To stop the doors clattering into the cabinet every time they're closed most doors will come with a little pack of transparent round pads. You just unpeel the cover on the back of these and stick them to the top and bottom edges of the door at the opposite side to the hinges.

To keep the clattering to an absolute minimum, you can fit a soft-close mechanism to the doors – see 'Fitting soft-close doors and drawers' (left).

Having fitted your doors and drawers the odds are you're going to have to adjust them to get a perfect fit. Have a look at Chapter 6, 'Adjusting doors with modern hinges' and 'Levelling drawer fronts'.

FITTING OVERLAY DOORS ONTO A FACE-FRAMED CABINET

As a general rule, this is exactly the same as 'fitting overlay doors onto frameless cabinets' on page 59, so have a read of that section first. The only difference between the doors on frameless and framed cabinets is where the hinge attaches to the cabinet and how the hinge looks as a result.

Sometimes these hinges attach to the door and cabinet exactly the same way as for a frameless door, although the hinge mechanism is slightly different. But often the hinge attaches to the edge of the door frame, in which case the only distance we need to work out, if we're not reusing the old mounting plates, is the height of the mounting plate positions from the top and bottom of the cabinet – see step 11 in 'Fitting overlay doors onto frameless cabinets'.

FITTING INSET DOORS ONTO A FACE-FRAMED CABINET

Inset doors give a kitchen a very traditional look and often the hinge itself is used as a decorative feature. Alas, these doors can be very awkward to fit and, while I'll give you some direction here, you really need to get yourself a good woodworking manual, gather an array of good woodworking tools and be prepared to spend a lot of time practising if you are to have any hope of avoiding an array of expensive mistakes. Below is a list of things to consider and to be aware of:

- With inset doors, the first question you really ought to consider is if you'd be better off replacing them with overlay doors. This will change the look quite dramatically, which might not be a bad thing, and it is also going to be so much easier to tackle on your own.
- The chances are you will have to trim an inset door to get it to fit an existing cabinet. You can only do this if the door is made from solid wood, or is at least framed in solid wood. This will invariably mean that the door is going to be expensive, so swapping to an overlay-style door might save you money, as well as heartache.
- If you're still determined to fit inset doors, bear in mind that the doors will expand and contract over the year, meaning that they might get stuck from time to time. To reduce the chances of this, purchase or make the doors well in advance and store them in the kitchen for a month or so to let them adjust to the humidity. If you have MDF doors this isn't an issue, but you'll have to ensure the MDF is sealed properly, as water will make them expand and fall apart.
- If you have surface-mounted 'butterfly hinges' then you may want to retain them, as they are decorative as much as anything. If you had old-fashioned butt hinges (also called mortised hinges), where you can see only the edge

Above: A butt hinge.

of the hinge when the door is closed, or completely concealed hinges, then I'd advise that you make life easier for yourself and replace these with the modern adjustable hinges that we discussed earlier. When purchasing these, you'll need to specify that you want hinges for 'an inset door on a face-framed cabinet'.

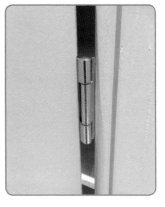 

- The easiest way to deal with inset doors on a face-framed cabinet is to remove the entire frame and then sort the doors out from the comfort of a workbench. Occasionally this is feasible, but often they are well and truly glued onto the cabinet and aren't going to move without damaging things.

If you can see any brackets or screws holding the frame to the cabinet, remove them first. If the frame is still held solid it's probably glued and stapled in place. Take a block of wood, put it against the back of the frame inside the cabinet and give it a decent smack

with a hammer. If it starts to come away from the cabinet, just repeat this process all around the frame until it's free. If it doesn't budge, don't keep trying because you'll damage the whole cabinet.

■ The inset door will need a consistent space between it and the frame. Most DIY stores sell plastic spacers (often called 'packers' or 'shims') that come in different colours, depending on their thickness.

These work great but, by happy chance, the laminate samples that most DIY stores provide free of charge are exactly the right thickness. Use these to hold the door in the right position in relation to the frame.

■ To make sure the inset door fits flush with the cabinet when it's closed, they usually come with some little brackets that you can screw to the doorframe. If you're renewing your doors these brackets should be in place already and should stop the door moving too far into the cabinet when it's closed.

■ If there aren't any already in place it's best to fit some at this stage – they just screw to the back of the frame, and the magnet variety work best as they also help keep the door shut. On wall units you usually set them in the top corner on the opposite side to the hinge where they're out of the way. For base units the top corner is often still best, but check first – you don't want to be snagging yourself every time you use the cupboard.

■ You'll be moving the door in and out of the frame as you adjust it. To ensure you always fit it the right way around, mark one corner of the door. For example, add a pencil mark on the top right-hand side of the door and make sure this is there every time you fit the door into the frame.

■ The chances are you will have to trim an inset door to get it to fit. If this is the case, trim the longer sides of the door first. This is because any tapering of the door edge is much harder to see on the longer edges. It's most important that the hinge side of the door fits perfectly square with the face-frame opening. If this isn't the case, trim this side first to get this side of the door perfect, then, if required, trim the longer handle side of the door, then the top and then the bottom.

■ How you go about trimming the door is dependent on what tools you have. A bench saw works really well and quickly, as does a surface or bench planer (also known as a jointing planer). These can be hired, but if you can't get access to either of these you could use a router, which would also allow you to bevel the edge of the door after you've cut it. In desperation, you might try using a hand or electric planer, but it is difficult to get a perfectly straight cut with these tools.

■ If you're unfamiliar with the tool, take the time to practise on some old doors before attempting to cut your nice new door.

■ If you're using butt hinges, it's better to use a small router or 'trimmer' to create the depression (or mortise, hence the alternative name for this hinge) you need to inset the hinge into the door.

■ You can make a mortise template from MDF, remembering that it needs to be clamped securely onto the door when you're using it. Always fit one door first to make sure your template is sound before moving on to the rest of the doors. The reason for not using a hammer and chisel to create the inset mortise is that the hinge needs to be perfectly flush with the door to get a good fit, which is difficult to do consistently with these tools. If you opt for this approach, remember to mark around the edge of the inset area first with the chisel, making the cross-grain cuts first, then the cut with the grain. If you do it the other way around the wood tends to split in the direction of the grain.

■ Visible hinges are decorative, so you'll need to place them consistently. With this in mind, it's best to make a template for the hinge and handle positions.

FITTING DOOR AND DRAWER HANDLES

We've already talked about making the templates for the handles. When it comes to drilling the holes bear the following in mind:

■ To reduce mistakes, always hang the doors first and open them before you drill any holes, just to make sure you've got the holes marked in the right place.

■ If you have handles that need two screw holes you're going to have to be very precise with the distance between the two holes. To give yourself a bit of 'wiggle room' use a wood drill bit that is a little bit wider than the screws

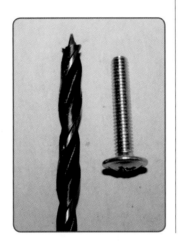

you're going to use. Don't go too big, though, or you'll be able to see the holes when the handle is in place.

■ To get a clean drill hole never just drill straight through the door into thin air. Always hold a block of spare wood firmly against the face where you're expecting the drill to emerge – this is especially important when you're drilling through laminated surfaces. Use a block of wood for this that is thicker than your drill bit is long, just to make sure you don't end up drilling into your hand. Better still, use a clamp to hold this block of wood in place.

■ Loosely fit both screws into the handle then draw the handle back to the door. Again, this is to just make life easier if you haven't drilled the holes the exact distance apart.

Renovating existing doors and drawers

Buying new doors can be an expensive business, so if you're on a tight budget it's always worth at least investigating what you can do to improve the look of your existing doors.

That said, it's not a given that restoration will be cheaper than replacement, so before you rush out and spend money on sanders and paint, have a read of this section and work out the prices before you start the project. Remember to factor in time – it can take an awful lot of hard work to renovate a single door.

How you can go about renovating drawers is affected by what type of drawers you have. In fairly modern kitchens the drawers are three-sided and the fronts can be removed relatively easily. In this case, you can just buy new drawer fronts to change the look of your kitchen, as we discussed earlier. In old kitchens the drawers can be three- or four-sided.

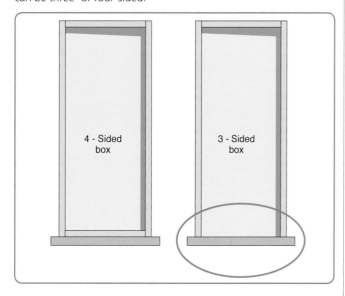

With a three-sided drawer, the drawer front is usually held to the rest of the drawer unit by glued wooden dowels. These can be next-to-impossible to remove without badly damaging the drawer itself. An alternative to removing them is to just cut the drawer front flush with the rest of the drawer.

You now have a four-sided drawer that you can just stick a new drawer face to. To make things neater you can reverse the entire drawer to use the old back as the new front, and stick the drawer front to this. This will mean taking off the drawer slides and reversing everything, but since you'll probably have to adjust the sliders anyway, it's worth doing.

If you think this conversion from three-sided to four-sided might be the easiest route for you, bear in mind that the new four-sided drawer with a drawer front stuck on it is going to be a little longer. So, before you start hacking anything to pieces, check that there is space behind the drawer when it's fully closed so that the new drawer front will still fit flush with the cabinet.

Left: When fully closed there needs to be at least a 25mm (1") gap if we are going to convert to a 4-sided drawer

On older four-sided drawers the drawer front is usually just screwed to the drawer and the screws are clearly visible when you open it up.

Occasionally, they will have used a bit of glue as well, so you might have to give the drawer front a sharp tap with a hammer to remove it completely.

If you can remove the existing drawer front then buying a lovely new replacement is an option. If you can't, then have a look at the renovating options that follow to see how you can at least change the way they look.

The simplest way of renovating inset drawers is to convert them to overlay doors by just buying a new drawer front and screwing it over the old one.

However, before you can even think about renovating your drawers you'll need to get them out of the cabinet, and this is often not as straightforward as you might think. For some insights into the labyrinthine mechanisms employed by various kitchen companies, have a read of 'Removing the drawers' in Chapter 4.

NEW DOOR HANDLES

This is a relatively cheap and easy way to change the look of your kitchen. The first thing to do is to remove the old handles, which is usually very simple (see 'Removing the door and drawer handles' on page 91).

If you've got door knobs (connected to the door via a single screw), you can replace them with pretty much any handle, although you'll want to reuse the screw hole created by the old knob.

If the old handle uses two screw holes then you'll need to take the handle off and measure the distance between the two holes. You'll want to buy replacements that have the same spacing. If this doesn't look realistic you can buy faceplates that cover the old holes. These give you more freedom, but they are very much a feature in themselves, which might not suit everyone.

Above: Some handle designs will cover the old holes

To fit the new handles take a look at the 'Making a template' section. Unless you're using the exact same holes from the old handles, making a template will save time and reduce errors. The section 'Fitting door and drawer handles' earlier in this chapter will step you through the process of actually fitting your new handles.

PAINTING

If you have a lot of time and not a lot of money this might be a viable option, but it is hard work and it'll take time and patience to do it properly. On the other hand, this is a wonderful opportunity to create a truly unique kitchen look. We're going to walk through painting doors, but the same rules apply if you want to paint face-framed cabinets.

Unless you're feeling extremely confident I would always advise going through the following step-by-step process with just one door; ideally the back of one that isn't highly visible. Firstly, this lets you practise without the world falling on your head if you get it wrong. Secondly, there are a number of finishes – usually melamine and high gloss – that can be very difficult to get paint to stick to. Finally, most paints will change colour as they dry, so paint one door, let it dry completely – give it at least a few days – and check to see is this really if the look you were expecting. You can use sample pots to do this on a small drawer front.

1 If your doors are solid wood and in good condition then painting or staining is feasible. If they are laminated, especially if the laminate is melamine, then check that the laminate and the wood (or often chipboard) underneath is in good condition. Most laminated doors have a base of chipboard or MDF that will expand and fall apart the moment it gets damp. In this case it's pointless trying to paint it; you need to replace the door.

Melamine is a type of plastic used to create a hard decorative laminate on many kitchen doors and drawers. It goes by a lot of different names: Arborite, for example, or the poetically whimsical 'high pressure decorative plastic laminate'. In truth, all we're really interested in is recognising that we don't have a natural wood finish, so we're going to have to treat it a little differently. Be aware that some modern kitchen doors are coated in a thin film of plastic or a very hard lacquer. In these instances, it's best to treat them as if they are melamine.

2 If your doors are in good condition, remove them from the cabinets and then remove the handles and hinges (see 'Removing old doors and drawers' on page 89).

There is a school of thought that says you should leave the doors and drawers hanging on their cabinets and paint them in situ, as they are effectively being held in place for you – don't listen to this! A kitchen without doors looks untidy but is functional. A kitchen that has doors with wet paint on them is an accident just waiting to happen. It's also much easier to paint a door or drawer that's lying flat on a workbench in a nice quiet area where it won't be disturbed or covered in dust, flour, sugar or whatever else is flying around the kitchen at the time. A quick word of warning though, a kitchen without doors can be a dangerous place for young children, so keep all dangerous items away from tiny hands.

3 We can't paint onto a dirty surface, so use sugar soap or detergent to remove all traces of grease and grime. Wipe them down afterwards with a damp cloth to remove any detergent residue and leave them to dry.

If the doors/drawers are very greasy you could try using a TSP- (Trisodium Phosphate) based product. This will remove the grease but it can also burn your skin and do serious harm to eyes, to say nothing of its effect on the environment. So, always use gloves and goggles when using it and start off using an ordinary detergent, only resorting to TSP if that fails.

4 If the doors are solid wood or have a wooden laminate surface, you'll need to sand them down a bit. The aim here is to create a good surface for painting (also called 'keying'). With that in mind, avoid coarse grain sandpaper and start with medium, finishing off with a nice fine grain.

Powered sanders will make this job a lot easier and quicker, but don't use anything too big and powerful or you'll remove far too much surface and damage any decorative effects. A good orbital sander is fine for plain flat doors, but if your doors and drawers have a decorative effect you're better off using a small detail, eccentric sander.

Either way, you'll create a lot of dust, so wear a dust mask. If you opt to undertake the sanding by hand, buy a sanding block and try to sand with the grain of the wood.

TIP *Many modern primer and paint tins will proclaim in large, Day-Glo script that you don't need to sand or even use a primer to get a wonderful effect. This may be true in some cases, but the truth is that sanding and priming will invariably result in a better finish. If you forego the initial sanding you should still sand the door lightly after the first layer of paint or primer, just to remove any raised grain, before applying further coats.*

5 During the sanding process you'll probably notice dints and imperfections in your doors. For larger scratches you're best off purchasing a good

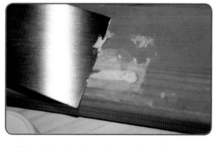

wood or general purpose filler, ideally a latex-based one that won't crack or shrink. Use a putty knife to apply it, pushing it in to the hole as hard as you can to ensure it fills it completely and binds properly with the door surface. Once you've applied the filler, let it dry completely and then sand the door down again.

With melamine surfaces most dints will be small and will probably disappear during the painting process, however, if you do need to fill one, try using a product along the lines of 'Colorfill' or 'SeamFil', or a latex caulk product. To use these, clean the area with a solvent – one is usually supplied with the filler – apply the filler and then use the solvent to remove the excess. If you opt for caulk, just use a fine-grade sandpaper to gently remove the excess.

6 Once you've completed your sanding, clear up your work area and remove as much dust as you can with a vacuum cleaner. Use the brush that the vacuum usually comes with to remove most of the dust from the doors and drawers

themselves. To remove any residual dust, apply white spirit to a microfibre cloth and wipe the door down thoroughly.

7 Next, you need to prime the surface. For wooden doors just get a good wood primer. For melamine doors you need a primer specific for this surface. It's very important that you cover every part of the wood or melamine surface with primer to avoid your paint peeling away.

To get a really smooth finish it's always best to put a coat of primer down, let it dry completely, and then lightly sand the surface to remove any raised grain before applying a second coat.

TIP *Most paint, varnishes and stains will give you a list of finishes that they will and won't work with. Alas, trying to discover what's been applied to your existing kitchen*

cabinets, doors and drawers isn't that easy. However, there are a few basic tests you could undertake. There's no guarantee that they'll work but they should give you a big clue:

- *If it's a wax finish, you ought to be able to just scrape a bit off with a fingernail.*
- *If you apply a drop of linseed oil to an inconspicuous area of a more remote door it will either be absorbed or it will form a droplet and run away. If it's absorbed it has an oil finish; if it runs away it's shellac, varnish, lacquer or polyurethane.*
- *Now dip a cotton swab into some acetone –nail varnish remover, for example – and apply it to an even more discrete area of a door. If it just beads up and runs away you probably have a polyurethane finish. If it doesn't bead up, leave it for a few minutes. The acetone will cause shellac and varnish to become sticky to the touch and it will dissolve lacquer completely.*
- *To discover if you have varnish or shellac, grab a bottle of methylated spirits (denatured alcohol) and another cotton swab. Dip the swab in the methylated spirits and apply a dab to yet another hidden area of your kitchen. If the finish is shellac it will turn tacky and start to dissolve almost straight away. If it's varnish it will only slowly react.*

Be aware that all the chemicals we're using here are flammable, so do the tests away from naked flames in a well-ventilated area.

Painting itself is a bit of an art form. Fortunately, it's relatively easy to become competent at it, although mastering it can take time. Just follow these guidelines and you won't go too far wrong:

- New paints are coming out all the time so it pays to do some research rather than just picking up the first tin you see. Internet forums and discussion groups are great sources of information and first-hand recommendation.

- High-gloss paints are generally the hardest to get a perfectly smooth, brush-mark-free, finish with. With this in mind, you might want to look at satin finishes and eggshell paints, which will hide imperfections much better.
- If you've got your heart set on a high gloss finish, consider spray paints. There are a number of products available that claim to be simple to use, but test them before use.
- Ensure your painting area is free from dust and is well ventilated.
- Avoid cheap paintbrushes. The easiest way to get a good paint finish is to use good brushes and rollers. Synthetic bristles are usually best for modern paints and a 50–75mm (2–3in) wide brush should be about the right size. The brush should always be narrower than the surface you're painting. Square-cut brushes should be fine, but you might want to consider a smaller 25mm (1in) sash brush for any detailed work on more ornate doors. More expensive brushes tend to have tipped bristles that come to a very fine end, rather than just being

Angled bristles of a Sash brush

cut to length, which leaves a square-cut end. The fine tip gives a smoother finish. If you can, run the brush over your hand – you can feel the silky smoothness of a tipped brush.

- If you're not planning on painting the back of the doors or drawers, cover the back edges with newspaper and masking tape to keep them clean.

- Lay the doors down flat to paint them. For ease and comfort, lay them on a workbench. If you put a bit of 12mm (½in) plywood underneath the door, you get a good solid platform, but one where you can paint the front and edges at the same time and lift the door off afterwards, without getting fingermarks on your paint. An alternative approach is to make or buy a nail board – a piece of wood into which you have knocked a series of nails to support whatever you're painting.

- Set aside an area where you can leave the doors to dry. A worktop, covered in newspaper that's held in place with masking tape with two thin batons of wood over the top makes a good resting place that will accommodate quite a few doors at the same time. If that's not possible, a floor area that's pet free will do, again using two batons to raise the doors off the floor.
- If you opt to paint both sides of the door, wait until the front of the door is perfectly dry, place a few microfibre cloths over the plywood we mentioned earlier, put the door on your workbench with the painted front protected by these cloths and paint the back.
- Before you use any paint or primer, always shake the tin for at least a few minutes. After this, open the paint tin using a large flat-headed screwdriver – ease up one edge of the lid, then go around the lid with the screwdriver, just easing up the edge of the lid every 2cm (¾in) or so until it lifts off.
- Once well shaken, give the paint/primer a good stir for a few minutes with a clean baton of wood.
- With all painting, the golden rule is not to apply too much in one go. Having to do three coats might take more time, but it will result in a much better finish than one overloaded coat, which is very likely to run and/or show your brush marks.
- Small rollers are usually easier to work with than a paintbrush and generally create a smoother finish. However, it's usually easier to use both a brush and a small roller. Use the brush for the edges and the decorative effects and 'cut-in' to the main part of the door before using a small roller to finish off the larger, flatter areas.

Use a brush to do the edges and then 'cut-in' to the main area

- An overloaded brush or roller is also going to drip paint everywhere. Don't dip brushes too deeply into the paint, and wipe away the excess before applying it. Run a roller up and down the paint tray a few times to squeeze out the excess.

Right: Start in the middle, half a roller width away from the previous paint and spread the paint to the edges and the previous roll.

Right: A coloured stain

STAINING

In many ways, this is the same as painting (see above), but, of course, you can only stain a natural wood surface. Staining is designed to enhance the natural beauty of the wood, its grain pattern in particular.

Stains can be applied with sponge brushes or even just a clean rag, so it can be a much easier process to get the hang of. If you do have good quality wooden doors it might be worth investigating staining ahead of painting.

The downside of staining is that the final colour can be affected by a number of things, so it can be difficult to get a consistent finish right across the kitchen. With this in mind, a timer and a methodical approach are essential. Also, while the staining process itself can be simple, the overall process is still time-consuming.

- Always start a brushstroke or roller near the centre of the area to be painted. Spread the paint out over the middle area and only once you have a nice even spread of paint should you take it to the edges. This ensures you don't end up with excess at the edges where it's more likely to drip and run. With a roller, start the next roll about half a roller's width away and spread the paint out towards the previous layer of paint.
- With brushes, try to use long brushstrokes and 'feather' the end of the stroke – apply less and less pressure before lifting it off the surface altogether. With rollers, once you've finished, lightly roll over the whole door again with almost no paint on the roller just to remove any texture and ensure a nice even layer of paint.
- After every painting session, immediately clean the brushes and rollers. Most modern paints can be simply washed off the brush in warm water. Once the brushes are clean, squeeze the bristles to remove any excess water or white spirit, and wrap them loosely in cling film to keep them moist and flexible.

VARNISHING

In most respects, varnishing and painting can be treated the same way, so have a read of the painting section above. Varnishing melamine and other plastic coatings is so close to pointless that I will not mention it further, which leaves only one other difference between varnish and paint; how you go about filling in any dints and blemishes on the doors. Not only is the colour of the filler you use critical, but also the colour it looks before you apply varnish is rarely the same as the colour it looks afterwards. Always test the filler and your varnish first – the back of a drawer front, for example, is a sensible place to do this.

Right: Clear varnish

- It's quite common for a solid wood door to be covered in shellac or a very hard lacquer finish. Neither makes staining an easy option, so it's important to discover what finish your door currently has – start by asking the manufacturer – and always check the suitability of any staining product against this finish. See the previous TIP for the basic tests.
- It pays to research what staining wonders of the modern world are currently available. For example, there are modern 'gel' stains that act more like paints. These new stains still let you see the grain of the wood, but generally offer far more intense and consistent colour options that are less affected by the wood type. For example, they tend not to blotch as readily as traditional stains on woods like cherry.
- The final colour of the stain is invariably affected by the quality of your sanding, even more so than with paint, as those areas that haven't been as thoroughly sanded will take up the stain differently. This can actually look good if you plan it out – as a general rule the sanded areas will appear slightly darker than the unsanded parts – but you do need to practise this effect first, always remembering that different woods will react differently. For stains you usually need to remove the old finish completely and get down to the natural wood. With this in mind you might want to start off using coarser sandpaper (100–120 grit) before dropping to a 'medium' and then a 'fine' to finish.
- The type of wood your doors are made from, their age and moisture content will all influence the final colour, so don't just

look at the tin description and take the final colour for granted. Get some sample pots and apply the stain to the back of a door or drawer first – before and after sanding.

■ Some woods don't like being stained – cherry, pine, etc. They either take up the stain too quickly or unevenly, giving a blotchy finish. You can get around this by applying a pre-stain conditioner. Be aware that these will also affect the final colour, so test first.

■ Many stains need to be applied and then wiped off. The length of time they are left between applying and removing is critical for the final colour. In a kitchen, where you want uniformity of colour if nothing else, this can be a problem, and I'd avoid the 'wipe-off' stains if possible. If you have your heart set on them, then make sure the setting time is consistent across all the doors and drawers and cabinet fronts.

■ Water-based stains tend to 'raise' the grain after they've been applied. If this is the case you'll need to sand it down lightly after the first coat and then apply a second.

■ Traditionally, you apply a stain and then apply a 'seal' to protect the wood. Some stains come with a 'built-in' sealer. If yours doesn't, have a read of the tin – it will undoubtedly point you in the direction of a suitable sealant. The most common sealer is polyurethane. Shaking the tin up beforehand causes tiny bubbles to get caught up in the polyurethane, which can ruin the finish, so restrict yourself to a gentle stir.

TIP *How do you know if you've sanded enough? Well, try putting your hand inside a nylon stocking or a pair of tights and running your hand over the surface. If the stocking snags, sand a bit more with fine-grade sandpaper.*

REFACING

If you have a traditional-style kitchen with face-framed cabinets, this is something you might want to look at. If you have a more modern kitchen with frameless cabinets then there's generally not enough of the cabinet frame visible to warrant refacing them. As a general rule, you only reface the cabinets and then fit new doors and drawers over these, so have a read through Chapter 6 first to familiarise yourself with removing and fitting doors, drawers and handles.

You shouldn't even consider refacing unless your existing cabinets are structurally sound. If they are and they aren't too badly damaged you might want to have a look at painting or staining as an alternative to refacing them, although by using a modern veneer kit, it's probably much quicker and easier to reface.

Refacing involves applying a very thin veneer – usually wooden veneer, just 1–2mm thick – over the existing surface. These days there are lots of companies offering start-to-finish refacing solutions; just give them all the dimensions and they'll supply you with everything you need, including new matching doors and drawers and a veneer in the colour of your choice that comes with self-adhesive backing.

You can buy veneers without any peel-and-stick glues on the back, but while they might save you a bit of money, they're more difficult to apply. You can also buy smaller sample sheets of veneer that can be used for practice.

In terms of preparation, it's much the same as painting; degrease it (avoid strong solvents as they can damage the surface), fill in any holes with wood putty and sand it down until you have a good smooth surface. Now use a fine sandpaper to 'key' the entire surface. Remove any dust with a vacuum cleaner and a tack cloth – white spirit can damage the surface so it's best avoided.

Apply the veneer so that any cut edges are hidden from view. The best way to do this is to veneer the sides first and then do the front.

To join sheets of veneer, overlap the sheets slightly and then cut through both sheets together with a fresh-bladed utility knife. You

can use scissors to trim the veneer roughly to size and a craft knife to carefully remove the excess.

If you use self-adhesive veneers they should come with a PSA (Pressure Sensitive Adhesive). If you are applying the glue yourself, opt for this type of adhesive, as it allows you to position the veneer but take it off and reposition it if you make a mistake. You only press it down hard to activate the glue when you're sure that it's positioned correctly.

Use a rolling motion to apply the veneer to the surface, as this reduces the chances of air getting trapped underneath. Smooth it down with the palm of your hand and then use something like a car ice scraper to press it down fully. If you do get air trapped under your veneer try piercing the bubble with a fine needle and pressing the trapped air out.

Be aware that you might have to adjust your cabinet doors afterwards to compensate for the slightly thicker surface.

MOVING CABINETS

If your kitchen is basically sound but you're not overly happy with the layout then moving the cabinets around would be a cheap and effective way of changing things (see 'Removing base cabinets' on page 94). Another issue that affects many kitchens is that, while the bulk of the kitchen is fine, the cabinets supporting the sink have been badly damaged by water and would benefit from being replaced.

Changing the countertops

The countertop, or kitchen worktop, is one of the first things people notice when they walk into your kitchen. As a result, it's also one of the easiest ways to change the look of your kitchen.

Well, I say 'easiest' but this largely depends on what you have in place to start with. If you currently have a solid granite worktop, then changing it is going to be a trial. On the other hand, if you have a fairly standard laminate worktop, changing it can be relatively straightforward. Whatever you have, you're going to have to rope in some friends to help, as handling most worktops is at least a two-person job.

If you're thinking of making up your own worktop, using tiles for example, you don't have to remove the existing one at all. If this is the case, have a read of the 'New countertops' section opposite. If you're going to remove the old worktop, see 'Removing the existing worktop' on page 92.

Below: Tile spacers create a perfect expansion gap.

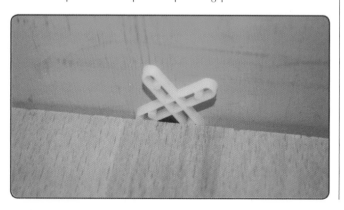

NEW COUNTERTOPS

Having removed the old countertop, the easiest approach to revitalising your kitchen is just popping out and buying a new laminate kitchen worktop, which is discussed in detail in the chapter 'Countertops – Installing a Laminate Countertop'. If this is outside of your budget, or just seems a bit boring and ordinary, you might want to think about making your own.

A TILED COUNTERTOP

In terms of price, this is probably going to be more expensive and time-consuming than fitting a standard laminated worktop. However, it's also going to be far more unique and it can be quite easy to do; it's not essential to even remove the old worktop – just screw or glue a 5–6mm (¼in) sheet of cement 'backer board' over the existing worktop and away you go.

The downside of tiled countertops is that the grout line is ideal for collecting dirt and developing stains. The upside is that it's a feasible way of the DIY enthusiast fitting a granite or natural stone work surface that won't break the bank.

1 Cover everything in the kitchen that you want to remain clean with plastic sheeting, secured in place with masking tape.

2 If you don't have a worktop in place that you can use as a base, you're going to need to fit one. Plywood makes a good base, but avoid anything less than 18mm (¾in) thick and buy marine ply (or exterior grade) just to ensure that if the wood does get wet, it doesn't fall apart or warp.

The finished worktop should be between 600–610mm (23½–24in) wide, so add the thickness of any concrete board and edging tiles to work out the width of your plywood. You'll also want a small overhang at the end of the worktop and a small gap between the plywood and the wall to accommodate any expansion – tile spacers are handy for this.

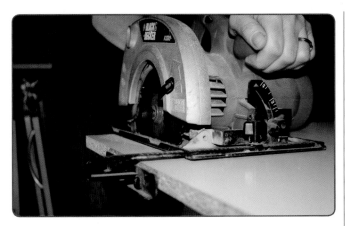

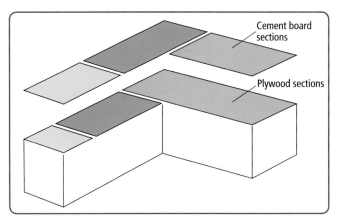

Cement board sections

Plywood sections

For a nice clean edge use a circular saw or a bench saw with a fine wood blade to cut the ply. A jigsaw and a steady hand should also suffice.

3 Check the cabinets are secure and level. If they aren't level use some small shims underneath the plywood. If the cabinets are nowhere near level you're better off taking them off the wall and levelling them (see 'Fitting new cabinets' on page 107).

Screw the plywood base to the cabinets. You can screw down, but it's going to be easier to renew in the future if you screw up from inside the cabinets. With that in mind, if you can't just screw up through the cabinet, it's better to use brackets inside the cabinet to secure the ends of the plywood.

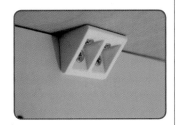

TIP *Always drill a pilot hole first before screwing into anything, as it reduces the chance of the screw splitting the material. Use a drill just a little narrower than the screws you're intending to use and either fit a stop to the drill bit to prevent you from drilling too deeply or get a pilot drill that comes with a countersink attached to it – this gives you depth control and lets you countersink your screws at the same time.*

Above: Countersink Pilot drill bit

4 Cut out holes for the sink and hob, etc. (see 'Fitting the sink' on page 54).

5 To make things more secure and to keep everything level, use a joining plate underneath the plywood to join different sections together.

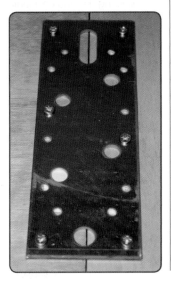

6 Use 6mm (¼in) cement backer board over the top of your plywood to create a good surface for tiling. To give more strength to the finished surface, avoid joining the sections of backer board in the same places you used for the plywood. It's best to leave a small gap between the backer board and the wall and between the sections of backer board to accommodate any expansion – again, small tile spacers are good for this.

You can cut backer board to size with a jigsaw or circular saw or just snap it by scoring it on one side with a utility knife, placing the edge close to a baton of wood, with the scoring at the top, and applying pressure to the scored line.

7 Cut out the holes you need for the sink and hob, etc. The easiest way to do this is to lay the backer board in position, secure in place with a few screws and then, from inside the cabinet, use a pencil to mark the edges of the hole in the plywood that you made earlier. Now remove the backer board and cut out the hole exactly as you cut out the hole in the plywood earlier.

8 If you're going to tile the front edge of the countertop you'll need to cut out some backer board for this edge as well. Remember, it's not essential to tile this front edge, you could use wooden or metal edging here, but now is when you'll need to make that decision.

9 You can just screw the backer board directly to the plywood,

but you get a stronger, more stable surface if you apply thin-set mortar or flexible floor tile adhesive to the plywood first, stick the backer board onto this and then screw it into the plywood.

10 If you're going to tile the worktop, the odds are you're also going to tile a splashback. You can do this by just applying the tiles directly to the wall, but it's easier to get a perfectly smooth, even finish if you

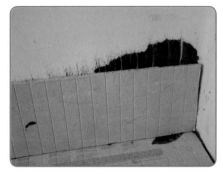

secure a section of backer board to the wall using the thin-set mortar or floor tile adhesive you used earlier and tile directly onto this.

11 Secure all the sections of the backer board together by applying tile adhesive to the gaps. Cover the gap with a strip of fibreglass backer board tape, before smoothing over some more tile adhesive.

12 You now have a secure surface, ready for tiling on. If you're tiling the edge of your worktop, think about using cap-tiles to create a neat, smooth edge. The downside of these is that they aren't always available for the tile range you want to use.

An alternative is to just use a tile that has a nice, finished edge, but the dilemma is which edge to show.

If you set the top tiles over the edge tiles, you get a stronger finish, but everyone sees the edge. If you set the edge tiles in front of the top tiles you get a neater look, but the edge tiles are far more likely to get damaged during day-to-day usage and fall off.

We'll cover tiling in a bit more detail in the 'Tiled splashbacks' section on page 161, but bear the following points in mind:

■ Take time to determine the best layout. Ideally you want full tiles for the front edge of the worktop and cut tiles at the back – this cut edge will be hidden by the tiled splashback. Try to avoid ending up with tiny slivers of cut tile, especially near an exposed edge.

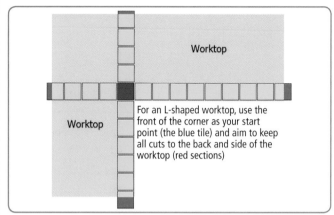

For an L-shaped worktop, use the front of the corner as your start point (the blue tile) and aim to keep all cuts to the back and side of the worktop (red sections)

■ Dry lay: cut and lay out all your tiles before you stick them down. This will show up any layout issues while you're still able to do something about them.
■ The grout line is the most vulnerable part of a tiled countertop. It'll stain more readily and is more prone to being cut and scratched. With this in mind, don't go for a thick grout line, avoid sanded grouts – non-sanded grouts are essential for fine grout lines – and use a good sealer afterwards (make sure it's 'food-safe').
■ You can get grout additives that help with staining and strength. Most of these make the grout slightly harder to work with, so be careful and practise first.
■ White grout will show up stains more readily than any other colour. You might want to consider ivory instead, or a colour that closely matches the colour of the tiles.
■ You want to use hard – ideally, porcelain – tiles for a worktop. Most ceramic wall tiles are too soft and one or more will just crack before the year is out. Softer stone tiles hide scratches quite well, but they need to be sealed and are more prone to cracking.
■ High glaze tiles are going to show scratches far more readily.
■ Larger tiles mean fewer grout lines, which to my mind at least is a very good thing.
■ It's essential that the tiles are flat and aligned with each other. If needed, use a wooden block and a rubber mallet to tap the tiles down.

■ You can polish granite and marble tiles, which is a good idea on any visible edges. Use polishing discs and a grinder to achieve this.
■ Screw a wooden baton, or the remains of your plywood, under the front edge of the countertop to support the tiles as they dry.

A CONCRETE COUNTERTOP

In terms of creating a unique look on a reasonable budget, you can't go far wrong with a concrete countertop. Here are some dos and don'ts and basic practices to help you:

■ Unless you've done this before, the first thing you need to do is set aside time to practise. The basic ingredients for a concrete worktop are relatively cheap but the options available in terms of mixes and effects are vast, so play around for a while. If you set up some test moulds bear in mind that the size of the mould is going to affect the rate at which the countertop dries, which in turn will affect the strength. With that in mind, you might want to build some test moulds about 600 x 600mm (24 x 24in) that are the same depth as your final countertop.

■ A concrete countertop will be heavy, so you need to ensure that all your base cabinets are sound, secure and able to take the weight. If you have any doubts, replace and/or secure those cabinets now.

■ There are two basic approaches: cast the worktop in situ, i.e. build the moulds on top of your base cabinets and pour the concrete directly into them, or make your countertop in the garage, for example, and bring it into the kitchen when you've finished.

Casting in situ means you can check your mould before you pour the concrete and be sure it's right. There's no heavy lifting and the danger of breaking the resultant worktop is reduced. On the other hand, your kitchen is going to be out of action for some time and you're going to throw up a lot of mess and dust in it. It can also be a lot more awkward to work on a countertop that has walls and cabinets hard up against it and as a general rule it's best to forget about polishing a concrete countertop that's been built in situ.

If you make the countertop in your garage you can ensure that you have the space needed to work on it. You can cast it upside down, which is much better if you want to embed various items in the concrete – coloured glass, shells, pea gravel, etc. – as these will settle to the bottom of the cast and be visible in the final worktop. You can also polish the final worktop without making a complete mess of your kitchen. On the downside, it's easier to get your mould wrong and you're going to have to get it back into your kitchen, which will require friends and either casting the countertop in sections or cutting them into sections before moving them.

■ The biggest problem is ensuring that the finish you get is the finish you wanted and that the resulting concrete mix is strong enough to survive day-to-day life in your kitchen. The easiest way to reduce these worries is to buy a kit. Lots of online companies sell these, they come with their own installation instructions and you can buy various decorative mouldings. The real upside of a kit is that you get the results of someone else's hours and hours of testing; the downside is that you'll be paying for that experimentation and Sod's law states that two weeks after creating your own 'unique' countertop, you'll walk into someone else's kitchen and see the exact same thing.

If you're feeling brave, or broke, or both, then experiment with your own mixes, but bear the following in mind:

☐ The amount of water you add to the mix is critical. As a general rule: the drier the initial mix, the stronger the resultant concrete and the lower the risk of shrinkage and cracking during the curing process. So measure the ratio of concrete mix to water very carefully and be consistent.

☐ A mix without much water doesn't flow very well, so you end up with lots of holes in your countertop. Reduce this by adding a 'plasticiser' to the mix, which will increase the fluidity and make the mix easier to work with, without changing the water content.

☐ You'll need to embed some sort of reinforcing wire/plastic into the mould. Many kits will provide these, but you can buy reinforcing mesh – chicken wire will do – from most builder's merchants. You should aim to embed any reinforcement into the centre of your concrete. If you buy your own, you can use crossed nails to support the mesh. Alternatively, pour half your concrete, place your mesh into position and pour the rest - this requires a fairly dry mix to ensure the mesh doesn't just sink.

☐ You can also add reinforcing fibres to the mix. These don't do much for the final strength of your countertop, but they do reduce the risks of cracking due to shrinkage and as such let you add more water to the mix. These fibres may well be visible in the final product and it will be up to you to decide if this is decorative or not. Casting the concrete the right way up from the outset will reduce the chances of these fibres being visible.

☐ You'll want to add an 'aggregate' to your mix – usually about 60–80% of the final mix will be aggregate. The most common is sand or gravel. These are added primarily as a 'filler', i.e. to reduce the amount of cement you're using, but they also affect the strength, colour and shrinkage rates.

☐ In addition, you may well want to try using 'decorative' aggregates; coloured glass, shells, gravel, sand, crushed rock, metal shavings, etc. How much of these you add and how large the 'chunks' are will affect the concrete, changing the strength and the shrinkage rates. With this in mind, it's important to document how much you add and to be consistent with the size of the individual 'chunks'.

- Soft water-absorbing aggregates are best avoided, as they weaken the mix and are prone to 'pop-outs' – they absorb water, swell up and pop off the concrete above them, causing a hole in your lovely new countertop.
- Check the properties of your decoration. For example, shells might look nice but they also dissolve in mild acids such as vinegar and lemon juice, which is not ideal for a countertop surface.
- It's best if the aggregate is fairly round, as it will make your concrete flow better, but if you opt for large decorative aggregate then go for thinner pieces.
- If you're casting your concrete the right way up you might find that your 'decoration' just disappears below the surface, never to be seen again. Making your mix drier will help to reduce this, but you can also experiment with sprinkling your decorative aggregate over the surface after you've left the mix to dry for a while.
- The basic colour of the concrete is determined by what cement you use and what your basic aggregate 'fillers' are. So find a basic colour you like – usually the lighter the better – and stick to it. However, you're not stuck with this base colour, you can add pigment to the mix when you make it up or you can stain the concrete afterwards. Pigments can be in power or liquid form. If you use a liquid pigment just bear in mind that it usually counts as water in your mix, so you'll need to reduce the amount of water as a result.
- You can get really clever by adding different pigments to different batches of concrete to try for a marbled effect!
- Play around with the depth of the countertop. The thinner the countertop, the lighter it will be. On the downside it will also be weaker, so strike a balance.
- Measure the 'yield' you get from your mix so that you can work out exactly how much of everything you'll need to complete your worktop.

If you're making your countertop in situ then you'll need a solid, sturdy base for your worktop. You can use plywood for this, but pick exterior grade or marine ply as you don't want it warping if it gets damp. Use at least 18mm (¾in) thick plywood, partly for the strength but also to reduce how thick your worktop needs to be and, as a result, how light it will be. It's always best to cover the ply with a diluted wash of PVA glue (about one-part glue to five-parts water) just

to make the surface less absorbent.

If you're making the countertop elsewhere then look to reduce the weight of the finished product by embedding foam into the mould. It's best to do this by applying a layer of cement, letting it dry a bit and then adding your 'filler'. Don't overdo it, as there's a balance between reduced weight and reduced strength.

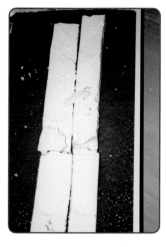

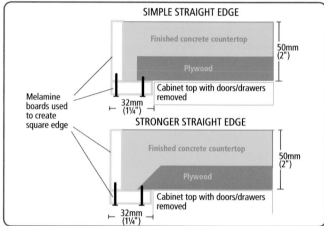

SIMPLE STRAIGHT EDGE
Finished concrete countertop
Plywood
Cabinet top with doors/drawers removed
50mm (2")
Melamine boards used to create square edge
32mm (1¼")

STRONGER STRAIGHT EDGE
Finished concrete countertop
Plywood
Cabinet top with doors/drawers removed
50mm (2")
32mm (1¼")

- Are you going with homemade edges or have you bought a decorative moulding kit? If it's the latter, you ought to have some instructions with the mouldings. If you're going to make the edging yourself, create a base that extends about 10mm (⅖in) around the front and sides of the cabinets and make a square edge just using two strips of melamine board screwed together. You can make this edge stronger if you go around your plywood base with a jigsaw set to a 45° angle.

- Melamine board makes a very good mould, as the finished surface is very smooth and concrete struggles to stick to it. Just to make sure your concrete doesn't stick, give it a rub down with some vegetable oil before pouring the concrete into the mould – it's usually easier to do this after you've sealed the mould, but before you've added the reinforcing mesh (see below).

■ Remember, your mould needs to include holes for the sink, taps, cooker hobs, etc. You can use melamine board for much of this and plastic sheeting and plastic bottles to create the rounded edges and tap holes.

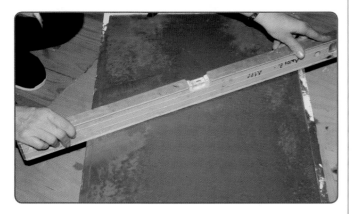

■ The mould should be about 50mm (2in) thick. We're going to use the edge of the mould to get a level surface on our countertop, so it's essential that the depth is consistent and you have a good, level edge all the way around.

TIP *Most timber merchants will cut wood to the right depth for you free of charge, so if you don't have a bench saw, buy your melamine board from your local timber merchant and ask them to cut it to size.*

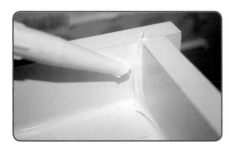

■ Make sure that the mould is sealed so that the concrete doesn't run out of it. Use ordinary silicone sealant for this task with a spreader to get a nice smooth edge. It's essential that there are no holes in your mould that your concrete can run out of.

■ To make sure the concrete gets into every corner of your mould, and to release any air trapped in the concrete, you need to vibrate the concrete. You only need to vibrate the exposed edges, as they'll be the only visible air bubbles. You can hire a concrete vibrator, but you can also just go around the edge of your mould giving it a good tap with a wooden baton. Alternatively, try vibrating it using a detail sander with no sandpaper attached. It's best to experiment on your practice moulds and see what works best, but bear in mind that vibrating the concrete too much can also be a problem.

■ Once you've filled your mould use a long straight edge – a spirit level is ideal – to get the surface of the concrete level with the frame of the mould. A sawing action works best as you slowly move the straight edge across the mould.

Now leave the concrete to dry out a little. When you can press your finger into the surface and leave a clearly defined fingerprint, go over the surface with a wooden float. Keep the front edge of the float lifted to stop it digging into the concrete and use semi-circular strokes to smooth it. Don't start at the edge, as this will just pull the concrete away from the mould. Instead, start a bit away from an edge and finish the stroke by going over the edge.

If you're casting your countertop upside down that's all you need to do, but if you're casting it in situ, wait until it's almost dry and then go over it again with a steel float. Dampen the float with a water spray and use the same semi-circular motions to bring out the 'cream' of the concrete – this is an almost pure cement surface with all the larger aggregates hidden underneath. The advantage of this is that you can create a countertop surface that doesn't need polishing. The downside is that you lose any 'special effects' from any decorative aggregates.

■ Leave the concrete to dry (cure). To stop the concrete drying out too quickly, close any curtains or blinds in the kitchen and open a few windows a fraction to create a little breeze. It's better that it takes an age for the concrete to dry rather than that it dries too fast, so try and keep the room at a fairly constant temperature, between 5°C (41°F) and 23°C (73°F) – the ideal temperature is about 10°C (50°F).

■ Once the concrete is almost dry, start to remove the mould edgings. You then need to leave it for a few days to dry completely. If you've been running your own experiments, the drying time will be longer due to the larger scale.

■ You can polish the finished surface with wet-and-dry sandpaper and an ordinary orbital sander, or you can hire a special polisher – these are usually designed for polishing concrete floors, but a small one can be used on a countertop. The grit rating you start off with is dependent on your surface, but you should always aim to finish on at least 200 grit.

■ You can get rid of any small holes using 'slurry'. This is the same concrete mix you used originally, but with no aggregates in it. If you fancy something different, try filling the holes with different-coloured slurry. Once you've filled all the holes, let it dry for a few minutes and then scrape off any excess and sand it down once it's dry – again, this is a process best practised beforehand.

■ You can use water-based and acid stains to create some very interesting finishes. Cure time is important when using stains.

■ Another approach is to use epoxy resin paints to create colourful finishes, although you lose some of the feel of the concrete in this process.

■ Your concrete will need sealing. Usually you do this before the staining and painting process, but check with the product you are using first. Make sure that the finishes you use are food safe.

EPOXY RESIN COUNTERTOPS

There are two approaches to using epoxy resin. You can either use it as a very hard, durable paint to transform an existing countertop, or you can actually make a countertop out of it in much the same way as we approached the use of concrete.

The latter approach comes under the umbrella term of an 'encapsulating' or 'casting' resin, and most of the materials and equipment you'll need can be found in your local craft store rather than a DIY outlet.

⚠ **WARNING**

Always wear gloves when working with epoxy resin and use it in a well-ventilated area. It's got quite a whiff about it and the hardener is a 'sensitizer', which means that if you use if often enough you can suddenly become very allergic to it, with dramatic and potentially dangerous effect. Always read the label and follow the manufacturers guidance.

Most of these projects will use a clear resin. You want to buy one that is very hard but does not take on a colour when exposed to sunlight – some turn yellowish. You can buy resins specifically designed for countertop projects. Set aside time to have a play around with various ideas and make up some small-scale templates until you feel confident enough to tackle the kitchen.

To keep costs down, you want your design to incorporate a lot of the 'interesting' stuff and very little of the epoxy resin. To achieve this there are two basic approaches you might want to consider. The first is where you cover the surface with, for example, slices of wood and then pour resin over the top. The second is where you mix the epoxy with, say, decorative gravel and then spread this mix onto your countertop, level it, and once it's dry, finish it off with a thin coating of epoxy. Which method works best for you is obviously going to be linked to the material you're encapsulating.

You'll need to make up a base for your countertop. Your earlier experiments should have determined what depth of resin works best, so use this to work out the depth of your base. A standard kitchen worktop is 38mm (1½in) thick, so work out what thickness of base you'll need from this. Plywood and melamine board make good bases, but your main aim should be to have something perfectly flat and clean to reduce the chances of bubbles forming in the resin.

You may want to paint this base material so that it's either hidden in your final design or plays a role in it. If you paint plywood, it's best to sand it down after the first coat to get a smooth surface, which will reduce the chances of bubbles forming. For melamine, avoid sanding first and use an appropriate primer.

If you use a translucent resin you might want to use lighting under the countertop to create a unique effect. Again, practise first to see quite how this will work and see Chapter 10, 'Lighting', for the properties of different lighting options.

You need to decide how you're going to handle the edges of your countertop. If you're applying only a very thin coat of epoxy over a fairly thin decorative effect (no more than 1–2mm thick), you could just stick the decoration on the edge using some contact glue and brush them over with epoxy – using dimes or pennies as the decoration is the classic example of how this method can be used. An alternative is to fit a permanent decorative edge to your countertop at this stage (wood or steel, for example) and then fill up the countertop with the epoxy to this edge.

Finally, you can apply a temporary edge just to act as a template. This can be removed once the epoxy is hard and a permanent edge applied – you could make this edge from the same material as your countertop. Make sure the temporary edge doesn't stick to the epoxy. Most craft shops will sell 'release agents' that can be sprayed onto the edging to ensure the resin doesn't stick. Rumours abound of various homemade approaches that include WD40, furniture wax, vegetable oil, silicone spray, etc. but whatever you opt for, try it first on your tests moulds to make sure it works for the epoxy resin you have chosen.

Epoxy resin usually comes in two bottles: a bottle of resin and a bottle of hardener. Mix these together exactly as the manufacturer says, but try not to get too much air into the mix as it can be very difficult to get out again.

If the decoration you're using is fairly thick it pays to cover it in a number of thin layers of resin. Once the decoration is completely submerged you can apply a thicker 'flood' layer.

Once you've applied the final layer, run a blowtorch over the surface. This flattens the resin and helps release trapped air. Again, practise with this approach until you're happy with how it works.

RENOVATING AND ADAPTING EXISTING COUNTERTOPS

If your existing countertop is damaged, there are a few things you can do to save the situation.

DAMAGED LAMINATED COUNTERTOP

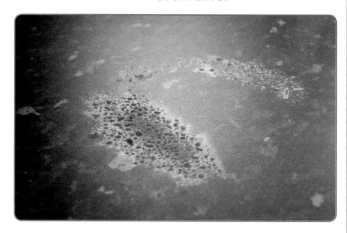

There are two common issues with laminated countertops. The first is that someone took a pan off the cooker and put it straight onto the laminate, causing it to blister. The second is that the laminate, usually on an edge, is starting to peel away.

For the heat damage you have the following options, although none are that great:

■ Try cutting out the damaged section and then replacing it with a new piece of laminate. However, the odds of getting a perfect match are quite small and it could end up costing roughly the same amount as fitting a new countertop – in which case just do that. If you want to have a go at just repairing the damage, see the steps opposite.
■ Fit something like a draining board or a chopping board over the damaged area. This process is covered in Chapter 7, 'Countertops'.

If the damaged section is not where you'd fancy fitting a chopping board, you could see about cutting out a chopping board area and then reclaiming the laminate and using it to cover the damaged area.

1 To release the laminate from the chipboard that makes up the actual countertop, heat it up using an iron. Keep the iron moving over the whole area and use a sheet of brown paper to just  separate the iron from the laminate, reducing the odds of damaging the laminate, or the iron. Use something like a paint stripping knife to try to lift an edge once the adhesive has warmed up and is tacky.

2 Once you have a section of laminate you'll need to cut it to size with a craft knife. The easiest way to do this is to roughly cut out the damaged section and mark the edges of the damaged area with some masking tape.

3 Lay your new section of laminate over the top of the damaged area and secure it in place with some more masking tape.

4 Now use a craft knife and a straight edge to cut through both the new section and the damaged area at the same time, thus ensuring a perfect fit.

TIP *Many materials can be scored, either to break them cleanly or to create neatly fitting joints. Regardless of the material you should always start off by concentrating on ensuring a straight line and you do this by applying very little pressure to the knife. Repeat the light scoring a few times until the knife has started to make its own groove, at which point it's usually safe to apply more pressure.*

5 Use an iron to warm up the old laminate on the countertop surface so that you can peel it off.

6 Position your new section of laminate in place and use your iron to stick it back down – if the iron doesn't work, just apply some contact adhesive instead. Weigh this section down for a while to ensure it's stuck down fully.

7 To hide the edges use a tube of laminate colour match joint sealant – ColorFill Worktop Joint Sealant, for example. A straight-edged putty knife or scraper will let you remove most of the excess.

8 Use the supplied solvent to remove any remaining excess.

If an edge of your laminate worktop is coming away you can use an iron, as described above, to heat up the laminate. This will make the adhesive tacky again and ought to stick the piece back down. If this doesn't work, try applying a small amount of contact adhesive to both the chipboard edge of the countertop and the back of your peeling laminate. Follow the instructions that come with the can, but as a general rule, use masking tape to cover the top of your worktop to prevent getting adhesive on it, apply your adhesive to both the countertop edge and the back of your laminate edge, wait until the adhesive has become tacky – usually a few minutes – then stick the laminate to the edge and use a roller or a towel-wrapped hand to press it down.

DAMAGED GRANITE COUNTERTOP

The most common issue with granite and stone countertops is that they develop a mass of small scratches over time, making the countertop look old and tired. If the scratches are small, they'll generally become invisible when you dampen the countertop surface. If this is the case, you could just use a granite colour enhancer to mask the scratches altogether. To apply this you need to use a solvent – usually acetone (nail varnish remover) – to remove the layer of sealer that should already be covering the granite. With the sealer removed, just apply a few coats of colour enhancer until the scratch has vanished and when it's dry, reapply some sealer. Bear in mind that you can make the scratches look worse with these colour enhancers, so always test a discrete area first.

If the scratches are deeper, try colour matching them using a permanent marker or one of a host of proprietary colour match products. If the scratches are numerous and deep then you have little choice other than to polish them out. This is a long and messy business, and you really ought to at least get a quote from a professional before you even think of doing it yourself. Bear in mind that you could completely ruin your countertop if you get this process wrong and that the correct tools are expensive to buy, although they can usually be hired.

Stone is not renowned for its flexibility, so it's not unknown for it to break. Fortunately there are now a lot of adhesives around that can fix the broken bit back in place with a join that is pretty much as strong as the original granite. Again, you need to weigh up the pros and cons of how much your granite countertop is worth versus how much you'd save by doing this work yourself. That said, it is fairly straightforward; namely buy a good glue and follow the instructions.

Adhesives that come with a glue and a hardener generally give the strongest bond and are easiest to use. You will probably need to put some sort of support in place to ensure your broken section is aligned properly and to hold the section while the glue sets. The easiest way to do this is to use some clamps to hold a small bit of wood or granite in place under the break.

PAINTING A GRANITE OR LAMINATE WORKTOP

You can buy epoxy resin paints, either in pre-coloured cans of spray paint or as tubs of clear resin and hardener, to which you add your pigment of choice. You can also use plain old-fashioned acrylic paints and then cover your finished masterpiece with a glaze of clear epoxy resin. This is essentially an artistic process, so you really need to practise and practise until you're comfortable with the process.

Here are some basic pointers, but use the products and processes that work best for you:

- Practise on small samples to keep the cost of learning to a minimum.
- With laminated tops it's usually best to lightly sand down the laminate surface first to give your paints something to bond to and highlight any areas where the laminate is damaged. Ensure the old laminate is firmly glued in place before you start anything.
- If you're using a variety of colours, it's best to buy them all from the same company so you're sure they'll blend and mix together evenly.
- Make sure you cover all the areas where you don't want epoxy with masking tape, old newspaper and dust sheets.
- Epoxy is a self-levelling liquid, but to get it truly flat it's best to go over the finished surface with a blowtorch as the heat really does help to flatten the final surface and blend colours together.

The alternative is to buy an off-the-shelf painting kit.

STAINING OR PAINTING A WOODEN COUNTERTOP

Again, this is a process that can create wonder or disaster in equal measure, depending on how much time you give yourself to practise and how expensive any mistakes might be. The general approach is the same as for painting and staining cabinet doors (see 'Renovating existing doors and drawers' on page 66).

Bear in mind that, while painting might look nice, you'll probably have to finish it off with epoxy resin to create a surface hard enough to meet the day-to-day demands of a kitchen worktop. Staining is more common for a solid wood countertop, but make sure the products you use are food safe.

Changing the splashbacks

REMOVING THE EXISTING SPLASHBACK

If you're renovating your kitchen you might want to remove the splashback, or part of it, replace the worktop and then refit the splashback. This isn't going to be easy, so think about whether it's better to rip out the splashback completely and replace it with new, as the odds are high that the existing splashback will get damaged during the removal process.

If you're determined to at least try to get the existing splashback off cleanly, follow the steps below. If you're just going to throw away the old splashback, still follow most of the steps below, but do so with a lighter heart and a heavier hammer.

REMOVING A LAMINATE SPLASHBACK

If the splashback is made from the same materials as the countertop, the odds are that it's held in place by sealant and caulk.

1 Where the splashback and the worktop meet there will be a watertight seal, usually created by a line of sealant. Again, this can be cut through using a utility knife.

2 Once dry, sealant is a very good adhesive, so you're going to need to lever the splashback off the wall and you'll need a fair amount of luck to do so without damaging it. Lever it off using something wide and thin – a bolster, for example.

If damage is not an issue for you, grab yourself a crowbar, although you might want to put a strip of wood behind the bar to reduce wall damage.

3 If you want to reuse the splashback you'll need to remove the sealant that was used to attach it to the wall. There's no easy way of doing this, but a utility knife blade fitted into a scraper makes it a little easier.

REMOVING A TILED SPLASHBACK

If you have a tiled splashback you'll need to remove at least the bottom row of tiles. Before you start, decide if you are going to retile the entire splashback and, if not, see if you can acquire suitable replacement tiles for those that are almost certainly going to get broken during the removal process. Tiles are lethally sharp when broken, so before you remove them, get yourself a pair of stout gloves and some eye protection.

1 Where the tiles meet the worktop there should be a line of sealant creating a watertight seal. This can be cut through with a utility knife.

2 To increase the odds of removing a single row of tiles cleanly, you need to remove the grout between the bottom row and the row above. You can do this with a utility knife or a  grout remover – a multitool can speed up this process. If you're removing all the tiles, ignore this step.

3 Ideally, start the removal at the end of a row, where you can get access to the tile edge. If this isn't possible, you'll need to sacrifice at least one tile by using a hammer to crack  open one tile and an old flat-headed screwdriver to remove the tile shards.

4 Now you have a clean edge, use a bolster and a hammer to carefully force the bolster behind the tile and lift it away.

TIP *If the tiles are affixed to a 'stud-wall' it can be difficult to remove them without ripping off the plasterboard and leaving great gaping holes in your wall. If this happens, just cut out a neat section of the damaged plasterboard to reveal the wooden batons or 'studs'. Cut out some new plasterboard to fit inside this hole – check the new plasterboard is the same thickness as the original*

board and screw the board into position. Secure the edges with plasterboard tape and then 'bond' the plasterboard by washing it over with PVA glue that's been diluted with roughly one-part glue to five-parts cold water – you can buy it already diluted, but it's cheaper to just make up your own. Once this is done, you can tile directly onto the plasterboard.

5 If you want to reuse the tiles, you'll need to get the old adhesive off them. This is easier to do if you place the tiles in a washing-up bowl filled with hot, soapy water and leave the tiles to soak for a few days. You can then scrape off the old adhesive with a putty knife or a paint scraper.

Making your kitchen childproof

As the father of a young child, the best advice I can give you is to complete this work before your child arrives. Yes, for the first six months or so your child is unlikely to move very much, but you'll also have little or no time to do this work. Another reason for doing the work early is that for the first month at least you'll forget that you've childproofed your kitchen and will rip out whatever device you have lovingly installed at least once a week or, if you are like me, almost daily.

CHILDPROOFING KITCHEN CABINETS AND DRAWERS

When people talk about childproofing kitchens, this is what they're usually talking about – keeping children out of cabinets filled with toxic cleaning chemicals and sharp utensils. There is a vast array of options available and they come in a vast array of price brackets. My advice would be to select something that is cheap enough to replace when you break it, won't break the cabinet when it does gets broken and doesn't rely on a key.

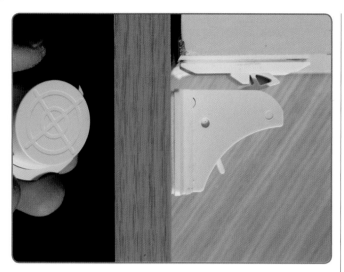

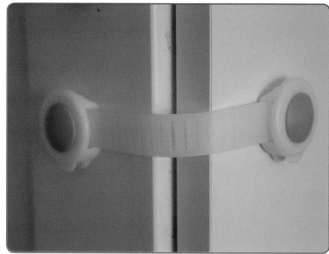

MAGNETIC LOCKS

These, as the name would suggest, use a magnet to open them, i.e. they use a key. They're completely hidden from view when the cabinets are closed, they keep the cabinet firmly closed and the magnetic key fits umpteen drawers.

The obvious downside is that you have to have the key on you all the time, therefore I'd avoid these for any cabinets that are in regular use during meal preparation – you can hang the key from your belt but it's still hassle you don't need when cooking. Restrict their use to infrequently used cabinets that hold dangerous cleaning chemicals – the cabinet under your sink, for example.

Fitting these is generally just a matter of marking your holes using a bradawl to get your screw hole going and making sure you use screws that aren't going to go right through your door. Simpler still are the self-adhesive versions, although they are not as secure.

HANDLE TIES AND STRAPS

These all work on the principle that if you can hold the cabinet handles together, the cabinet cannot be opened. If there is only one handle then you secure this handle to the next cabinet along using a strap. The upside is that there is no screwing involved with their fitting – the straps are usually self-adhesive. The downsides are that they can look awful, they might not fit the cabinet door

handles you have, the self-adhesion eventually fails and they can get annoyingly awkward to use.

You can use the strap-type locks to keep fridges and cookers locked. Yes, the glue eventually gives way but, if you get fairly cheap ones, you can just replace them as and when required.

SPRING-RELEASE LOCKS

In my experience, these are the easiest to use on a day-to-day basis and they're fairly cheap. On the downside, they can be awkward to fit and you may have to adjust the cabinet door hinge and drawer mechanism fairly regularly to keep them working (see 'Adjusting doors with modern hinges' on page 122). They also aren't that secure and a determined child can eventually overpower them.

The only issue with fitting them is getting the two parts of the latch to line up properly and the fact that the inner part of the mechanism often has to be attached to the top of the cabinet or drawer, which is just plain awkward.

Personally, I'd fit magnetic locks to those cabinets holding dangerous stuff that I can't move out of reach, strap locks to all the appliances and spring-release locks to everything else. I'd also check that all hinges and drawer mechanisms in the kitchen are solid, firmly in place and working correctly – if they're moving or loose then no locking mechanism is likely to work for long, if at all.

OTHER THINGS TO CONSIDER

To fully childproof a kitchen you need to try to put yourself into the mind of a short but stubbornly determined vandal with plenty of time on his/her hands, boundless energy, the sort of curiosity that would kill off all the cats within a three-mile radius and a gritty refusal to acknowledge any form of Health and Safety regulation. Do this and you quite quickly realise just how dangerous the home, and especially the kitchen, is.

CHEMICALS

An awful lots of kitchen products are downright dangerous. Locking them away is fine, but it also pays to think about moving them to a cabinet that is out of reach of the kids. Remember that dishwasher tablets are quite sweet-like to look at but are poisonous. It's not a good idea to leave them in the dishwasher for any length of time if the dishwasher door is not locked with some sort of strap-type lock.

ELECTRICITY

Most modern gadgets in the kitchen are electrical. This means interesting switches to entice your child and cables and leads all

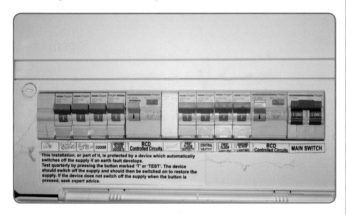

over the place that can be chewed or pulled. Personally, I'd look to change my main electrical consumer unit to one that uses RCDs – residual current devices.

An RCD-controlled circuit will turn off the electricity the moment anything untoward happens, so a child can actually chew through the kettle lead and live to tell the tale. You can buy a number of different types of switch and plug guards. The plug ones usually just blank off the socket and the switch guards either

Below: Fitting a plug guard.

fix a switch in the open or closed position or require, say, a pencil to turn the switch on and off.

Leads are more difficult to deal with. Avoid long leads that a child can reach up to and tug, bringing a kettle or blender crashing down on them. Using plastic ties to keep leads as short as possible helps, but making sure all electrical appliances are pushed to the back of the countertops or put away completely when not being used is better. Pay special attention to the kettle, as this is both a heat and an electrical hazard.

HEAT

This is the one that terrifies me. Heat is something you have to have in a kitchen and it's difficult to make its use entirely safe. With regards to the cooker and the hob there are a few things you can do.

Firstly, use some of the strap-type handle ties to stop little ones opening the oven door.

It also might be the right time to think about either buying a cooker where the gas can only be turned on if the burner ring is lit – they have a thermocouple on each burner ring; if the gas goes out it stops the flow of gas, and if the gas hasn't been lit it doesn't matter if little fingers play with the dials as it doesn't turn the gas on. Alternatively buy a cooker than has a lid – when the lid is down, the burner rings cannot be lit. With an electric cooker, it might just be an idea to turn it off at the main switch, which is usually at the back of the countertop and therefore well out of reach of small children.

In day-to-day usage it pays to only use the back burner rings when children are around and to always turn pan handles to the back or side.

OTHER DANGERS

Most kitchens have tiled floors, which are easy to keep clean but can be very slippery when wet. It makes sense to put non-slip mats on the floor to reduce the chances of them slipping and ensure there's nothing too sharp at ankle height, so that if they do slip they're not going to hurt themselves too much.

Don't leave things on the edge of your countertops where a child can reach up and pull the items down on top of themselves. The biggest advantage you have over a small child is height, so put the most dangerous items in your kitchen on the top shelves of wall cabinets.

4 DISMANTLING THE OLD KITCHEN

This is the fun bit! If you do nothing more in your quest for a lovely new kitchen, at least experience the sheer joy of ripping out the old one. Alas, it can also be a quite dangerous pastime, so have a read of this complete chapter beforehand.

Planning ahead

I cannot repeat this enough. If you don't plan things properly you will run into disaster sooner or later. So before you take up a hammer and wield an attitude upon your old kitchen, ask yourself, 'Have I got everything ready for the new kitchen?' To help you figure that out, have a read of the next chapter where we go through the basic kitchen installation process step-by-step.

I guess the most important thing to ask yourself before you do anything is 'how long can we last without a functioning kitchen?' This is going to vary wildly depending on your circumstances. There was a time in my life when all I needed from a kitchen was a fridge and a kettle. Now, I live half my life in our kitchen and I'd need the process to be quick and smooth, i.e. well planned. I'd also need an extensive list of take-away restaurants and somewhere to safely store my young boy out of harm's way in the interim. Take the time to think all of these issues through before you start.

LIVE TO FIT ANOTHER DAY

Removing a kitchen invariably involves removing tiles. Broken tiles are extremely sharp and can inflict a vicious cut with little or no encouragement. The rest of the demolition process isn't exactly risk free either so, before you start attacking your kitchen, make sure you have all the basic safety equipment to hand – gloves, safety glasses, heavy-duty work trousers, knee pads, ear protectors and at least a basic first aid kit.

THE RIGHT TOOLS FOR THE JOB

Have you got the right tools to hand? Not just for the ripping out stage, but for putting everything back again? We've covered all the basic tools in earlier chapters, but have a read through the rest of this manual to make sure you have everything you need before you start.

THE RIGHT PEOPLE LINED UP

As part of the budget process, you should have already decided if and when you're going to need to bring in a professional. There are also parts of the process that will require a partner to help lift and hold things. Make sure you have confirmed the dates with all of these people in advance.

You wouldn't believe the number of calls we get from people who have ripped out their kitchen and only then realised that they need a plumber to help put the new one back again. Most decent tradesmen will have work booked weeks, if not months, in advance, so make sure you have arranged a date for their work BEFORE you rip everything out.

The demolition process

There are two basic approaches to removing the old kitchen:

- **Option 1:** Remove it carefully so the components can be reused or resold.
- **Option 2:** Purchase a large hammer and vent life's frustrations upon your old kitchen until it has been reduced to rubble.

I tend to go for option 2 for the very simple reason that it's far more fun! However, I'm going to assume that we all know how to hit things very hard until they break, so we'll concentrate on the more decorous approach to kitchen removal. This might do little to improve our mood, but it should allow us to recoup some of our money – with a bit of luck.

Regardless of if you use an enormous hammer or a loving embrace, the actual steps to removing your kitchen are much the same:

1 Either prepare your car ready to transport the waste to the local tip or hire in a skip for the duration of your kitchen project.

2 Everything that's staying in place or has resale/reuse value needs to be covered to protect it from damage and dust. It also pays to tape up the doors into the kitchen to stop dust spreading throughout the house.

TIP *Taping plastic sheeting over everything will protect things but can leave unsightly tape adhesive residue on walls, doors and windows* 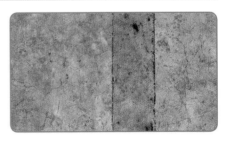 *afterwards. You can avoid this altogether by using masking tape, but often this just doesn't stick things down well enough. If you do get residue marks, try using warm soapy water on them. If this isn't working, help the process along by warming everything up with a hairdryer or make a gentle abrasive paste – baking soda with water or coconut oil, for example.*

3 Remove all the old doors, shelves and drawers (see 'Removing old doors and drawers' on page 89). This makes everything easier to lift and gets them out of the way.

4 Unscrew the electrical sockets – if you have tiled splashbacks, you'll need to loosen the electrical sockets to get all the tiles off. If you're going to reuse these sockets you might want to remove them completely – in which case you'll need an electrician – or you might want to cover the face of the sockets with masking tape to reduce the chances of them getting damaged. Either way, if they have electricity running to them it's a good idea to turn off all the sockets at the consumer unit first.

The wall cabinets will often have lighting underneath them. You'll need to remove the electrical cables before taking down the wall units. Again, this might be best left to a professional electrician.

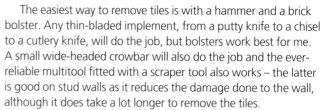

⚠ **WARNING**

The easiest way to get yourself electrocuted is to not tell people what you're up to; you turn the electricity off, someone watching the television wonders what's happening, sees the switch on the consumer unit has been tripped and turns it back on again, just as you're licking the live wire. So tell people what you are doing and put a notice on the consumer unit to warn people not to turn things back on again. If you can isolate a circuit with a fuse, always take the fuse out and put it in your pocket.

5 Knock off all the wall tiles. Be careful when you're doing this – gloves and safety glasses are essential. If you have stud walls (see 'A brief guide to walls and wall plugs' on page 44), you want to try not to rip holes into the wall when you're doing this, but you also need to accept that this is sometimes unavoidable and you'll just have to reboard it afterwards – see 'Reboarding and repairing holes in walls and ceilings' on page 101.

The easiest way to remove tiles is with a hammer and a brick bolster. Any thin-bladed implement, from a putty knife to a chisel to a cutlery knife, will do the job, but bolsters work best for me. A small wide-headed crowbar will also do the job and the ever-reliable multitool fitted with a scraper tool also works – the latter is good on stud walls as it reduces the damage done to the wall, although it does take a lot longer to remove the tiles.

Unless you're planning on reusing these tiles, don't bother about removing the grout on a plastered wall. Just work the bolster under an edge and give it a hit with your hammer. On stud walls, especially when they haven't been plastered, it can reduce the wall damage if you use a grinder or multitool to remove the grout first. Personally, I think it's quicker just to knock the tiles off and reboard the wall if the subsequent damage is dramatic.

6 With the tiles out of the way, remove the wall cabinets (see 'Removing wall cabinets' on page 91).

7 With the wall cabinets out of the way and the tiles gone you can remove the countertops. If there is a sink or a cooker hob in the worktop, have a read of the appropriate section below. If there's nothing set into the countertop then the only thing holding it down are the screws up from the cabinets below and a line of sealant which seals it against the wall – usually the worktop will have two lines of sealant; one creating a waterproof seal between the worktop and the tiles and another holding the worktop against the wall. How you go about removing the worktop depends on what it's made from and if you are planning on selling it (see 'Removing the existing worktop' on page 92).

8 All that remains of the actual kitchen are the base cabinets (see 'Removing base cabinets' on page 94).

9 That's the kitchen itself out of the way; all that's left now is the ceiling, the lighting and the flooring. For removing the existing flooring see 'Removing the old flooring' on page 97.

For the ceiling, you have the option of leaving it as it is – always remembering that if you change the ceiling light positions you are going to be left with holes that will need to be filled in – or you can get the ceiling 'skimmed' by a professional plasterer. The latter option is more expensive, but the finish is much better. If you opt to leave it as it is and just fill in any holes, have a read of the section 'Reboarding and repairing holes in walls and ceilings', on page 101.

If your ceiling has a 'textured' finish, you might wish to get the ceiling skimmed anyway. Check with your plasterer first, but it's often easier to overboard the ceiling and then skim it, in which case you can cut the price down a bit by at least doing the overboarding yourself (see 'Reboarding and repairing holes in walls and ceilings' on page 101). Be aware that old textured plaster finishes often used asbestos in their make-up.

REMOVING OLD DOORS AND DRAWERS

Remember that there's a market for second-hand doors, so even if you're planning on replacing them entirely, it's well worth getting the old ones off cleanly.

REMOVING FRAMELESS DOORS WITH QUICK-RELEASE HINGES

Most modern frameless door hinges come with a quick-release mechanism. These hinges can look horribly complicated and we'll be going over how these work later on, but for now just ignore their apparent complexities.

1 Start with the bottom hinge. Run your finger to the back of the hinge – the end set deepest into the cabinet – and feel for a little spring-loaded lever or bar.

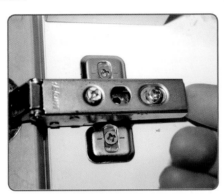

2 While these hinges all work on the same principles, the 'lever' will come in a wide variety of shapes and sizes and release in a slightly different way. To add to the confusion, many hinges will come with a metal or plastic cover plate that hides the mechanism from view. These can usually just be flicked off with a small flat-headed screwdriver – see below.

So, we're going to have to play around a bit to figure out how our hinge releases. With this in mind, hold the door securely, lift the lever up and give the hinge a little tug. The hinge should now separate from its base plate. If it doesn't, try pressing the lever down, or pushing it in, all while giving it a little tug and a wiggle.

If there doesn't seem to be a spring-loaded movable bar or lever, you probably don't have a quick-release hinge, so jump to 'Removing frameless doors with sliding hinges' below.

3 Repeat Step 2 for the upper hinge.

Below: Removing the base (or mounting) plate.

4 If you're planning on reusing the old hinges and cabinets, you can just leave the hinge base plate attached to the cabinet,

but you'll need to remove the rest of the hinge from the old door.

If you're replacing the hinge completely, just unscrew the base plate from the cabinet – there are usually two screws, one at the top and one at the bottom.

Above: Removing the hinge from the door.

Below: Hinge cover plate.

You should be able to see two screws holding the actual hinge to the door. If you can, just unscrew them and lift the hinge off. If you can't, there's probably a cover over the hinge, so slide a small flat-headed screwdriver under the cover and lift it up to expose the screws.

REMOVING FRAMELESS DOORS WITH SLIDING HINGES

Older frameless doors don't have the quick-release system, so if you can't find any moving bar at the end of the hinge, you probably have one of these.

1 Hinges often have a cover over the adjustment mechanism that clips onto the hinge and can be removed by just flicking it off with a small flat-headed screwdriver.

2 Using a Pozidriv or Phillips screwdriver, loosen the screw at the back of the lower hinge. You should now be able to pull the base of the door outwards and slide the hinge apart – you might have to give the door a bit of a wiggle first.

3 Repeat with the upper hinge.

REMOVING OVERLAY AND INSET DOORS ON FRAMED CABINETS

Doors on framed cabinets usually have much simpler, more traditional hinges. The only problem these pose is that the screws have often been painted or varnished over in the past. If this is the case, carefully remove the offending material using a craft knife.

1 Remove all the screws, except for one, from both upper and lower hinges.

2 Supporting the door, remove the final screw from the lower hinge.

3 Remove the final screw from the upper hinge and remove the door.

4 Remove the rest of the hinges from the door and set them aside if you're planning on reusing them.

More modern 'framed' doors will have a variation on the 'quick-release' hinges that we discussed earlier, often adapted so that the hinge can be mounted on the side of the frame. Again, you can

either lift a little spring-loaded lever at the back to release it, or just unscrew the single screw securing it to the base plate and lift the door away.

REMOVING THE DRAWERS

How straightforward this is going to be is largely dependent on the age of your kitchen. In older, traditional kitchens, you can usually just pull the drawer right out.

The problem with old drawers was that people kept pulling them out completely by accident. To prevent the chaos that this caused, modern drawers come with a variety of mechanisms to ensure that the drawer will only come out so far and then stop. Alas, there are lots and lots of these mechanisms and few are easy to fathom.

If you are having problems releasing your drawers, the most obvious place to look for clues is on the internet – there are umpteen websites showing how the various drawers work for different manufacturers. So, if you know the manufacturer of your kitchen, just enter 'removing [manufacturer name]kitchen drawers' into your search engine. If this doesn't work try the following:

1 Pull the drawer open until it reaches its stop. If you're lucky you'll see a runner on the side of the drawer with wheels. With these you can lift the drawer unit up slightly and it should pull farther out and come away.

2 Another common approach is to have the drawer rail set under the drawer. For these, pull the drawer out till it stops and have a look under the drawer.

3 If you move the drawer back and forth you can see

how the mechanism runs and what it stops up against. Often there is a little catch here and by pulling the drawer up or down a little, you can slip the drawer off its rail.

4 If pulling up and down doesn't work, look for levers or buttons to press. These are often a different colour so they stand out, and they're usually quite close to the front of the drawer. There'll be a button or lever on each side of the drawer and they'll usually both need to be pressed at the same time.

REMOVING THE DRAWER FRONTS

If you're renovating your kitchen, you can often just get away with removing the drawer fronts rather than the entire drawers.

1 Most modern drawers with metal drawers and wooden drawer fronts have a mechanism that lets you remove the drawer front completely. This is handy, as it makes both replacement

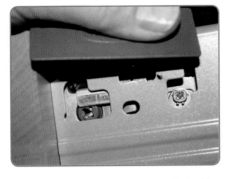

and renovation much easier. First look for any covers on the inside or outside of the drawer close to the drawer front and carefully remove them.

2 This ought to reveal some sort of mechanism. If you can see a screw head it usually means the drawer front can be removed by just giving this screw a quarter turn. Bear in mind that the 'mechanism' you have revealed will have two basic functions: to release the drawer front completely and to allow you to level and adjust the drawer front. Keep an eye on what's happening when you turn any screws: if things just seem to be moving up and down then you have found the adjustment mechanism, so continue your search for the release screw.

3 If there are no covers on the side of the drawer then the release mechanism will usually be a button or lever under the drawer, close to the drawer front. Press this button or lever and the drawer front should come away.

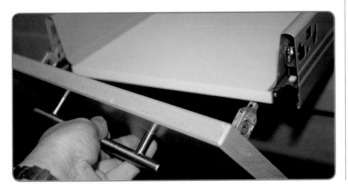

REMOVING THE DOOR AND DRAWER HANDLES

If you look behind the handle you'll usually see the screw, or screws, holding it to the drawer or door. If this is the case it's just a simple matter of grabbing the appropriate screwdriver and removing the screws.

Occasionally, you'll look behind the doorknob and there's nothing there. In this instance the screw is actually a part of the knob and you just need to turn the knob anti-clockwise to unscrew it from the door or drawer.

REMOVING WALL CABINETS

1 If you haven't already done so, remove the doors and shelves (see 'Removing old doors and drawers' on page 89).

2 Cabinets are usually screwed to their neighbours to make them more rigid and stable. To remove the units, we'll first need to remove these screws.

There are usually two screws at the front of the cabinet and one or two screws at the back. If you're lucky, these screws will be clearly visible but, more often than not, they're hidden away, often under plastic caps. If you still can't find them, it's common practice to hide them behind the hinge base plate or for them to be set at the same height as any shelves so that the shelves hide them once fitted.

Below: Flick these caps off to reveal the screws

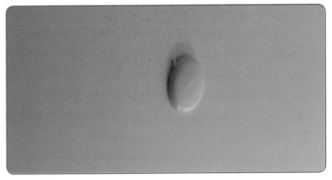

Often, the manufacturer will supply cabinet connector bolts to hold the cabinets together. To get

these out you need to unscrew them until the screw is almost out of the bolt and then lightly tap the screw with a hammer to knock the bolt out – you may also need a pair of pump pliers to pull the bolt out altogether.

3 Often the wall cabinets will be attached to a cornice at the top and a pelmet at the bottom. Occasionally, you can just undo the screws holding the cornice/pelmet to the cabinet you want to remove, but most of the time you'll need to remove the entire length of cornice/pelmet. These are usually held in place by screws – just find them and carefully remove them.

4 Check that your cabinet doesn't have any lighting inside or underneath it. If it does, just remove the screws fixing the lights and cabling to the cabinet. Make sure no electrical cables are passing through holes in your cabinets. If they are you might want to have an electrician disconnect the cable from the light so the cable can be removed.

5 Occasionally, the cabinets are simply screwed into the wall behind them. If this is the case, just remove those screws, while a friend supports the cabinet from underneath.

More often, the units are held in place by two brackets set on either side of the unit, near the top. These are invariably hidden behind covers, so as not to offend the eye. Remove these covers – they usually slide off.

While supporting the cabinet from below – you'll need a friend for this bit – loosen the screws. By loosening the screws you can

now lift the cupboard up off the brackets and away from the wall.

Sometimes you'll remove the cover to reveal a system with two screws. One screw, usually the uppermost screw, tightens the cabinet to the supporting bracket, whilst the lower screw is used to get the cabinet level. Since we're removing the cabinet it doesn't really matter what screw we turn, so start with the top and, if that doesn't work, try the bottom screw.

REMOVING THE EXISTING WORKTOP

If you have a laminated particleboard worktop then removing it is pretty easy, but there's little to be gained by removing it neatly – they don't have much, if any, resale value. On the flip side, a solid stone or laminated stone worktop does have resale value but – as a result of 'Sods law', clause 2, subsection 6 – is markedly more difficult to remove cleanly.

Solid stone can be so difficult to remove cleanly that it really does make sense to get a quote from a professional company to remove it for you.

Above: Tiled splashback on top of worktop.

1 Most kitchens will have a 'splashback'. If you're dismantling your kitchen entirely then you'll have removed this splashback already. If you're renovating, you need to be aware that a correctly fitted worktop is fitted underneath this splashback, meaning that it's close to impossible to remove the worktop without first removing the splashback (see 'Changing the splashbacks' on page 81).

2 Before you can remove the countertops you need to disconnect any cooker hobs and sinks that may be set into them (see 'Disconnecting the sink' and 'Removing the hob' on page 96). Most hobs, gas or electric, will have an electrical supply that will also need to be disconnected (see 'Electrics' on page 96).

The holes where your hob and sink were are the most likely places in which your worktop will break. If you're planning on reusing your worktop, you need to be very careful around these areas. For stone worktops you might want to think about cutting the worktops in the middle of these holes with a grinder or a circular saw so that you at least have a clean cut that can be joined up later with epoxy resin.

Right: A grinder with a depth setting will ensure you don't cut through the cabinets

3 The worktop will be attached to the cabinets underneath. With wooden and standard laminated worktops there will be screws coming up from the cabinets below. If this is the case just find the screws – usually a few per cabinet – and remove them.

Stone or tiled worktops are often glued onto a substrate of plywood or cement board. If you're lucky, this was screwed up from inside the cabinets, but often they're screwed down and the worktop itself then covers the screws. In the latter case, you have no option other than to try to prise the countertop off with a crowbar, which will almost certainly damage the cabinets as well as the countertop, or use a multitool to see if you can cut through the glue and screws.

The multitool is the best option, but it will take some time. Try to cut through the glue or sealant holding the countertop base

to the top of the cabinets. Bear in mind that there may be some screws holding the worktop down, so use a blade that can cope with metal. Cut along the back of the countertop to break any seal holding it against the wall.

An alternative to the multitool is to use a crowbar to lift one edge of the worktop enough to get a small shim between the base of the worktop and the top of the cabinet. Now work your way all along the worktop, putting more shims in place. Once you've lifted the entire length of the worktop, go back to the start, lift it a little more and put a thicker shim in place – or use a hammer to

tap a wedge deeper underneath the countertop. The aim here is to slowly lift the worktop off the cabinet until the seal finally breaks. This approach does work, but the cabinets are usually damaged in the process.

4 While laminate worktops are usually light enough to just be lifted out whole, life is going to be much easier if you can cut the worktops into sections. For solid stone worktops, cutting them into sections is pretty much essential, as they are just too heavy to lift otherwise – that weight can also cause them to break apart when you attempt to lift them off the cabinets.

Fortunately, these worktops were usually too heavy to fit as a single section as well, so there will already be joints. Carefully go over the worktop and identify these joints. Having done that, check under the worktops to see if any brackets or plates are holding the joints together.

TIP *A quicker, though messier, approach to removing the worktop is to forget about separating the sections neatly at the existing joints and just go at them with a grinder or a circular saw. A circular saw, set to the depth of the worktop, will quickly go through a wooden worktop. It might not get right to the edge that's hard against the wall – although you should be able to slide the worktop out far enough to make a clean cut – but it will cut through enough of the worktop to allow you to break it apart.*

This approach will also work with stone worktops, but you'll fill your home with stone dust. To keep this to a minimum, seal the room first with plastic sheeting and masking tape, open all the windows, use water to keep the dust down at the cut and a vacuum close to the cutting blade to remove as much of the dust as you can at source – this entire operation will involve a number of friends. The most important aspects of this approach are to use the right cutting blade for the materials you have and to wear eye protection, gloves and masks at all times.

5 Remove any brackets, either by unscrewing them or using a grinder/ multitool to cut through them.

6 Now use a multitool or a utility knife blade to cut along the joint. The worktop is usually held together by glue or a sealant and, with a modicum of luck, the joint is wide enough to get a blade into. For laminate worktops, you don't need to cut right through the joint; you're just trying to weaken it enough to allow you to break the worktop at this point for easier removal.

7 To separate the worktop cleanly, place a series of shims under one side of the weakened joint – an alternative is to push a baton of 50 x 25mm (2 x 1in) underneath one side of the joint.

8 While a friend holds the supported section of worktop, push down on the unsupported section and use it as a lever to break the joint. With a bit of wiggling, the worktops should separate cleanly at the joint.

For stone worktops, the joint is usually held together by an epoxy glue, which can sometimes be stronger than the stone itself. If you score the joint with a utility knife and then use a heat gun to soften the seal, you can sometimes get the joint to break open.

9 Once the worktop is free from the cabinets and cut into sections, they can be removed. Bear in mind that stone countertops can be enormously heavy. Also, stone is very brittle, so if you hold the sections horizontally there's a good chance they'll just break in the middle when you lift them. As such, you need to lift them and get them edge on as soon as possible.

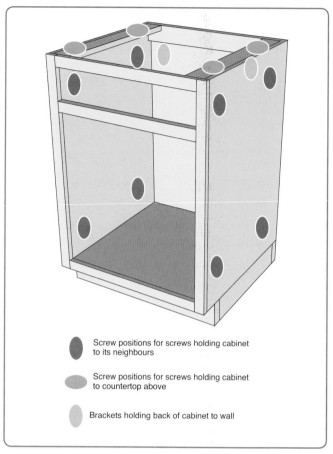

Screw positions for screws holding cabinet to its neighbours

Screw positions for screws holding cabinet to countertop above

Brackets holding back of cabinet to wall

REMOVING BASE CABINETS

Base cabinets are generally held in place by brackets that hold them against the wall, by screws that hold them against the neighbouring cabinets and by more screws that hold them to the countertop above.

1 Remove all the doors first (see 'Removing old doors and drawers' on page 89). As with wall cabinets, the base cabinets are usually screwed to their neighbours and we'll need to remove all these screws (see 'Removing wall cabinets', step 2).

2 The cabinet will also be held to the countertop above it, usually by two screws at the front and two at the back.

3 The unit should also be held against the wall, usually with two screws in the top corners. Often they're screwed directly to the wall and you'll see the screws quite clearly; occasionally they'll be hidden behind covers that can be slid or flicked off with a flat-headed screwdriver.

Most kitchen base units have a 'false back', in that there's a space about 50mm (2in) deep behind the back of the cabinet and the wall. It's common practice to secure the base unit to the wall by fitting brackets into this gap and then screwing the cabinet to the wall via this bracket. If you're removing the worktop as well as the base unit this poses no problem, as these screws are clearly visible with the worktop removed. However, if you just wish to remove the base unit on its own, you might have trouble getting to these 'hidden' screws.

If this is the case, your best option is to cut a hole into the top

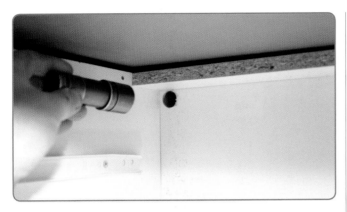

corners of your base cabinet using a hole cutter. Shine a light through these holes and, with luck, you should be able to see these securing brackets and unscrew them from the wall.

4 The unit should now be free, but if the worktop is still in place, you'll need to lower the legs to remove it. On most basic units

the legs are simple plastic legs hidden behind a plinth or kickboard.

Removing a plinth without damaging it can be a tricky business. Most plinths are held to the cabinet legs via plastic clips that are simply pulled off. In older kitchens the plinth is actually screwed into place. The screws will often be hidden under caps or recessed and covered with wood putty.

If it looks like the plinth is screwed into position, remove all the

screws you can find, except for the ones at either end. Just unscrew these about halfway, then get a grip on them with a set of pump pliers and use the screw head to tug the plinth out. If there are no screws, the plinth is probably held by these plastic clips. If you're lucky there will be a slight gap between the top of the plinth and the cabinet base. To find this you'll need to get down on the floor and explore. If you find a gap, try to get a flat-headed screwdriver in behind the plinth and gently lever it out.

If there are no gaps, have a look at the end of the length of plinth and see if there are any gaps there that you can exploit with a flat-headed screwdriver. Often pushing and pulling the plinth or its neighbour where they connect will reveal a gap big enough to get your fingers in, so try pushing the plinth at the ends.

If you can't get behind the plinth to ease it out then find yourself a small screw – a 1in, size 6 screw should do. Screw this about 12mm (½in) into the plinth, grip the head of the screw with a set of pump pliers and pull the plinth out. With the plinth removed you can now lower the cabinet legs by just turning the base of them anti-clockwise – you might need to use a set of pump pliers to get this going.

If you've removed all the screws holding the cabinet in place it should now start to lower, making it easier to remove without damaging anything.

PLUMBING

I'm not going to go into kitchen plumbing in any depth here because there's already a truly wondrous book on the subject entitled *The Haynes Home Plumbing Manual*, which covers pretty much everything you'll ever need to know about kitchen plumbing. However, you'll need to at least understand the process at this stage. Remember that your old sink and hob are probably connected up in much the same way as the new ones you'll be fitting later, so it pays to take the old ones out carefully to see how the fitting process works.

TURNING OFF THE WATER IN YOUR HOME

Before you can tackle any plumbing work you'll need to turn off the water. In an ideal world you'll look under the kitchen sink, follow the pipework from the base of the taps and quickly discover two 'isolation valves'. These come in many guises: some have a little lever you can turn; with others you insert a flat-head screwdriver into a

slot and turn it. In most cases it just needs a quarter turn to turn off the water and you can easily test this by opening the taps afterwards and checking that little or no water emerges.

The beauty of isolation valves is that you can just turn off the water to each individual tap or appliance, but if you can't find any then you're going to have to turn off the hot and cold water to the whole of your house. How you go about this varies, depending on where you live and what kind of water system you have in your house.

As a general rule, the stop tap for the cold water is under the sink, close to the floor. If you close this – turn it clockwise – the

cold water to the house will be turned off and, for many homes, all the hot water will also be turned off.

If your hot water is still running, go and find your hot water cylinder – usually in the upstairs airing cupboard. There is a tap, which usually has a round red handle, just above the cylinder and if you close this, the hot water will stop running.

Sadly, many of these taps have not been turned off since the house was first built, so they often won't turn at all. If this is the case there should be an emergency tap set outside your home, close to the property line, usually hidden under a cover set into the pavement. Turn this tap off and it turns off the cold water. If the hot water is still running despite you turning

off all the taps in the airing cupboard then just open these taps again and wait, eventually the storage tanks will empty and the hot water will stop running as well – this often takes about 5–10 minutes.

If all this has failed then bite the bullet and call in a plumber, or buy *The Home Plumbing Manual* – you know it makes sense.

DISCONNECTING THE SINK

1 With the water turned off, you need to disconnect the sink from the waste pipework. If you look under the sink you'll see the sink waste, or plug hole,

is connected to the waste pipework via a nut – usually made of plastic. This needs to be turned anti-clockwise and you can usually do this by hand. If you can't, a pair of 'pump pliers' should do the trick.

There is a section of curved pipework called a 'trap' below this nut and this will still contain water – usually fairly dirty water – so just be aware of this.

2 We now need to disconnect the taps from the hot and cold water pipework. This pipework is usually made from copper and is best cut using a 'pipe slice'. If you've only isolated the water for the kitchen taps and not turned off all the water in the house you need to make sure you cut the pipe between the base of the taps and the isolation valves. To use a pipe slice, attach it to a straight section

of pipework and turn it in the direction of the arrow marked on it. If you haven't got a pipe slice you can use a hacksaw to cut the pipework, although this will leave a sharp and often uneven edge, which will need to be smoothed down with a file afterwards if you wish to reuse this section of pipe for your new sink.

3 The sink is usually held in place by brackets underneath it that hold it onto the worktop. You just need to loosen these off with

a screwdriver. Once they are loose they can be bent back, away from the worktop.

4 The only thing now holding the sink in place is a seal. Often, this is just a foam strip and the sink can just be lifted out of the worktop. However, the seal is usually a line of sealant and you'll need to cut through it with a utility knife to break it.

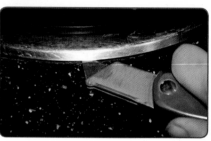

You can now lift the sink and its taps up and away from the worktop.

REMOVING THE HOB

1 A gas hob set into the worktop will be connected to the gas supply via a pipe underneath it. It's very easy to disconnect this yourself, just as it's very easy to disconnect a freestanding gas cooker from the gas supply pipework. However, without the right equipment, you cannot be certain that the gas pipe is not now leaking. A tiny leak of gas, given a bit of time, can create an impressively large hole in the exact spot your home once stood. So, please, just leave the gas pipework well alone. Get a professional in, check he or she has the correct qualifications, and let them do the job safely.

2 With the gas disconnected you can look under the hob and see that it's held in place by a bracket at each corner. Just loosen these off with a screwdriver and remove them.

3 As with the sink, the hob is often sealed to the

Above: Unscrew the brackets.

worktop with a line of sealant that needs to be cut through with a utility knife. Once you've done this, the hob can be lifted out.

ELECTRICS

Don't touch any of the electrical outlets in your kitchen until a professional electrician has come in, disconnected them and made them safe. Once you know for sure that there is no danger of electrocution, it should be fine to remove the old electrical sockets and, if you're planning on moving them, removing the old back boxes from the wall.

GAS

As mentioned already, don't disconnect any of the gas appliances yourself. Although it's easy to disconnect cookers and hobs, it's nowhere near as easy to tell if the system is completely leak free afterwards.

REMOVING THE OLD FLOORING

How you go about this depends on two things: what your flooring is and what the actual floor underneath it is made from. Jumping up and down in your kitchen is usually enough to figure out if you have a solid concrete or wooden floor. This affects how you go about taking up some flooring types, but it also affects how you go about laying any new flooring. So have a good jump.

REMOVING OLD FLOOR TILES

Floor tiles are usually hard and in many cases, very, very hard. Removing them cleanly from a kitchen floor can be a sweaty, potentially hazardous, and above all time-consuming task. Not only do you need to remove the tiles, but you also need to remove the adhesive, which is often more obstinate than the tiles ever were.

First off, this can be dangerous work so make sure you have donned your ear defenders, safety glasses, gloves and dust mask.

If the base floor of your kitchen is wood, the tiles are often laid onto thin sheets of plywood or concrete board. If this is the case, it's easier to lift this board and the tiles in one go – the board is usually held in place by fairly short screws and can be lifted with a crowbar and/or a claw hammer.

If the tiles are on a concrete floor, things can be a bit more difficult and you might want to ponder just applying the new flooring directly over the existing tiles. If the old tiles are basically sound, this could work a treat and save a lot of time. If you're changing the layout of your kitchen and need to apply the new flooring over areas that weren't covered by the old tiles, you'll need to get the non-tiled area level with the tiles you're going to use as your new floor base. The easiest way to do this is to mix up some floor tile adhesive and use it to stick down some sheets of concrete board over the non-tiled areas. If you've decided that it's best to start afresh regardless of the sweat and toil involved, read on.

Usually the tiles don't go to the edge of all your walls, so find yourself an end tile as your start point. If you can't find an already exposed tile edge, grab a large hammer and smash the tile of your choice into pieces. Remove these pieces, and you should now have a nice tile edge to get to work on.

You can just use a hammer and a wide-edged chisel to do this job, but it's much easier and faster if you buy yourself a tile-removing chisel, which is just a wide-bladed chisel with the blade set at an angle. Fit this into an SDS drill set to hammer action and get to work. Just place the chisel under a tile edge and hammer away.

If you're lucky, you'll be left with a nice, clean, even floor. If the adhesive is really obstinate, see if you can hire a heavy-duty tile scraper, which is really just a bigger version of the tile chisel and

SDS hammer drill. If you can't, then consider using 'self-levelling' compound to smother the remains of the adhesive and leave you with a flat, smooth finish. You

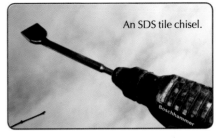

An SDS tile chisel.

can do this yourself, but it's usually best left to a professional. If you're going to do it yourself, just remember that you need to ensure the levelling compound can't just run away through any holes, and that you usually need to encourage it to self-level by smoothing it a bit with a fairly large metal trowel.

REMOVING VINYL TILES

This was the kitchen flooring of choice for many decades. Fortunately, because it's been in place for

⚠ **WARNING**

Old Vinyl floor tiles often contained asbestos, so you might want to just leave them well alone or call in an expert for advice.

so long, they are often in the process of removing themselves and only need a little encouragement.

If yours are more obstinate, you can hire or buy a floor tile stripper. The cheapest of these is just a wide, thin blade, attached to a handle. They do work, but they also break quite quickly – you can buy replacement blades though. You can also hire more heavy-duty versions – often motorised ones that will do the job quicker, although they're often too unwieldy to use in a small kitchen.

Alternatively, you can just use the tile chisel and SDS hammer drill approach that we talked about above, although the chisel blade is usually a little too thick to work well. Or if you're a glutton for punishment, a hammer and a thin bladed paint scraper will do the job, albeit slowly.

It's often easier to

do this job when it's quite cold. This makes the tiles very brittle and they'll shatter and come away relatively easily. If this isn't working for you, consider the exact opposite approach. Get yourself a paint stripper heat gun and use this to start heating up the tiles while a partner operates whatever tile stripper you've opted for. The heat softens the glue holding the tiles in place and can make them much easier to remove.

REMOVING LAMINATE FLOORING

This is the easiest of the lot. Just find an edge you can grab and bend the laminate section upwards. The entire row should lift and when it gets to an angle of about 75° you can usually just pull it away. Older laminate was often glued together. If this is the case you might have to grab a hammer to 'encourage' the sections to part.

If you're considering laying your own laminate in the future, it pays to take your time removing the old stuff just to see how it works. It also pays to retain the underlay beneath the laminate.

Kitchen Upgrade Manual

5 FIRST THINGS FIRST

In this chapter we'll step through the overall process of putting the new kitchen together to get a feel for what we need to do, what other people need to do and what order it all ought to be done in.

Planning your installation – the work schedule

We're only discussing the way we're going to tackle the actual kitchen installation here; we've assumed that you have actually got a plan of your proposed kitchen layout and, if the kitchen hasn't actually been delivered, it's at least on its way at this stage.

> **TIP** *People never like to see pipework and cabling, so the temptation is to bury or 'chase' everything into your walls. This is fine, but by doing so you're potentially weakening those walls. With this in mind, a horizontal channel should be no more than one-sixth of the depth of the wall and vertical channels should be no more than a third of the depth of the wall. This is usually sufficient to bury your water pipework and electrical cabling but not enough, as a general rule, to allow you to hide your waste pipework in the wall.*
>
> *Water and electricity don't play well together so never put them in the same channel, no matter how tempting you might find this idea.*

The 'work schedule' below is not exhaustive, and you can move some of the items around a bit. For example, you can move Stage 13 back, but it makes sense to get the water finished in the kitchen as soon as you can. Stage 8 can also be moved, but it's easier to paint a blank ceiling rather than having to cut in around light fittings etc. and it makes sense to wait until you have finished all the really dusty work before you even think of painting things. As such, use this list as a guide, not a set of rules.

1   Arrange for all the gas work to be moved into position and tested (see 'Moving the gas services').
2   Move the plumbing ('the first fix').
3   Move the electrical sockets.
4   Move cables for ceiling lights into position.
5   Repair any holes in your ceiling.
6   If you have stud walls or 'drylined' walls (see Chapter 2) it's a good idea to mark out exactly where you're planning on fitting your wall cabinets and fit wooden batons into the walls to ensure you have a good fixing point for the cabinets (we discuss this more in Chapter 6). You ought to have at least one wall cabinet available to you so you can work out exactly what height the fixing batons need to be.
7   Plaster the ceiling and walls. Always remember that your plasterer will have to have access to water. It's better if this is outside the house or in the kitchen.

8   Paint the ceiling.
9   Drill ceiling holes and fit ceiling lighting.
10 Fit base cabinets (see Chapter 6).
11 Fit worktops (see Chapter 7).
12 Fit wall cabinets (see Chapter 6).
13 Fit sinks and hobs and finish off ('second fix') the plumbing work and gas work – if you're fitting a freestanding cooker, you might want the leave the gas work for this until the end.
14 Make sure all 'under-cabinet' lighting cables for your wall cabinets are in position.
15 Complete splashbacks (see Chapter 8).
16 Lay new flooring (see Chapter 9).
17 Finish off the electrical work – fit sockets and under-cabinet lighting, etc.
18 Fit all doors and handles.
19 Have tea and biscuits.

MOVING THE GAS SERVICES

A professional with the appropriate qualifications must do this work – in the UK this means they are 'Gas Safe Registered'. Bear in mind that a gas engineer can be qualified to fit a boiler but not a cooker, so always double-check their qualifications before work begins.

For a gas hob you'll need the pipework brought roughly into position at the start of your project so that the base cabinets can be fitted. If you have a freestanding cooker, the pipework and fittings for this can also be completed at this stage. Near the end of the project the gas hob can be fitted completely – and any freestanding cooker can be connected up and tested.

MOVING THE PLUMBING

Once the old kitchen has been removed you can start moving the hot and cold water and the waste pipework into their new positions. Bear the following in mind:

- Push-fit fittings are much easier to use than compression or soldered fittings.
- Push-fit fittings work with standard copper pipework. Using them like this gives you a slightly more rigid finish and can work out cheaper, but you really do need to use a pipe slice to cut the pipework to size, as sharp edges will damage the rubber seals used in push-fit fittings.
- If you use plastic pipework remember that you need to push a pipe strengthener into the pipe before you push the fitting on.
- You can buy plastic pipe in 25–50m rolls, which can save on fittings and reduces the chances of any leaks.
- If you're running pipework in your floor it's best to use plastic pipework. If you do use copper it needs to be protected, as cement corrodes copper.
- Plastic pipework 'chased' into a wall is notoriously difficult to detect afterwards. Avoid using it altogether if you can and, if you can't, consider covering it with metal channelling (see overleaf). This will give it a bit of extra protection, but it mainly makes it easier to find the pipework later on.

Above: Inserting a pipe strengthener.

■ If you're installing an island it's best to use 110mm (4in) pipework for all the underfloor waste, as it reduces the chances of the pipework getting blocked. If this isn't feasible then don't drop below 50mm (2in). If it does get blocked you'll thank yourself if you've fitted a 'rodding point' to the pipework, which allows you to remove any blockages without having to dig up your kitchen floor.

■ Most kitchen cabinets have a gap between the base of the cabinet and the wall. This is usually about 70mm (2¾in) deep and allows you to run all your pipework behind the cabinets without having to channel

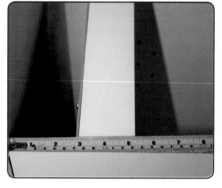

out the walls. However, not all cabinets have this feature so check them at this stage. If your cabinets go back hard up against the wall then you'll probably have to channel out the wall to accept the waste pipework or run this pipework through the cabinets – remember the maximum channelling depths we talked about above. Hot and cold pipework can be run under the cabinets and then come up into them where the sink is to be fitted.

■ All kitchen waste pipework should be at least 40mm (1½in) in diameter.

■ To avoid having to make large holes in your kitchen cabinets, bring your pipework straight out of the wall and terminate them with push-fit 'stop-ends' or 'isolation valves'. You can now turn the water back on and fit the cabinets by just cutting relatively small holes with a hole cutter. Once the cabinets and worktops have been fitted you can finish off the pipework connections ('second fix').

■ Finish off the 'first fix' work by providing a usable cold water supply. An isolation valve and a flexible tap connector is the simplest way of achieving this.

MOVING ELECTRICAL OUTLETS AND CHANGING THE LIGHTING

There's no reason why you can't reduce the cost of the electrical work by channelling out all the walls, fitting the sockets yourself and running all the cables into position. Once that's been done get an electrician in to connect everything up and test it all.

The caveat to this approach is that you don't do all of this and then look around for an electrician. Make an agreement in advance that this is the way you're going to go about it. Get the electrician to set the size of the cables and to confirm quite how he or she wants the cabling arranged. Also have them verify that your proposed socket positions are acceptable, without breaking any local/regional regulations. Often this arrangement won't lead to a massive reduction in cost, but being able to do much of this 'donkey work' yourself can save time and hassle.

Before you start, have a read through the following bullet points and check them off with your electrician:

■ If you opt to channel out the walls yourself, hire or buy a large hammer drill and a channelling tool, as doing it by hand takes forever.

Always don safety glasses, ear defenders and a dust mask before starting this task.

An alternative approach is to use an angle grinder to cut two lines into your wall and a chisel to knock out the bit between your lines. You can also buy or hire a channel cutter (wall chaser); essentially two angle grinders stuck together.

■ Always try to channel out your walls vertically or horizontally. Avoid diagonal runs, as this just confuses people and increases the risk of someone putting a nail through your nice new cable later on in the project. All cables hidden in walls need to be protected. You can buy lengths of channel profile, as plastic or galvanised steel, to cover your cabling. Neither will save your cables from a determined attack, but the steel covers do at least give it a go. Most importantly, covering your cabling with a metal channel makes it a lot easier to detect with a standard cable and stud detector.

- Use large-headed nails (clout nails) to secure your channel profiles into place.
- Metal profiles or conduits must be earthed, which is the main reason the plastic versions are now more popular.
- You can buy plastic or metal 'back boxes' for sockets that can be channelled into your wall. The easiest tool to use for this work is a hammer and a 'scutch' chisel.

Above: A scutch chisel.

- Use a short 'boat' level to make sure you have your sockets level and, if you're planning on a run of sockets right across your kitchen, you might want to make a simple template just to make sure they are all level with each other.
- Be aware that you can buy 'back boxes' specifically for stud walls.
- For ceiling lighting the usual approach is to lay the cable in position with about 500mm (20in) excess. Mark down this position on a plan but don't actually cut your holes yet. Once the ceiling is finished, come back with your plan and carefully cut your holes. Now reach into the hole and drag your cable out. This method isn't suitable for all lighting, so check how your electrician wants to go about this and work it into your schedule.

REBOARDING AND REPAIRING HOLES IN WALLS AND CEILINGS

REPAIRING HOLES IN PLASTERBOARD

The easiest way to repair a hole in the ceiling is to first fit a new piece of plasterboard into the hole and then skim this with ready-mixed 'finishing' or 'patch repair' plaster.

1 Plasterboard comes in different thickness, so it's an idea to make your hole a little bit bigger in order to get a sample that you can take to the merchants. A full sheet of plasterboard is 2400 x 1200mm (8 x 4ft) and, while you can buy half sheets, you're invariably going to have lots of plasterboard left over, so making the hole a bit bigger isn't going to cost you any more.

2 It's not essential that the patch of plasterboard is an exact fit for the hole, although it's obviously better if it is. You can make a rough guess or trace the hole by

holding a sheet of paper over it and rubbing the edge with a soft pencil.

3 Use a hard pencil to transfer the trace onto a piece of plasterboard.

Cut out the plasterboard with a utility knife or 'pad saw'. To see how to cut plasterboard in a straight line, see 'Reboarding the ceiling' (step 4, page 103).

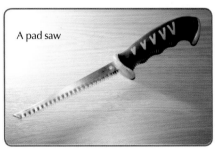

A pad saw

4 To reduce the chances of your plasterboard section breaking as you push it into the hole, it pays to cut the board at a slight angle. The narrower edge goes into the hole.

5 If you're fixing the hole from an old lighting rose, the odds are there is a joist running across the hole. If this is the case you can just screw your patch of plasterboard directly to this joist.

If you just have a hole, you'll need to put some wood over it to give you something to secure your patch of plasterboard to. It doesn't have to be a big piece, as it's not going to be supporting any real weight, just ensure that it's longer than the width of the hole and small enough to push into place from below.

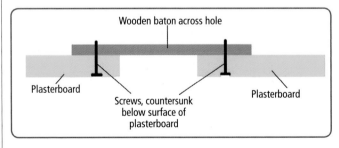

Wooden baton across hole

Plasterboard

Screws, countersunk below surface of plasterboard

Plasterboard

Push the baton into the hole. Hold it in place with your hand and then screw up through the plasterboard and into your wooden baton. Repeat on the other side of the hole. Ideally, you should use plasterboard screws for this, as they don't rust and discolour the final plastered finish. The most important part of the screwing process is that the screw is countersunk slightly below the finished ceiling surface and you haven't used an excessively long screw, which just increases the risk of you going through a pipe or a cable. You only need to go through the plasterboard and into the baton, so a 1in, size 6 screw should be more than enough.

6 Now screw your plasterboard patch into your baton to make a nice repair patch that can be plastered. Put a dust sheet over the floor under the hole to catch any drips of plaster.

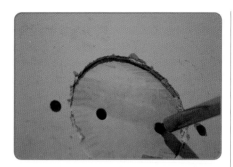

7 To hide your repair it's easiest to just buy a small pot of ready-mixed plaster – it's usually called 'finishing' or 'patch repair' plaster. Use a paint scraper, small pointing trowel or putty knife to roughly apply the plaster. It doesn't need to be flat – at this stage it just needs to cover the hole completely and to be a little proud of the surrounding ceiling finish.

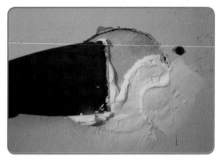

8 Now use a metal plastering trowel (also called a 'float') to get the surface completely flat. It's not essential that you use this exact tool – the most important thing is to get the plaster patch flat so that the edge you use is non-absorbent, hard, perfectly straight and wider than your hole.

Dampen your trowel with water spray and draw it across the ceiling and the hole to flatten the plaster. Don't start before the hole and draw it right across the entire hole in one go as this usually pulls the front edge of the plaster away from the hole. Instead, start just inside the hole and draw it right across the hole, holding it hard against the ceiling. Now go back the other way, again starting a few centimetres in front of the hole edge. Keep the trowel damp at all times and make sure the front edge of the trowel is always just above the surface. After every sweep, wipe the trowel clean with a damp cloth.

Try not to overwork the plaster. It doesn't have to be perfect at this stage, but it's very important that there are no holes or depressions in your finished plaster.

9 Check the instructions that came with your plaster but, as a general rule, leave it about 20 minutes to start drying and then go over it again with a damp trowel. This will smooth the finish that little bit more.

10 Once it's dry, go over it with an orbital sander fitted with fine-grain sandpaper and give it a coat of paint. The paint usually emphasises any imperfections, so you might want to give it another sand after the first coat.

REBOARDING THE CEILING

Most modern houses contain an awful lot of plasterboard so, even if you're not planning on reboarding your ceiling, you might still want to have a read of this section just to familiarise yourself with cutting and replacing plasterboard.

If you're changing your lighting it's easier to have all the new cables run into position before you reboard the ceiling. As a general rule, the electrician will run the cables into the rough position and leave about 500mm (20in) of spare cable loosely coiled in place. They will mark down where these positions are and, once the ceiling has been reboarded and plastered, they'll return, bore out a small hole in the new ceiling where the light is to go and then reach through and pull this coil of cable through the hole. It is best to double-check that this is how your electrician is going to approach the lighting before reboarding the ceiling.

1 Using full-size 2400 x 1200mm (8 x 4ft) sheets of plasterboard is usually a two-person job. If you're going to have to do this by yourself then you'll need to hire or buy a set of support arms to hold the plasterboard in place.

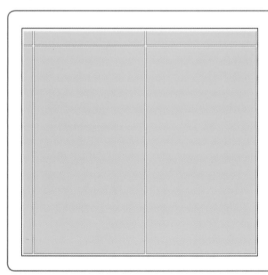

←The bad way of boarding a ceiling. By using two full sheets we are left with slivers of plasterboard around the edges and all plasterboard edges are lined up.

→The better way to board a ceiling. We have cut the full boards back a bit so we're not left with slivers and we have staggered the boards so that the edges don't all line up.

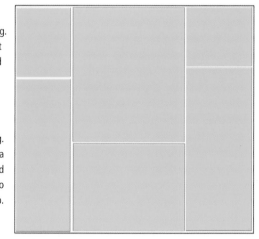

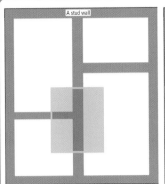

This patch of new plasterboard is not fully supported on any edges and will be weak and probably crack before too long.

We may have used more plasterboard here – it comes in big sheets anyway, so it's unlikely to cost more – but the board is fully supported on three edges and partially supported on the fourth.

2 Measure your ceiling. In an ideal world, you won't have to cut your plasterboard at all, but that's highly unlikely. Try to ensure that you don't have a sliver of plasterboard at one end of your run. If you look at the example diagram you can see that cutting back the boards avoids small, fragile slivers of board at the edges and by staggering the boards you avoid lining up all our edges, which can create a line of weakness.

If you're reboarding a stud wall or have removed the old plasterboard from the ceiling you need to cut your boards to match up with the studs and joists. It's not always possible to have every edge of the plasterboard supported and screwed into a wooden stud, but you should always try to get at least three sides supported, especially the long sides.

3 If you are over-boarding the ceiling it's not essential that the edges of the new boards are resting on the ceiling joists. However, it's handy to know where these joists are so that you can screw up into them. You can approach this in the old fashioned way: stick something sharp up through the existing ceiling and repeat until you hit a joist, or you can use the modern approach: buy a stud detector. These days, the standard detector finds quite a few different things, so it's a good idea to have one at home for general DIY.

Once you've found your joists, use a pencil to mark their positions on the wall about 25mm (1in) down from the ceiling so that you can still see your mark when your new boards are in place.

4 To cut plasterboard in a straight line hold a level – or any other hard, straight material – in place and then lightly run a utility knife along this edge. Repeat this two or three more times.

5 With the board marked, just hold the plasterboard

steady and give it a smack with your palm roughly where you've scored it. It will crack fully along your mark.

6 The board is now only held together by the paper on one side. Bend it over most of the way along your cut line and run your utility knife along the crease to cut though this final bit of paper.

7 You'll generally need a friend or a set of support arms to help you with this bit. Lift your cut plasterboard into position and quickly drive a few screws into it near each corner – it's not critical where, you just want the board held against the ceiling by itself as fast as possible. Once it's held in place you can take your time driving screws through and into the joists. You'll need to go through two layers of plasterboard and into some wood, so 38mm (1½in) should be long enough. Remember, it's important that the screws are countersunk so that they're just below the surface of the plasterboard. If you're using an electric screwdriver with variable power, it pays to turn the power down so the screw will counter-sink, but not drive right through the plasterboard.

TIP *The easiest way to stop the edges of the boards breaking as you push them together is to use a pad saw or utility knife and angle the edge slightly so that the narrow side goes in first.*

8 Once all the boards are in place use 'plasterboard jointing tape' to cover all the edges. You need to cover where the boards join together and where they join to the wall.

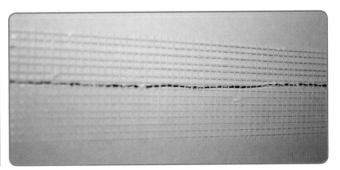

6 CABINETS

When buying a new kitchen, this is the area that will consume most of your money. With that in mind, it's always worth thinking about renovation as opposed to out-and-out replacement, so you might want to have a flick through Chapter 3.

Types of cabinet and what to consider

While there are always bargains to be found, the reality is that if one cabinet is cheaper than another there's usually a very good reason for the price difference. When talking about price we're talking about the cabinet with its doors, as they are almost always sold together. The materials used are the obvious cause for the price difference: solid wood cabinets last longer, have better resale value and can usually be restored. Cabinets made from wood veneer give a great look for a fraction of the price, while cabinets with a plastic veneer can be much cheaper. That said, plastic veneers can offer far more design options, with brightly coloured high gloss finishes very popular right now.

The actual cabinet design also has a big impact on the price. Most modern kitchens have 'overlay' doors and 'frameless' cabinets. These are easier to make – and to fit – and allow the manufacturer to use cheaper materials without that having a big visual impact on the finished kitchen. The more traditional 'face-framed' cabinets are far more expensive because the 'face' is visible and, as such, has to be made from higher-quality materials.

Other ways of reducing the price of cabinets is to make the backs of them out of thin, compressed cardboard, usually only about 6mm (¼in) thick, with a thin plastic veneer over the top. Yes, this reduces the price, but the cardboard nearly always warps – especially if it's under the kitchen sink – and it damages easily. With that in mind you might want to go for cabinets with more robust backs.

Another way of reducing the price of a cabinet is to supply it flat-packed. From a consumer's point of view this is often a terrific thing, in that you can purchase high-quality cabinets at much cheaper prices. Another real bonus of flat-packed kitchens is that you can buy the entire kitchen and store it in a corner of your garage until you're ready for it. The downside is that building flat-pack cabinets is far more time-consuming and can test your patience to the limit.

The other big determinant on price is the design. Basic cabinets either with shelves or drawers are much of a muchness, but outside of these basic cupboards is a world of wondrous design. From a DIY point of view, the big problem with designer cabinets is that they are often very awkward to fit and are expensive, so just one slip of a screwdriver can leave you with a very big bill. I'm not going to delve too deeply into this area, other than mentioning those designs that save and utilise space better.

CORNER UNITS

The cheapest way to deal with a corner is just to push two cabinets up against each other to make the 90° angle, put some filler pieces in to stop the doors and drawers hitting each other and then put a worktop over them to hide the great big gap that you're left with. If you have a huge kitchen this might not be a problem, but in smaller kitchens the space you lose costs far more in the long run than the cost of a unit that can utilise that space better.

BLIND BASE CORNER UNIT

This is a simple way of utilising far more of the corner space. The downside is that, although you have this extra cupboard space and a far smaller void, the space itself is very difficult to get at.

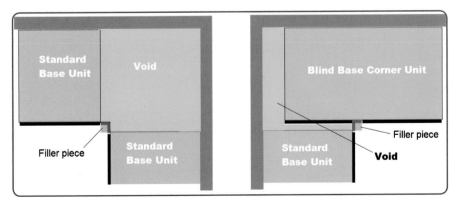

this type of unit, so if you have your heart set on one of these, you'll have to accept that your choice of kitchen is going to be quite severely limited.

PULL-OUT SHELVES AND DRAWERS

LAZY SUSAN

This is an easy way of making better use of the space provided by the blind base unit. In essence, it's a rotating shelf or basket that you can swing out to bring those items hidden in the dark recesses of your blind base unit out into the glorious light of day. There are umpteen variations on this theme; the general rule being that the simpler to use and the more space they save, the higher the price.

DIAGONAL CORNER UNITS

These are by far the best way to utilise the corner space in your kitchen, but in terms of 'look' you either love them or hate them. The downside to these units is that in order to provide more usable corner space, they take up more space in your actual kitchen. The other big downside is that very few kitchen ranges actually have

Once again, there are umpteen options available but they're usually only available for a particular range, so setting your heart on one will often reduce your options further down the line. In my experience, it pays to be sitting down before you ask how much some of these cabinets cost.

PLINTH DRAWERS

These are a neat way of getting more space from what would otherwise be a dead area under the cabinets. They are not the easiest drawers to reach and they aren't suitable for storing food in. Most kitchens don't have perfectly level floors and, as a result, you may have to shave off some of the drawer front to get them to fit properly, so check that this is feasible before you buy them. It is, of course, quite easy to make these up yourself – some old drawers, a bit of plinth, some castors, and a bit of time and imagination should suffice.

Fitting new cabinets

The first stage of fitting a new kitchen is to fit the base units. There are umpteen different types of kitchen cabinet but, in terms of fitting, we'll concentrate on the design most commonly sold at DIY stores: frameless cabinets.

WHAT TYPE OF WALLS DO I HAVE?

You'll need to secure both the base and wall units to your walls. How you go about doing this depends on your wall type (see 'A brief guide to walls and wall plugs' on page 44). It may take some time to discover exactly what type of walls you have, but it's worth the effort. Once you've enlightened yourself, go out and buy the appropriate screws and wall plugs for your wall type or have a read of the sections at the end of this chapter entitled 'Fitting batons into stud walls' and 'Fitting a supporting baton to a drylined wall (dot and dab)' if you'd rather strengthen the walls themselves.

Since your base units are held up by their legs and by each other, they don't need any heavy-duty fittings to secure them to the wall. Alas, the same cannot be said of wall units, but we'll discuss that particular bridge when we come to it.

Tools

We discussed tools in depth at the start of this manual, so have a flick through Chapter 2 again if you need a refresher.

- ■ A variety of levels: ideally, a laser level, a 1.5m (5ft) long level, a shorter 500–600mm (20–24in) level and a short 'boat' level.
- ■ A screwdriver set, or an electric screwdriver with a selection of bits.
- ■ A drill with hammer action and a selection of masonry and wood drill bits
- ■ A set of clamps – G-Clamps and Spring Clamps - ideally ones with rubber feet. If you can't get these you'll need some wooden batons to put between the clamp and the cabinets to prevent damaging the cabinets.
- ■ A jigsaw with a selection of fine wood blades and a downward cutting blade.
- ■ A soft pencil.
- ■ A tape measure.

SETTING THE HEIGHT

As a general rule, most kitchen worktops are about 900mm (3ft) high. If the kitchen users are particularly tall or short you might want to change this height – the ideal height is when the ball of your wrist is level with the top of the worktop. If you're

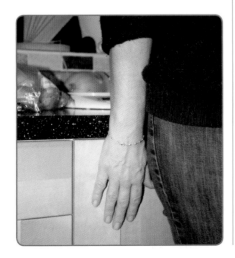

thinking about increasing the worktop height, just remember that this will also mean increasing the height of the wall cabinets – usually set 500mm (20in) above the worktop. The cabinets themselves will also place limits on their final height – although there is usually a way around this.

For ease of fitting, we're going to aim to set the cabinets so that the kickboard fits underneath them, on top of the finished floor surface, without the need to cut down the kickboard or have a huge gap between the base of the cabinets and the top of the kickboard. Note that, because the kickboards are set back a bit from the front of the cabinets, you can have a gap of 5–10mm (¼–⅜in) between the base of the cabinet and the top of the plinth and no one will be any the wiser.

1 Work out how much higher your finished floor will be compared to how it is now. For a tiled floor, this is the thickness of the new tiles plus about 5mm (¼in) for the adhesive.

2 Add the height of the kickboards, usually 150–190mm (6–7½in). Now add on the actual height of the base units and then another 5mm (¼in) to give you 'wiggle room'. The final result should be about 865–870mm (approx. 34½in) above the finished floor surface. Most worktops are about 38mm (1½in), which brings us to the standard 900mm (36in), or thereabouts.

3 This calculated height is going to be the highest you can set the cabinets above the floor without leaving a big gap between the plinth and the units. However, before you can safely use this height you need to know if your kitchen floors slopes, and if so, by how much. You can usually tell if your room slopes at all just by looking, but if you have any doubts just lay a long level on the floor and see where the lowest corner point is.

4 From this low point mark the wall with the maximum unit height you calculated in step 3 and use a laser level to mark this 'base line' right around your kitchen.

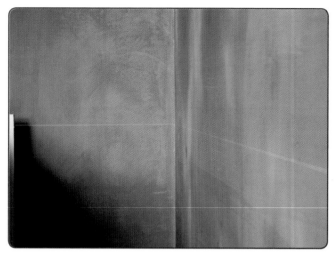

Once you have your base line marked out, consult your plans and use a tape measure to just check how high your units are going to be above the finished floor level at the most important work areas – mainly the food preparation area. Usually any slope in a kitchen is minimal, but if you do have a distinct slope you need to make sure that the worktop is going to be at a functional height all the way around. Remember that you can always make a slope work in your favour by using the lowest point as a baking area, as

the act of pounding dough into submission is easier if the worktop is usually about 50mm (2in) lower.

If need be you can use one base line for one side of the kitchen and another for the other side of the kitchen, just ensuring that each separate 'run' of units are level with each other.

If the slope really is distinct you can split your run into two or more levels, either by using full-height units to separate the 'runs' or just using an end panel and a separate worktop section.

FITTING THE BASE UNITS

You now have a base line marked around your kitchen and you should have an accurate plan of your kitchen to work from. One word of warning before we begin: most kitchen units have the back of the unit set in a bit, so as to leave a gap of about 70mm (2¾in) between the wall and the back of the unit.

This allows you to run pipes and cables behind the units without having to either recess all the pipework or cut out huge swathes of the units backs to accommodate them. Alas, one famous manufacturer of flat-packed units tends not to do this; the backs of their units are designed to fit flat against the walls. This means that you either have to run pipework and cables underneath the units – the gap for this is determined by the height of your kickboards – or you have to recess the pipes and cables into the wall, or run pipework through the units themselves. Either way, it's a real pain.

1 You should always start off in a corner, so decide which corner you like the most.

2 If you have flat-packed units, start putting them together, beginning with those in your preferred corner. You will have to lay the units on their sides and backs to build them up, so get yourself a nice soft, clean surface that you can put the units down on without fear of bumps and scratches occurring – the cardboard they come in is good for this. For the corner unit, fit the door hinge plates to the units, as you'll need to fit the doors to check some of your distances. For the other units, leave them off for now – we'll secure the units to one another by screwing them together and hiding these screws underneath these fittings. Do fit the drawer rails at this stage, as it's much easier to do so now.

If your units arrived already put together, then the biggest issue you will have is figuring out how to remove the drawers from the cabinets so that they don't get damaged during the fitting process. Most come with the drawer fronts fitted back-to-front to prevent damage, but it's still best to remove them entirely (see 'Removing the drawers' on page 90).

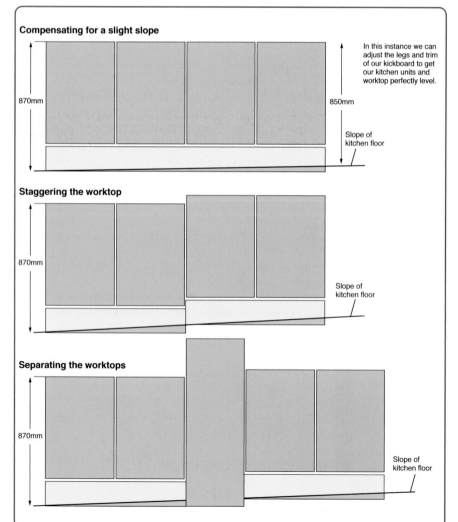

Compensating for a slight slope

870mm

850mm

In this instance we can adjust the legs and trim of our kickboard to get our kitchen units and worktop perfectly level.

Slope of kitchen floor

Staggering the worktop

870mm

Slope of kitchen floor

Separating the worktops

870mm

Slope of kitchen floor

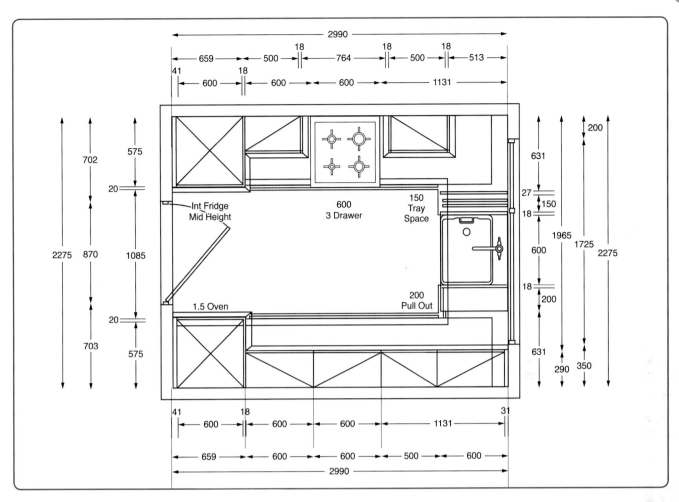

The diagram shows a kitchen plan with the following dimensions:

Top horizontal dimensions: 2990; 659, 500, 18, 764, 18, 500, 18, 513; 41, 600, 18, 600, 600, 1131

Left vertical dimensions: 702, 575, 20; 2275, 870, 1085; 20, 703, 575

Labels within plan: Int Fridge Mid Height; 600 3 Drawer; 150 Tray Space; 200 Pull Out; 1.5 Oven

Right vertical dimensions: 200, 631, 27, 150, 18, 1965, 1725, 600, 2275, 18, 200, 631, 290, 350

Bottom horizontal dimensions: 41, 18, 600, 600, 600, 1131, 31; 659, 600, 600, 500, 600; 2990

3 The legs of most base units come in three sections: the base, a fixed length section and a screwable section that allows you to adjust the leg height.

4 There will usually be holes already in place into which you can push the leg base and then secure it in place with a few screws. Note that the base is often not round. This is deliberate, as you want a

section of the base to overlap the sides of the unit to give the unit additional strength.

5 Fit the legs together and set them to roughly the height of your kickboard by screwing the end section up and down. Once you know you have the legs set to the right height use one leg as a template to set the height for all the others.

6 Lift the units and lower them into position. Be aware that the legs are pretty fragile and if you try to drag the units across the floor the legs will just break.

7 Starting with your corner unit, adjust the legs so the unit is level with your base line. To adjust the legs, screw them up and down. You can do this by hand or use a set of pump pliers to make it a bit easier. When

you're looking down on the leg, turning it clockwise will raise the unit and anti-clockwise will lower the unit. Now use a level to verify that the back of the unit is level and that the unit is also level front to back.

8 Once you have your corner unit in place and level, move onto the next unit that makes up your corner. To get this unit into position you'll need to fit the 'corner filler piece' that comes with the corner unit. To fit this, you'll need to hang the doors onto the corner unit – see 'Fitting doors and drawers' on page 121 and 'Fitting corner pieces' on page 119.

With the corner piece fitted, you can set the next unit in place to complete the corner. It's best not to attach the other unit to your corner until you've finished putting all the other units in this row into place.

9 Now carry on fitting the rest of your base units until you have all the units for one wall set up. They should all be level with each other, with the tops touching your base line and they should all be in place as per your plans, but not yet fixed in place.

10 If there are any gaps in your run, to accommodate a freestanding cooker or washing machine, for example, decide if you're going to be fitting end panels to the units on either side of this gap. If you are, you don't need to fit them right now – it's usually easier to tile the walls and floors then fit the end panels (see 'Fitting end panels' on page 120) – but you do need to take their thickness

into account when setting the size of the gap between the units. Also, check for any filler pieces. These should be marked on your plan and, while you don't have to fit them at this stage, you do need to mark them on the wall and set out the units accordingly.

11 You can now see if there will be any issues. These usually consist of pipework and cables, etc. that are stopping the units fitting back against the wall and doors that will bang into things when they're opened.

Occasionally, you'll need to move the pipework, but usually you can adjust the units by cutting out sections of the back to accommodate the obstruction (see 'Cutting around pipes and cables' on page 115). Once you've made all your cuts you should be able to place all the units into their designated positions and they will all fit snugly against the kitchen wall.

12 With all the base units in place, mark the walls at the inside edge of each unit so that you can put them back into their exact places later.

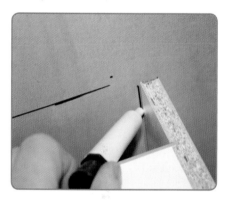

13 Now start to secure the base units in place. Most kitchens come with the fixing brackets supplied. It's important that they don't poke up above the height of the units, so position them a few millimetres below the top of the units and, using a pencil, mark the hole position on the wall.

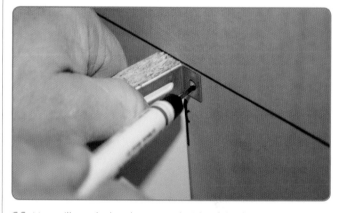

14 You will need a bracket on each side of the first unit. Once these have been marked it's usually easier to lift the unit aside, drill the holes (6mm drill bit is adequate for base units), fit the appropriate wall plugs or fittings, depending on your walls, and then attach the brackets to the wall.

15 Put the unit back into position and double-check it's level in each plane. Most units will have a thin plastic protective cover over the front and sides to prevent them getting damaged during the fitting process. Often this is coloured blue to make it easy to see, but don't bank on that. Now is the time to remove this covering, so find an edge, scrape it with your nail and hopefully you'll be able to peel the rest of the covering away. You can now screw the unit to the wall brackets.

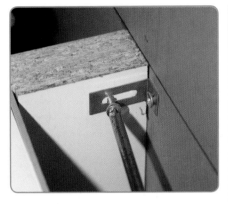

16 Place the next unit into position. To ensure it's up tight against your first unit, use clamps to draw the two units together. It's not essential that the front of the units are perfectly aligned at this stage, but it's good to get them fairly close. Note that we are using clamps with rubber feet, so that they don't damage the units, and two clamps, top and bottom.

The units are aligned when the front edge of both units are perfectly in line with each other, top and bottom. You can achieve this by adjusting the feet of the unit that isn't secured to the wall yet, but if you have the clamps set about right, it's easier to just use the palm of your hand to bump the unit up and down until it's aligned.

19 Double-check the units are perfectly in line with each other and then screw them together. Before doing this, check that your screw is not going to go right through both units – it should go halfway into the second unit. It's easier to screw into laminate if

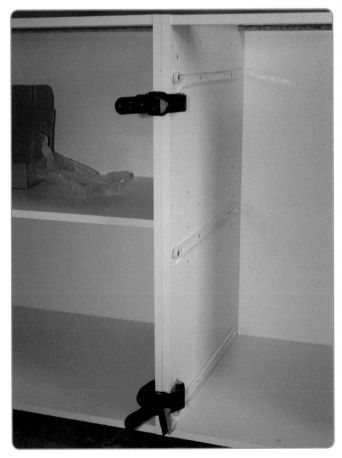

you drill a pilot hole first. It's also an idea to countersink the hole so the screw head is flush with the surface. Just drilling the screw directly into the unit will achieve this, but you can buy drill bits with a counter-sink on them. These let you set the depth of the hole as well and, while not essential, they're a handy tool to have around.

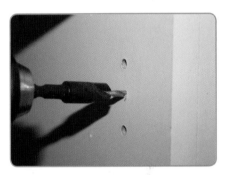

It's always nice to hide these screws, so the best place to put the front two screws is beneath the door hinge base plate. You only need one screw for the back and the best place for this is close to where you'd be putting the wall brackets. Be

17 You're going to screw the two units together in a minute, so you don't need to use two brackets to hold your latest unit to the wall. One bracket on the far side of the unit will suffice. Mark this on the wall and then remove the clamps, move the unit to one side, drill your holes and fit your wall plugs – or whatever other fitting you're using – and fit the bracket to the wall.

18 Now place the unit back into position and loosely fit your two clamps back again. You want the clamps to hold the units together, but also to have a little movement at this stage, so you can get the two units perfectly aligned. Note that we've used spring clamps, which are ideal for this purpose.

aware that placing this screw behind the back of the unit will hide the screw, but will also make it difficult to remove this unit at a later date without removing the countertop first.

20 Check the new unit is level with your base line and level front to back. Once you're sure it is, screw it to the wall bracket fitted in step 17.

21 So, that's the first two units in place. Now place the next unit into position, mark, drill and fit the wall bracket for this unit, and then repeat steps 16–20 until you either reach the end of the 'run' of units or you reach a gap.

If you're building a gap into your run of units you need to ensure that the gap is consistent at the top and bottom and front and back. If your units are perfectly level, this should always be the case.

Most freestanding appliances are 590mm (23½in) wide and are designed to fit into a 600mm (24in) gap between the units. You need to double-check this when you're setting out the gap, both by checking your plans and quickly measuring the appliance you're hoping to fit into this gap. You'll also need to decide if you are fitting end panels and, if so, adjust the unit positions so the gap is the right size with the end panels fitted. You can temporarily clamp the end panels onto the units just to ensure you have the width of the gap set right.

Use a level to bridge your gap and ensure the units on either side are level with each other.

TIP *Most cabinets are just plain white, which is not a problem because you see very little of the cabinets themselves. However, at the end of a run of units or where there*

is a gap you will be able to see this plain white cabinet side, which is rather unsightly. To make these ends and gaps look much nicer you fit 'end-panels', which are generally the same colour as your doors and give your kitchen a nice clean finish. One of the biggest mistakes people make when planning a kitchen is forgetting that they'll need these end panels and also forgetting that they have a width – they are generally 10–18mm deep. This oversight either results in the units no longer fitting the space between walls or the gap no longer being wide enough for the appliance you've bought.

You don't have to fit end panels on either side of a gap for a washing machine, cooker etc., as the appliance is designed to fit this gap with very little space on either side. However, if you're creating a gap for, say, a waste bin, the sides of the cabinets will be clearly visible so you'll need to fit end panels.

---

22 You should now have all your base units in place, but with no doors, shelves or drawers fitted. At this stage you can go straight on and fit the wall units, but it's generally easier to fit the worktops first (see 'Installing a laminate countertop' on page 137).

FITTING THE WALL UNITS

With the worktops fitted and covered over for protection, you can get to work on fitting the wall units. As a general rule, you want the base of the wall units to be 500mm (20in) above the worktop: any lower and the worktops are difficult to work at; any higher and they become more tricky to use for shorter members of the family. When you're setting this height, bear in mind any pelmets you're attaching to the base of the units, as you'll be measuring this 500mm (20in) from the base of these pelmets.

Pelmets aren't essential, but they do have two basic functions. The most obvious one is that they are decorative, especially in more traditional kitchens. Their other function is to hide any lighting system or flip-down TV you might have under the wall units.

Having decided if you're going to have any pelmets below your wall cabinets, you can calculate the height of the fixings you're going to use to secure the units to the wall. How you go about this will vary; however, most work on the principles we'll step through below.

If your cabinets came already built, then you'll be able to see two brackets in the top corners. These will vary from manufacturer to manufacturer, but they're usually covered in a plastic shroud to hide them from view and they have two screws; one to tighten the cabinet to the support bracket and draw it securely against the wall, the second to raise or lower the corner of the unit so that you can get the unit perfectly level. Occasionally, you'll just see one screw that's fitted into a slot, which provides both the levelling and fixing functions in one.

The fitting inside the cabinet will have a bracket associated with it. This bracket is secured to the wall to support the cabinet.

1 Draw two perfectly horizontal lines for your wall units: a top 'base line' showing where you want the top of your cabinets to be and a second line a little bit lower, where you'll fit your support brackets to the wall. To reduce mistakes, draw these lines in different colours.

To get your base line, measure the height of the cabinet and the height of the plinth, and add the distance above the worktop that you want.

For example. We would like the wall cabinet to be 500mm above the work surface. We know the wall unit is 700mm high and that we have a 60mm pelmet attached to the bottom of it. Therefore we set our base line at 700+60+500 = 1260mm above our worktop.

To get the height of the brackets, just put the support bracket into place on the cabinet while it's sat on your worktop and measure the distance from the top of the cabinet to the fixing holes in the bracket.

This distance is 60mm in our example, so we just measure 60mm down from our base line and draw – ideally in a different colour - another perfectly level line to mark the screw positions for the brackets. This height is often given in the fitting instructions that come with your units.

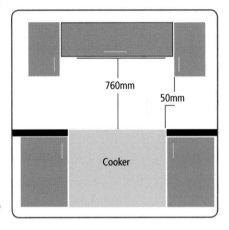

2 Bearing in mind that you've gone to great lengths to ensure your base units and worktops are perfectly level, you should only have to mark your height once and then use a laser level to extend the line around the kitchen.

3 More often than not, the wall units are directly above the base units, so you'll probably also need to draw a vertical line up from the edge of the base units to mark your start position.

4 It's a good idea to make up all the wall units you need for a single wall and lay them out on top of the worktop, just to make sure that everything is going to fit. Protect the worktop with some cardboard first.

Often it's only the act of laying things out right in front of you that causes the issues to suddenly leap into view. The three most common issues are: units too close to the walls, units too close to the cooker and assuming your walls are truly vertical when they aren't.

Remember that fitting units right into corners usually results in handles banging into walls every time the doors are opened. Avoid this by bringing the units a little away from the wall, filling the gap with a filler piece (see 'Fitting filler pieces, corner pieces and end panels' on page 116) and fitting door hinges that only open to about 110°.

You don't want wall units too close to a cooker hob. The regulations vary, so have a read of your cooker manual before finalising the position of your units – the golden rule with regulations is that the manufacturer is always right. That said, in the UK, anything even vaguely combustible that's being fitted above the cooker hob needs to be at least 760mm (30in) above the cooker top – if your cooker has

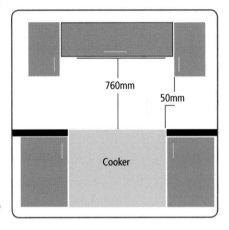

a lid, you're going to need clearance for this anyway. There is also a side clearance for anything below this height. Again, it varies, but a 50mm (2in) clearance to the side of the cooker for anything combustible and less than 760mm (30in) above the cooker is a good rule to go by – if needed you can get around these limits by fitting a non-combustible base to your wall units.

In older houses, walls are rarely perfectly vertical. This can cause issues if you've measured everything at one height and are now going to fit wall units much higher up – if the walls lean towards each other you might find that you don't have enough space; if they lean out slightly you might need to fit filler pieces to remove any gaps.

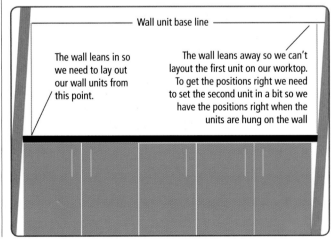

Wall unit base line

The wall leans in so we need to lay out our wall units from this point.

The wall leans away so we can't layout the first unit on our worktop. To get the positions right we need to set the second unit in a bit so we have the positions right when the units are hung on the wall

5 Before you start fitting the wall units you need to make sure your walls are going to be able to support them. If you have solid walls this shouldn't be a problem, but if you have stud walls or 'dot and dab' walls (also called 'drylined' walls), it's a bit more awkward. Many people just use a 'stud-wall' or 'dryline' fitting to secure the wall units to the wall and this isn't necessarily wrong but, bearing in mind how much weight wall cabinets can end up carrying, I think it's best to strengthen the wall itself (see 'Fitting batons into stud walls' and 'Fitting a supporting baton to a drylined wall (dot and dab)' at the end of this chapter).

If you have solid walls you're best off using 2–3in, size 10 screws to secure your wall brackets, which require a 7–8mm hole with a 7–8mm (size 8) brown wall plug.

6 Check with the documentation that came with your wall units for exactly where the support brackets need to go. As a general rule, they fit about 18–25mm in from the outside edge of the unit, so you need to mark the outside edge of our first unit

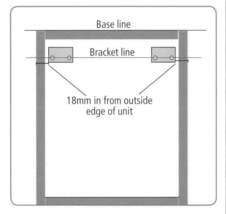

Base line

Bracket line

18mm in from outside
edge of unit

on the wall then mark 18mm (in our example) in from this edge. Hold your bracket up against this mark and mark the bracket holes with a pencil.

7 You now need to do the same for the other side of the unit. So measure the width of the unit, mark this width on your wall and mark the bracket position in from this outside edge. Mark the drill holes for this bracket.

8 Drill your holes and fit the brackets.

9 You can now lift the unit up onto the supporting brackets – you might need someone to give you a hand for this. If you've got the brackets in the right place the cabinet should just drop onto them. If you're a little out, most brackets come with slots rather than holes and so by just loosening off your screws a bit you can tap the bracket left or right a little, tighten the screws again and give it another go.

10 If you look at the top of your unit you should be able to see where the cabinet is in relation to your base line. It's rare to be exactly level first time, but the mechanism inside the units is designed with this fact in mind. Usually there are two screws. The one facing you is used to tighten the unit against the wall and the one underneath is used to change the height of this corner of the unit. Adjust this lower screw on both sides of the cabinet until your cabinet is perfectly aligned to your base line. Double-check it's level by putting a level on the top of it.

TIP *Don't screw your wall cabinets back against the brackets until you've finished the row – get the cabinets level with each other first. It's often easier to screw all the wall cabinets in a run together whilst they're sat on the worktop and then, with the help of a friend, lift the whole lot onto their support brackets in one go.*

11 Use your level to check that the unit is also level front to back. If the front is slightly higher than the back this is no real problem, so just leave it be. However, if your walls bow in a bit and, as a result, the front of your units are slightly lower than the back, you'll need to bring the base of the unit out a bit to prevent everything falling out of the cabinet.

You can make some wooden wedges from offcuts and use these to bring the base of the unit out a little until it's level front to back.

If the wall is very badly bowed you might want to consider fitting a wooden baton along the base of all your wall units to compensate for the wall. The gap produced can only be seen from the side and it can be hidden using a base-unit end panel – these are deeper than the wall units, so you can cut them back to hide your gap completely. Note that the wood/veneer covering the back of most cabinets is thin and fairly weak, so any support needs to be on the actual frame of the cabinet.

12 Repeat steps 6–10 for the next unit. Once you have the next unit level with the first, make sure the front edges are perfectly aligned – use spring clamps to clamp them together if need be – and then screw the units together with two screws at the front. As per the base units, the ideal place to screw them together is under where the door hinge base plates will go.

If needed, fit more wedges under the base of the new unit to keep it level front-to-back. Continue until all your wall units are fixed in place.

CUTTING AROUND PIPES AND CABLES

Hole cutter

The odds of fitting a kitchen that doesn't involve cutting out sections of the cabinets themselves is very low. At the very least, if you're fitting the cabinet under the kitchen sink, you are going to have to cut holes for the hot- and cold-water pipework and for the waste pipework.

To cut holes you'll need a 'hole cutter' or an 'auger'. As a general rule, augers are better for boring out deep holes in solid wood, while hole cutters are much better suited to kitchen fitting.

An auger

There are only two issues you need to be aware of. The first is that having your drill on hammer action is going to bring forth misery, so always make sure it's turned off. The second issue is that hole cutters have a nasty habit of ruining the back of the hole when used on laminated wood – the laminate rips away to leave a fair bit of a mess. With this in mind, it's always best to start cutting the hole from the side you're most likely to see once the kitchen is being used. Alternatively, you can reduce the chances of damage by following these steps:

1 Use a 6mm wood drill bit to go through the centre of your proposed hole, drilling right through the wood.

You can use the hole cutter drill bit to make the initial hole

2 On the side that is the least important to you use the hole you've just drilled to centre your hole cutter and start making your hole. You only need to go through the thin laminate covering.

3 Now go to the other side, use the hole you made earlier as your centre and cut right through to the other side.

Be aware that the wood you're cutting out gets lodged inside your hole cutter. This sets a maximum depth you can go before you need to dig this wood out of the cutter, and the act of extracting this wood can be a right pain. Some hole cutters come with a spring inside them to push this wood out. If your spring doesn't work then a flat-headed screwdriver can be used to work the wood out or you

can try unscrewing the cutter from the centre drill and using the drill bit to knock the wood out.

Often the pipes you are cutting around are affixed to the wall. In this instance it's best to use a hole cutter to make the hole and then use a jigsaw to connect the hole to the edge of the cabinet.

Most tools have a problem with creating a neat edge on laminated wood. Because the laminate is so much harder than the wood it's been stuck to, most cutting blades tend to lift and splinter the laminate, but usually only on one side. If they cut through the laminate and then into the wood below you usually get a clean cut; if you cut the wood and then the laminate above, the laminated surface is lifted a little by the cutting blade, and chips.

If you need a perfect cut on both sides of laminated wood then you might be better off using a router to make your cut. If this isn't feasible, you can prevent the laminate being lifted by either taping it down with masking tape (this tends to reduce chipping rather than eliminating it) or by clamping another piece of wood over or under it. In this instance

Above: L – a clean downward cut R – a chipped upward cut.

the laminate cannot lift because the other plank of wood is pressing it down. This would be great if it wasn't for the fact that a standard jigsaw blade cuts on the upward stroke, meaning that the side that gets chipped is the top side, the side facing you.

This tends to be a problem with kitchen fitting because it's usually easier to mark out all your cut lines on the side facing you, which promptly gets damaged by the jigsaw blade. Putting another block of wood over your cut line isn't going to work, so the easiest way around it is to buy some 'downward-cutting' blades. These will still chip the underside of your board, but this generally isn't an issue. If it is, you can put a spare sheet of board underneath the laminate you're cutting and by cutting through both sheets, you usually get a nice clean cut on both sides of your laminated board.

So why are standard jigsaw blades upward

cutting? Well the problem with downward-cutting blades is that they have a habit of jumping up and causing chaos when they do. To prevent this, always start the jigsaw blade moving and then present it to the wood you wish to cut once it's up to speed. Once you're cutting, keep your weight over the jigsaw to ensure it stays firmly in contact with the wood surface.

TIP *Another issue with jigsaws is that the shoe marks the surface as you push the jigsaw along. You can buy plastic covers for the shoe (the base) of the jigsaw to prevent this. Otherwise,*

use extra-wide masking tape to cover the surface of the board by about 40mm (1½in) either side or your cut line. It's also an idea to apply masking tape over the shoe of your jigsaw.

To cut a square edge with a jigsaw, follow these steps:

1 Cut both the straight lines.

2 Cut a curve that reaches your end line about halfway along.

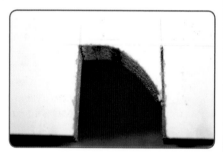

3 Now cut back the other way to get a nice square finish.

Most kitchen units are made of MDF or chipboard with a layer of plastic laminate over the top. This gives you a strong, waterproof product that isn't too expensive, but it does rely on the laminate being in good condition to maintain the seal. The moment you take a hole cutter or jigsaw to your laminate you risk water getting onto the now exposed chipboard, which causes the chipboard to swell up and misshape. To prevent this, seal all of the cuts you make, especially those made to the unit supporting your kitchen sink.

Everyone seems to have a preferred method of achieving a waterproof seal but I find silicone sealant is the easiest. Just apply a bead of it to your cut area and then use a spare piece of cardboard to smear it over the cut area, making sure the exposed chipboard is completely covered.

If you don't have sealant, varnish and PVA glue work just as well.

FITTING FILLER PIECES, CORNER PIECES AND END PANELS

If when you lay out your kitchen units you discover that the space you have turns out to be a few millimetres too small for the units you've bought, then you have a problem – sometimes a big problem. On the other hand, a little gap in your units is a simple thing to sort out. With this in mind, it's generally best to design your kitchen with the idea that you'll have a bit of free space and will require a few 'filler pieces' to hide these spaces.

The best place to put filler pieces is at the beginning of a run where the corner unit is, or at the end of a run, joining the last unit to the wall. Not only does the latter give more room for opening doors etc., but it also tends to be a little more discrete.

Right: A BIG filler piece.

MAKING AND FITTING FILLER PIECES

A filler piece is just a length of wood that matches your kitchen. Often they are just sections of plinth or kickboard, occasionally an end panel. The less cutting you have to do, the better, but all you really need is the right colour and size at the best price – one end panel might be cheaper than a 2m (6½ft) length of plinth, of which 90% will go to waste.

1 Once you've laid out your kitchen units you can determine what gaps you're going to have and where they will be. Mark the position of each unit and attach them to the wall until you come to your first gap.

2 Measure the gap between the two units – or the unit and the wall – at the top and bottom of the unit. If you're joining two units together, this gap should be the same top and bottom.

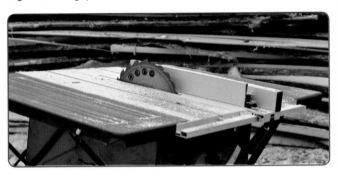

Above: Table or bench saw.

3 To get a nice straight cut you're best off using a bench saw with a fine-toothed blade designed to cut laminated wood. If you haven't got access to a bench saw, a jigsaw and a steady hand will do.

When you're making a cut, bear in mind that a cut edge at the top of your filler piece will be hidden under the countertop, whereas a cut at the bottom is far more likely to catch the eye. If you have to cut one side of your filler piece it's better to put the cut edge against the wall and the clean edge against the unit, as that wall cut can be easily masked with a bead of caulk. If you're joining two units and have to cut one side have a think about where people will generally be standing in the kitchen – it's always better if the cut edge is away from the observer.

4 It's easier to fit the filler piece to a unit that has yet to be secured to the wall, then to put that unit into position and secure your filler piece to the neighbouring unit or wall.

To get the bottom of the filler piece in the right position just clamp an offcut of wood to the base of your free unit and set your filler piece on top of this.

There are two common ways of securing your filler piece in position. We'll step through the simplest first and then look at the alternative.

5 Set the filler piece in place – you might need a friend for this – and drill a pilot hole through the top side of the unit and into the filler piece. Use a countersink to allow you to recess the screw a bit and then,

Above: Hide the screw behind your hinge plate.

holding the filler piece in position, secure it to the unit. Repeat this for the base of the filler piece so that it's fixed at top and bottom against one of the units.

This approach is easy, but the screw is very close to the front of the unit and can therefore be seen. You can often hide it by drilling it in the area where the door hinge plate will go or use either plastic covers or a dab of caulk to hide your screw head.

Above: Clamp a baton across the front of your unit to get your filler piece flush.

TIP *In some circumstances it looks better if the filler piece is flush with the doors, rather than flush with the edge of the cabinet frame. To achieve this, use brackets to attach a baton of wood to either side of your filler piece and then screw through the side of the unit into the baton. You can also use this approach to fit the filler piece flush with the edge of the cabinet, as discussed in step 5. The baton allows you to clamp the*

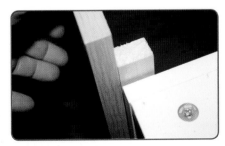

filler piece into position while you screw it into place, which can make life easier.

6 Now put the unit into position and check that all the brackets needed to secure the unit to the wall are in place.

7 If you're securing the other end of the filler piece to a wall, jump to step 8.

Make sure the filler piece is aligned correctly with both units and repeat step 5 with the unit already fixed into position. You might find it easier to use the baton of wood you had in Step 4, but this time use it to bridge both units and use one clamp in each unit.

With the filler piece in place, secure the free unit back to the wall. If you want to see the alternative approach to fitting a filler piece, read on.

8 If you don't want visible screws or if you're securing the filler piece to a wall use the following approach:

Put your filler piece into position and mark the inside of it, top and bottom.

TIP *As a general rule, a filler piece set back a millimetre or two from the front of the units looks fine. Alas, the same can't be said for a filler piece that protrudes past the front of the units. With this in mind, while you should always aim for it to be perfectly flush, if you feel perfection is in limited supply, err on the side of a little bit in.*

9 Now remove the filler piece and screw a bracket to the unit, using your marks. Make sure your screw won't go right through the side of the unit. Metal brackets often have slots that allow you to move the bracket forwards and back a bit, which is handy.

Plastic brackets tend to give a more rigid finish and give a more consistent 90° angle.

10 Place your filler piece into position and, ensuring your screws aren't too

long, screw through your bracket and into the back of the filler piece, securing the filler piece to your free unit.

11 Move your free unit into position. Again, if you're joining two units together it's easier to use an offcut of wood clamped across the base of both units to hold them in position while you secure your filler piece. Mark the inside, top and bottom of your filler piece against the secured unit or wall, as in step 8.

Make sure the brackets you're going to use to secure the unit to the wall are already in position.

12 Now remove the free unit and fit your brackets, top and bottom.

13 Move your unit back into position and, once you're sure everything is aligned properly, screw through the bracket and into the back of the filler piece. The top bracket is usually easy to do, but the bottom bracket can be a bit of a bind. If need be you can get to it from underneath, but if that proves impossible you can just put a few dabs of grab adhesive between the bracket and the filler piece and use a weight – wrapped in a cloth to prevent scratches – to hold it in place while the adhesive dries.

Below: Plastic hinges work best.

FITTING CORNER PIECES

In essence, a corner piece is just a specific type of filler piece. They are usually fitted to blind corner units and are designed to ensure that the units aren't so close to each other that the doors on either side of the corner keep snagging and banging into each other.

You fit corner pieces in much the same way as you'd fit a standard filler piece (see page 117). The only difference is that you want to determine where the corner piece should be and then secure the corner unit into position. As such, neither unit should be fully secured into place yet.

1 With the door on the corner unit in place and level, hold the corner piece in place. Note that this piece is usually flush with the doors – you want it close enough to the door so that you can't see the plain white cabinet behind it, but not so close that the door doesn't open cleanly. So, hold or clamp it in place and test that the door opens OK.

2 With the corner piece held in place, run a pencil or marker pen down the edge of the corner unit, so as to mark the back of the corner piece.

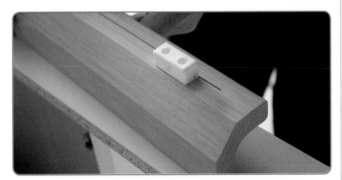

3 Use this line to set two brackets into position on the corner piece. Note that we've used plastic brackets because they create a far more consistent 90° angle. If you don't fancy using brackets you can just screw through the side of the unit and into the corner piece – use a pilot drill and a countersink, as per steps 4 and 5 in 'Making and fitting filler pieces' on page 117.

4 Now fit the corner piece back into position. Check your brackets are holding it in the right place and that the door on the

corner unit will still open and close freely. To get the height right, clamp a block of wood to the base of the corner unit to support the corner piece.

5 You can now set the unit that finishes the corner into position. Note that the corner piece sets a minimum distance between this unit and the corner unit, but you could make this bigger, if required, by attaching a filler piece to your corner piece. This is in no way essential, but if your row of units requires a filler piece, setting it here tends to work quite well.

6 You can set the other end of the corner piece flush with the unit or flush with that unit's door – the latter is more common. Decide which looks best, mark the bracket positions accordingly and then fit a bracket to the unit, top and bottom. You can now put the unit into position and, if you're ready to secure everything in place, screw the corner piece to the unit.

An alternative to using brackets here is to fit a baton to the back of the corner piece and then screw through the sides of the unit and into this baton.

FITTING END PANELS

The vast majority of wall and base unit 'carcasses' come in one colour: white. This keeps the costs down for the manufacturer and has little or no impact on the consumer because you get to see very little of the unit itself once it's been fitted. The exception to this rule is the units on the end of a run of units or on either side of a gap. In these positions we will get to see one or more sides of the units; a dull, boring, white side that will no doubt affront our eyes.

To get around this, the manufacturer will supply 'end panels', which will generally match the colour of your kitchen doors.

As a general rule, it's easier and looks neater if you complete the flooring and any wall finishes before you fit the end panels. Be aware that you can often buy two types of end panel. For base units you can get ones that just cover the side of the base unit itself or you can buy longer ones, designed to cover the unit and then reach down to the floor. For wall units they will often supply a longer version designed to match up to any pelmet you might attach to the bottom of the wall unit.

With this in mind, check the sizes of your end panels when you order them and make sure they will work with the plinth and pelmet you have opted for.

1 End panels come in two basic widths; ones that cover the unit and finish flush with the unit's closed doors, and ones that just cover the unit side exactly. I personally feel that the former looks best, so it pays to check that these are available for your kitchen.

2 The easiest way to position an end panel is to use spring clamps with rubber feet to hold the panel in place while you get it in position. Once you're happy with the position, use G-clamps with rubber feet or wooden blocks to ensure it doesn't move.

3 If your panel width is fine, jump to step 7.

If your panel is too wide then you need to turn it around so that what will eventually be the outside face of the end panel is pressed against the unit side and the back edge is up hard against the wall. Use clamps to hold it in this position and then use a pencil to draw across the front of your unit, marking the panel – it's often easier if you use a strip of masking tape over the area you intend to mark.

This approach will only work if the panel isn't too tall. If it is, then you'll just have to take careful measurements of the required width at the top and bottom of the unit and then transfer these measurements to the end panel, remembering that you want your cutline to end up hard up against the wall.

4 If you want the end panel to be flush with the edge of the unit then just cut along the line you've marked. If you want it to be flush with the front of the door you need to add the width of the door; 25mm for example.

Above: If you think you'll have to cut back your end panels it's easier to cut this width before the worktop goes on.

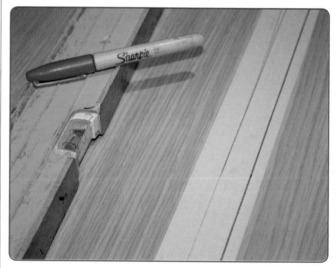

5 Remembering our earlier discussion on cutting laminate, use either a bench saw or jigsaw to cut back your end panel.

6 If you now turn the end panel around, the outer face will now be facing out and your cut line will be against the wall. Check the front edge is aligned with your cabinet and use spring clamps to hold it in position.

7 If you have to take something off the height of your end panel, always take it off the top. For the base units, this will leave the cut hidden under the worktop; for the wall units it's always best to avoid cutting the top or the bottom if you can, but if you must take something off, take it off the top – if you're fitting cornice above the wall units you can cover the cut edge with a section of this.

If you're fitting an end panel that will reach down to the floor you'll need to measure the height front and back, so as to compensate for any slope in the floor.

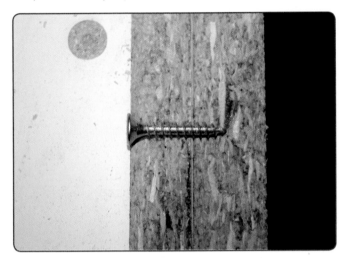

8 You should now have a correctly sized end panel that is clamped into position. You secure it to the unit by screwing through the unit side into the end panel. Before you do this, make sure you have the right-sized screws – ones that will go through the side of the units and then about halfway into the end panel. Always remember that you'll be countersinking the screw heads.

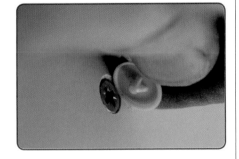

Right: Use plastic caps to hide your screws

9 You can hide your two front screws under the area where you're going to fit your door hinge plates. The two back screws can be recessed with a countersink and covered with plastic caps or white caulk to hide them.

10 Use a pilot drill with a countersink on it to go through the unit side and just into the end panel. Now carefully screw the end panels into place.

FITTING DOORS AND DRAWERS

As a general rule, this is the last thing you do to your kitchen, as you want to minimise the chances of the doors and drawers getting damaged. We discussed this area in some depth in Chapter 3, so here we're going to assume we're fitting standard 'quick-fit' doors with 'Euro-hinges', or as they call them in Europe, 'hinges'.

To make sure you have the process right, it's best to fit one door completely and then, to speed things up a bit, go through the steps below, en masse, for the rest of the doors.

FITTING THE DOORS

1 The door hinges come in two parts: a hinge plate (also called a base plate), which attaches to the cabinet, and the hinge itself, which attaches to the door. Let's start off easy and fit the hinge plates.

If you look inside your cabinets you should see that they come with two sets of fairly large, pre-drilled holes – about 5mm (¼in) in diameter – positioned close to the front of the cabinet – we've also been using this area

to screw our cabinets together (see above). Screw the hinge plate into these two holes, using the screws provided. The shape of the hinge plate differs but, as a general rule, they are roughly cruciform in shape and the longer 'leg' of the cross points into the cupboard – check this against the instructions that come with the hinge.

2 Place your door face down on a soft, clean surface – an old blanket, for example.

Your doors will be supplied with two large holes – about 35mm (1⅜in) in diameter – drilled halfway through them. Above and below each big hole are two much smaller holes, often pinpricks through the laminated surface.

Place the body of your hinge into this large hole and then screw it into position with the screws provided, using those tiny holes already marked out.

3 Modern hinges fall into two types: ones that clip on and off (quick-release hinges) and ones that slide on. The easiest way to tell the difference is by looking at the hinge plate – the slide hinges have a screw set into the top of the hinge plate. For both types, it's usually easiest to do the uppermost hinge first and then move onto the lower one.

Quick-release hinge
Flick back to Chapter 3, 'Fitting Overlay Doors Onto Frameless Cabinets' and read Steps 16-18 to see just how these quick release mechanisms work.

Above: A Slide-on hinge base

Main adjustment screw

Slide-on hinge
You should see a cup shape at the end of the hinge. To fit these hinges, slide the hinge onto the hinge plate until this cup slips under the screw on the hinge plate. Just tighten this screw and the hinge should be in place.

4 Now you'll almost certainly need to adjust the hinges to get the doors level and opening and closing smoothly (see 'Adjusting doors with modern hinges' next).

ADJUSTING DOORS WITH MODERN HINGES
In a utopian world you would just fit your hinges, close the doors and all would be well. Alas, this is rarely the case. More often than not the doors will need adjusting, but if you've used the latest hinges, this is a relatively straightforward procedure.

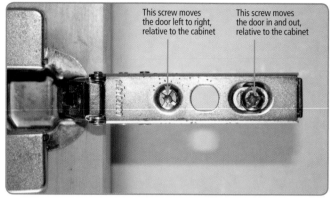

This screw moves the door left to right, relative to the cabinet

This screw moves the door in and out, relative to the cabinet

These hinges come with two screws on the hinge arm itself. Exactly where these screws are varies, but the back screw almost always allows you to move the door in and out – closer to and farther away from the cabinet – while the front screw moves the door left or right in relation to the cabinet.

You can also move the entire hinge up or down by loosening the two screws holding the mounting plate to the cabinet and sliding the whole plate up or down.

Alternatively, some hinges come with a third screw in the middle, which is used to move the door up and down.

The door isn't closing fully
The usual cause of this is that the door is just a fraction too close to the cabinet – as you close it you'll be able to see and feel the door edge catch the surface of the cabinet. Have a close look to see if it's the upper or lower hinge that's causing the problem – it can be both, of course.

On modern hinges, you can sort this out by turning the back screw of the misaligned hinge anti-clockwise. As you do so, you'll see the door slowly move out. If the door is standing too proud of the cabinet, turn this back screw clockwise to draw it in a bit.

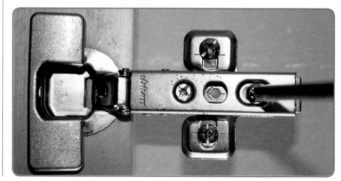

For older sliding hinges, turn this back screw anti-clockwise to loosen it and then just pull the door out a little before tightening the screw again to hold the door in position.

TIP *With slide-on hinges, if you adjust your doors, then take them off altogether it's not uncommon to discover they are miles out of alignment when you put them back on again. This is caused by the main adjustment screw on the hinge itself sitting on top of the hinge plate, rather than fitting into the grove at the front of the plate. If this happens, you might need to take the door back off, wind the adjustment screw on the hinge fully in. Fit the door again and then readjust it.*

The door drops a little

Sometimes you can resolve this problem by adjusting just one hinge, but usually it's better to move both hinges a little. To make the adjustment use the front screw on your hinge arm.

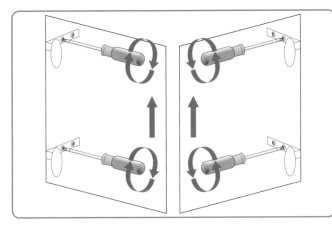

With a left-hand door, turning the front screw clockwise will draw the top of the door to the left, which will raise the right-hand side of the door a little. If you turn the front screw on the lower hinge anti-clockwise, you'll draw the bottom of the door to the right, which also brings the right-hand side of the door up. For a right-hand door, just reverse the way you turn the screws; anti-clockwise for the top hinge, clockwise for the lower hinge.

It's best to just give the screws a single turn on each hinge and then close the door to see what effect that's caused. If you're making the problem worse, then you're turning the screws in the wrong direction; if it's getting better, repeat the process until you have your door level.

The door goes up a little

This is just the opposite of the previous problem; so, for a left-hand door, turn the front screw on the top hinge anti-clockwise to move it to the right and turn the bottom hinge screw clockwise to draw it to the left until your door is level and the gap is correct.

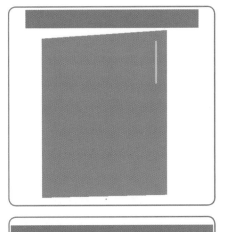

The gap between the doors is too big/small

This is more of an issue when the doors actually touch each other when closed. You need to move the left-hand door to the left – so turn the front screw on both upper and lower hinges clockwise by the same amount. To move the right-hand door to the right, turn both hinges anti-clockwise by the same amount.

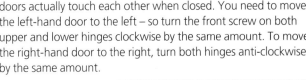

The entire door is too low/high

In this scenario you need to move the entire door up or down a bit by moving the mounting plates. Loosen the two screws holding the upper and lower plates to the cabinet and lift the door into the right position. Now tighten them up again.

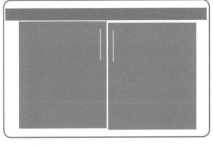

The amount of movement you have here is limited by the size of the slot in the mounting plate and where the screws are already, so you might have to move one door up a bit and the other down to get them level with each other. As previously mentioned, some hinge systems have a central screw on the mounting plate that allows you to move the plate up and down.

FITTING THE DRAWERS

If you bought a flat-pack kitchen, you can start building your drawers if you haven't already done so. If you bought a kitchen where the cabinets were delivered pre-built then the drawers would have already been in place and you would have removed them earlier. In this instance, all you have to do is remember how on earth they came out and try to put them back in again with the aid of any manufacturer's instructions.

Before you do this, it's best to fit the handles to the drawers (see opposite). If you don't want to fit the handles just yet, apply a bit of masking tape to the drawer front as a makeshift handle.

Often, to prevent damage in transit, the drawer fronts will have been turned the wrong way around and you'll need to take them off and turn them around. This is usually just a case of undoing a few screws.

LEVELLING DRAWER FRONTS

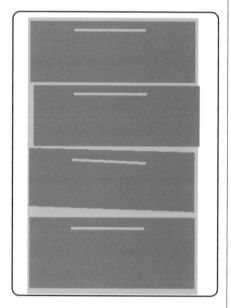

As with modern hinges, modern drawer fronts are also adjustable. Sadly, while there is a modicum of standardisation when it comes to hinges, it's a technical free-for-all with drawers.

Modern drawers usually come with three mechanisms: a screw, or some sort of bevel, that you turn to move the drawer front left and right; a similar mechanism for moving the drawer front up and down; and some sort of latch that will allow you to remove the drawer front altogether. These mechanisms are either under covers on the side of the drawers or are underneath the drawers – you can remove the covers with a flat-headed screwdriver.

If the mechanism you discover doesn't look vaguely comprehensible, and they often don't, try looking it up on the internet.

On older-style drawers,

the drawer front is usually just screwed directly onto the drawer. In this instance, it's just a matter of loosening the screws and giving the drawer front a wiggle to get it level. If that doesn't work, remove the drawer front completely and re-drill the holes on the drawer with an 8mm drill bit. Now fit washers to the screws and reattach the drawer front. You should now have much more 'wriggle room' to get the drawer front level.

FITTING DOOR AND DRAWER HANDLES

As a general rule, it's best to hang all your doors and then fit the handles. There's two main reasons for this: firstly, the doors are now held in place and are at a quite convenient height to work with; secondly, it reduces the chances of you fitting the handle in the wrong place. Conversely, it's usually easier to fit the handles to your drawers before putting them into their respective units.

TIP *Door and drawer fronts often have a protective plastic covering. This can be quite hard to spot sometimes, but you'll need to remove it before fitting your handles. After you've drilled the holes for your handles, scrape the edge of the hole with a fingernail to see if you can release and remove this protective covering.*

The handles will not usually be fitted to your kitchen doors and drawers. However, most manufacturers will put tiny, almost pinprick holes on the back of the doors and drawers, indicating where best to fit the handles.

Because the manufacturer doesn't know which handle option you've gone for, there may be a number of holes marked on the back. Find the ones that match your handles and use a coloured whiteboard marker pen to highlight the holes you're going to use on all your doors and drawers – doing this for all the doors at the same time reduces the chances of making a mistake.

If your doors and drawers don't come with any markings, you're going to have to decide the positions of the handles for yourself and ensure that each handle goes into the exact same place on each door. To do this, you're best off creating a template (see 'Making a template' and 'Marking hinge and handle positions' in Chapter 3). The act of drilling the holes for the handles is also covered in Chapter 3, 'Fitting door and drawer handles'.

SOFT-CLOSE HINGES

If you opted for soft close, your hinges and drawer mechanisms should come with the soft-close mechanism attached to them. If you want to retroactively fit a soft-close system, have a read of Chapter 3, 'Fitting soft-close doors and drawers'.

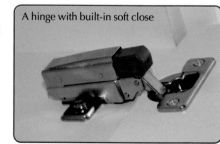

A hinge with built-in soft close

Fitting kickboards (plinths)

Kickboards are designed to create a nice clean finish that stops dirt accumulating under the units and allows the manufacturer to get away with fairly cheap, ugly legs on their units. As we mentioned at the start of this chapter, you can get or make kickboard drawer units that also add some valuable – albeit, quite awkward to reach – storage space to your kitchen.

We considered the height of our kickboards when first deciding what height to set our base units to. So, in a fairly level kitchen, you ought to be able to fit the kickboards without having to cut them down to size first. Alas, if your floor isn't level, you're almost certainly going to have to cut the kickboards down a bit.

In our example, we're going to fit kickboards in a U-shaped kitchen.

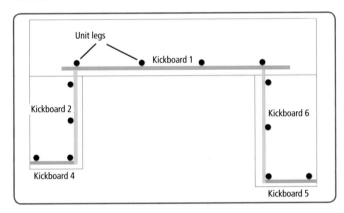

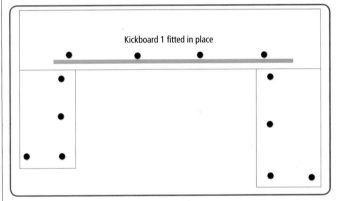

1 You can see that for kickboard 1, we don't have to be very precise with measuring the length because it can always extend under the units without causing any problems. With this in mind, we'll measure the distance from the front unit legs on the left and right wings of our U-shape and then add on 100mm to ensure our kickboard is long enough.

2 Having measured up, use a bench saw, mitre saw or jigsaw to cut the kickboard to the right length. Take note of which side is the front of the kickboard – for white kickboards this isn't as easy as it sounds.

3 Place the kickboard on the floor, up against the base of the units. If the units are high enough, the entire kickboard should slip underneath the units and rest against the unit legs. If this is the case, jump to step 9.

If the kickboard won't fit underneath the units, you're going to have to cut it down. You should always cut the top of the kickboard down, never the bottom. The easiest method is to just rest the kickboard on the floor against the base of the units, in the position

you want it to be in when fitted, and use a pencil to mark both the base of the unit and the kickboard in three places: the point at which the kickboard no longer fits under the units; the point at which it disappears under the units (at the end where the kickboard is too tall); and another point about halfway between the two.

4 Measure the distance from the base of the units to the floor at the end and middle points that you've just marked on the units.

5 Take 5mm off your two measurements – this will give a little 'wiggle' room (the gap can't be seen once the kickboard is fitted). Mark this new measurement on the kickboard at the points marked in step 3. For example, if the distance from the base of the unit to the floor was 180mm, we measure 175mm from the base of the kickboard and mark this on the kickboard.

6 Mark 5mm off the height of the kickboard at the point it no longer fitted under the units.

7 Use a long level, or any long straight edge to draw a line between your three points, extending it until it reaches the edge of the kickboard. Cut the kickboard along this line with a jigsaw. Note that you're making our cut at the top of the kickboard because the top will be hidden underneath the units and is unlikely to get wet.

TIP *In our example, you will not be able to get kickboard 1 into position to mark it if it's too tall to go under the units. In this instance, you can find the point where it will no longer fit under the units by just running an offcut of kickboard under the units until it reaches the point it no longer fits. Mark this position on the base unit then measure from this point to where your kickboard will start. Transfer this measurement to your kickboard – this will be where any cutting ends. Now take the same two measurements we described above, transfer these to your kickboard and make your cut. If you make this kickboard slightly longer than necessary you will have a good margin for error and will be able to move the kickboard left or right until you have the perfect fit.*

8 Put the kickboard back in place and check that it now goes under the base units.

9 Put the kickboard in position and then lay it on its side, hard up against the legs of the units. Use a pencil to mark the centre of each leg onto the kickboard and use that mark and a combination square to draw a straight line up the kickboard.

10 The units should have come with a bag of clips and brackets. Mark a position on the line you have just drawn that will be about three-quarters of the way up the kickboard when it's upright and in place.

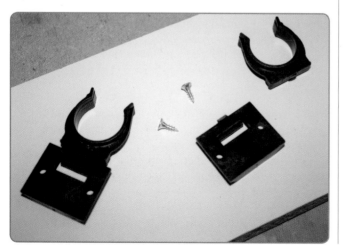

11 Centre the bracket on your line. Double-check you know which is the front and back and top and bottom of your kickboard, and screw the bracket into position using the screws provided.

12 Slide the plastic clip onto the bracket until it's centred on your line and repeat steps 10–12 for the rest of the clips.

13 Some kickboards come with a length of clear plastic that clips onto the base and provides a neat waterproof edge. This should just clip and hold in place by itself, but use a little line of clear sealant to hold it in position if need be. Also, if you did have to cut down your kickboard, it's best to seal that cut line with a bit of sealant/PVC glue/varnish to protect it from any water damage.

Above: From behind, the clips are gripping the leg.

14 Lift the kickboard into position and push it back against the legs of the units. If you've got all your clips aligned properly it should just click into place and hold there firmly. If one or more of your clips isn't aligned, you can move the clip left or right on the bracket until it's in the right place.

15 Repeat this process with the other kickboards.

If you look at our example layout above, you can see that the best way to go about fitting the rest of the kickboards is as follows:

■ Cut kickboards 4 and 5 a little longer than necessary. Follow steps 3–14 to fit these completely.

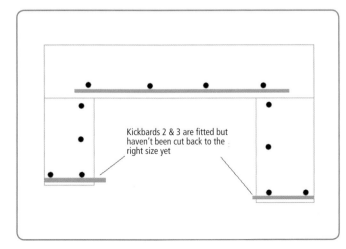

Kickbards 2 & 3 are fitted but haven't been cut back to the right size yet

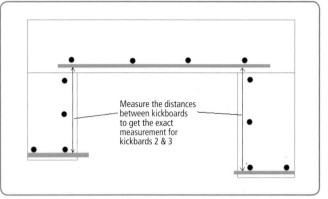

Measure the distances between kickboards to get the exact measurement for kickbards 2 & 3

■ Measure the distance between your kickboards and use this to cut kickboards 2 and 3 to size. Note that you have the option of cutting the kickboard so it goes up to or over the smaller kickboards.

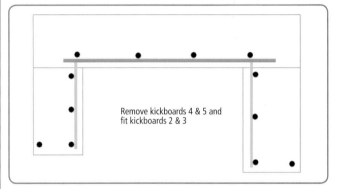

Remove kickboards 4 & 5 and fit kickboards 2 & 3

■ Cut and completely fit kickboards 2 and 3.

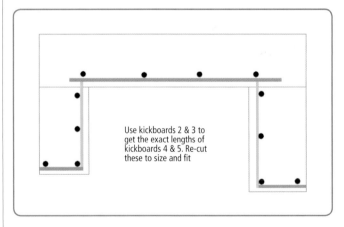

Use kickboards 2 & 3 to get the exact lengths of kickboards 4 & 5. Re-cut these to size and fit

■ You can now measure the exact lengths of kickboards 4 and 5 and fit these.

Exactly how you go about cutting and fitting your various kickboards will, of course, change depending on your layout, but the principles are the same. You also need to bear in mind where your cuts are going to be. Aim to have them hidden, either by being butted up to a wall or another kickboard. You can use iron-on strips of laminate to cover your exposed cuts – most kickboards come with a few of these and we'll cover using them in 'Iron-on strips' on page 153. This is never as neat as the edge the manufacturer supplies, so even these need to be hidden away where possible.

Fitting cornices and pelmets

These are the finishing touches to the kitchen, so by now you should have fitted all your units and worktops and all your cabinet doors/drawers and end panels should be in place. In a kitchen, 'cornice' refers to the decorative edging that goes on the top of the wall units and 'pelmet' is the decorative edge underneath the unit. The fitting of a pelmet is identical to that of a cornice, so we'll just walk through fitting the latter.

The easiest way to cut a cornice or pelmet is with a mitre saw, and the best mitre saw is a powered mitre saw with a circular

blade, deemed by the manufacturer to be suitable for the material you will be using – usually this is 'laminated particle board'. Your cuts will be far more accurate if your mitre saw comes with a laser that shows exactly where the blade will cut.

1 Exactly how the cornice is going to sit on your units is dictated by the shape and style of the cornice and by your own personal taste. However, how it sits is going to determine exactly how you measure the sections, so you need to decide here and now.

The easiest way to get a feel for how the cornice will look is to cut off a small section, a little longer than the depth of your wall units plus the width of the cornice itself. For example, if my wall units are 350mm deep and my cornice strips are 50mm wide, I would cut off a length of cornice just over 400mm long. Not only can we use this offcut to see how the cornice will fit, but we'll also use it as our first fitted strip.

2 Exactly how you get your measurements is going to be affected by the design of the cornice, but the following approach tends to work for most. Take the length of cornice you cut to size in step 1 and hold it up in place on the unit. Now use a pencil to mark the front edge of the unit onto the cornice.

3 Set the mitre saw to cut a 45° angle. There are two 45° angles you can cut: left-handed and right-handed. Bear in mind when cutting that the longer end will always be on the outside edge of the cornice.

Place the section of cornice into your mitre saw, making sure it's pressed back hard against the 'fence' – the metal ridge that runs across the base of the mitre saw.

4 If you have a laser on your mitre saw, make sure it's on, and move your cornice along the fence until the corner you marked is right under the cut position. If you don't have a laser you'll have to lower the blade – the mitre should be off at this point – closer to the cornice to see where this cut will be. Now cut the cornice at a 45° angle.

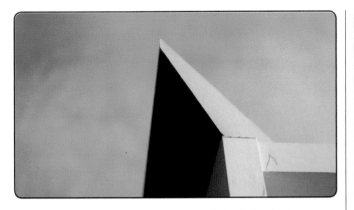

5 Present your cornice up to the unit and check that it's been cut correctly – the 45° angle cut should exactly meet with the edge of the unit. If it's right, measure the length of the cornice from the tip of your 45° cut to the base of the strip and compare that to the depth of the unit. For example, our unit is 350mm deep and our perfectly fitting length of cornice is 380mm. So we now know that if we measure the depth or length of our units we just need to add 30mm on to that measurement for every angle we're going to cut. Also, since wall units are usually the exact same depth, we now know the perfect measurement for all our left- and right-side pieces.

6 Using the calculation in step 5 we can measure the front of our unit, or units, from edge to edge. We will have two angled cuts, so in our example we will add 60mm to our measurement. In our diagram, we're showing pelmet only because it's easier to see.

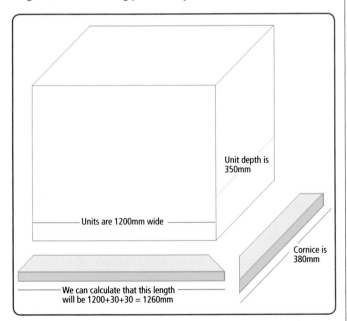

Unit depth is 350mm

Units are 1200mm wide

Cornice is 380mm

We can calculate that this length will be 1200+30+30 = 1260mm

7 It's best if you make up the cornice for the simplest area of the kitchen first – for example, a single unit hanging on the wall by itself. Then just lay out the pieces on top of this unit and make sure they fit correctly.

8 If you're fairly sure your cornice is cut correctly, bring all the pieces down and lay them out on a hard flat surface – a sheet of plywood, for example. The easiest way to secure the pieces together is with glue such as 'mitre adhesive'. This is usually a

two-part adhesive. You squeeze one part of the glue onto one piece of cornice, spray the second part of the glue – the activator – onto the other and then just squeeze the two pieces together. You usually get about ten seconds to get the two pieces perfectly aligned and you need to hold it in place for about another ten seconds – check the label for precise instructions. If you see any glue being squeezed out of the joint, wipe it off immediately.

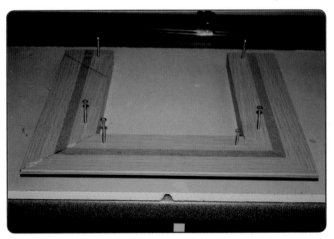

9 Once you have all your pieces stuck together, screw the cornice into position from the top. To do this drill pilot holes into your cornice, put your screws in – give them a few twists just to keep them in position – and then lift your cornice pieces onto the units. Once in position, you can screw them down.

10 Now complete the rest of the cornice and pelmet. If you find that one of more of your joints isn't perfect you could look at using a coloured filler to smooth out any gaps or deformities.

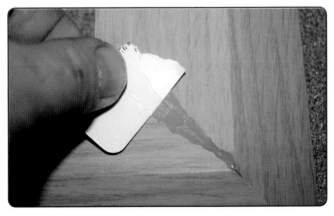

Fitting batons into stud walls

Your wall cabinets will potentially be carrying a lot of weight and, while many specialist fittings for stud and drylined walls claim to be more than up to the job, it's often better to play safe and strengthen the wall itself. That said, fitting batons to walls is not straightforward, so don't just discount the fittings now available. The biggest 'GripIt' fitting is designed for a safe shear load of 113kg. If you use these and then run a good grab-adhesive along the back edges of your wall units, I really would be shocked if your wall units didn't remain on your walls, regardless of what normal kitchen life throws at them.

If you're not sure about using glue and plasterboard fixings, you can just replace the plasterboard behind your wall units with 18–22mm ply or particleboard and attach everything to this. Again, this will work in most instances, but the most secure way of keeping wall units on walls is to fit a wooden baton behind your wall units and then screw your support brackets into this baton. The downside of this approach is that you might have to get the wall replastered if it's not all going to be covered by wall units or tiles.

Steps 1–3 in the section 'Fitting the wall units' takes you through the process of determining where your wall unit brackets are going to go. So, if you haven't already read that section, have a read now.

1 You should already have your base line marking the top of your brackets so it's easy enough to work out where the screw positions are going to be. To avoid losing your measurements, draw long vertical

and horizontal lines across the wall so that you can still see your marks once you've removed the plasterboard.

2 With your marks in place, use a plasterboard ('jab' or 'dryline') saw to cut away the section of plasterboard.

The odds are you'll have to extend the intended width of your hole, as you need to end the cut up against a stud. You'll also need to cut out a bit more of the plasterboard below where you're going to place the batons in order to screw them into place, but bearing in mind that plasterboard comes in 1200 x 2400mm (4 x 8ft) sheets anyway, it makes little sense to fiddle around with tiny holes – just make the hole depth small enough that the wall units will still fully cover the new plasterboard.

3 We'll need to fit a baton between each 'stud' in the wall (in the UK these batons go by the lovely name of 'noggins'). So measure the distance between the two studs and add a few millimetres.

4 For stud walls it's best to use a baton 38mm (1½in) thick by about 75–100mm (3–4in) wide, as this will usually match the dimensions of the stud itself. These are usually sold in 2400mm (8ft) lengths as 'CLS' (Canadian Lumber Standard). CLS comes in two standard widths: 75mm (3in) or 100mm (4in) – the 75mm (3in) should be more than enough for your needs.

5 It's easier if you cut the batons a few millimetres too long. Doing so means that you'll have to hammer the batons into position but once there they will stay in place all by themselves. Hammer the baton back until it is flush with the stud work and lined up with the line for your hanging brackets.

Below: Extend all your lines so you can still see them once the plasterboard has been removed.

6 Use a long pilot drill to drill at an angle through the bottom of the baton and into the studwork. Now use 4in, size 10 or 12 screws to secure the baton to the studwork. If you can get your hands on an impact driver, it makes sense to put at least one screw right through the studwork and into the baton. Repeat for all other batons.

Below: If you slightly angle your screws front to back it's easier to get a screwdriver into position

7 Cover the hole you made with a new section of plasterboard (see 'Reboarding and repairing holes in walls and ceilings' on page 101).

8 Redraw your base line across the new plasterboard.

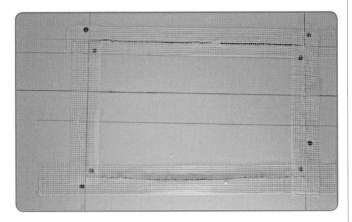

FITTING A SUPPORTING BATON TO A DRYLINED WALL (DOT AND DAB)

You usually don't need to go to these lengths to secure wall units to a drylined wall but sometimes the distance between the plasterboard and the wall behind is just too big for any dryline fixing to be relied upon. If you harbour any doubts you might as well fit a baton, for peace of mind if nothing else.

1 Steps 1–3 in the section 'Fitting the wall units' (page 113) took you through the process of determining where your wall unit brackets are going to go. So, if you haven't already read that section, have a read now.

You're going to remove the section of plasterboard where your base line is, so extend all your lines beyond the area you're going to cut out so they can be redrawn afterwards.

2 Use a dryline saw to cut out your section of plasterboard. You only need a cut-out section big enough to get your baton in. If you can ensure it all remains hidden by wall units you can avoid any issues with replastering the walls afterwards. The baton itself should be about 75mm (3in) wide and deep enough to be flush with the finished wall surface once fitted. Note that most timber merchants will plane your baton down to the right depth for little or no extra charge.

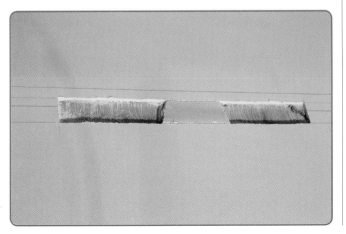

3 Use a hammer and bolster or chisel to knock out any lumps of adhesive so that you have a clean, flat section of wall exposed.

4 Cut your wooden baton to size. It's best to screw it to the wall every 500mm (20in) along its length. Aim for these screws to be close to the centre where you expect the wall units to be, so that they don't get in the way of your hanging bracket screws. Drill pilot holes for all screws.

5 Get a friend to help hold the baton in position. You should aim for the centre of the baton to be the right height for the hanging bracket screws.

Use a 5–6mm masonry drill bit to go through your centre pilot hole and drill the wall behind. Now remove the baton and re-drill the hole using an 8mm drill bit. Fit a brown wall plug into the hole and screw the baton back into position.

6 The baton should now be held firmly in place by a single screw. Take a moment to mark the baton with a pencil to indicate which side is facing you and which side is up. Use a 5–6mm drill bit to drill through the rest of your pilot holes and into the wall.

Below: Mark the top of the baton before drilling the rest of the holes.

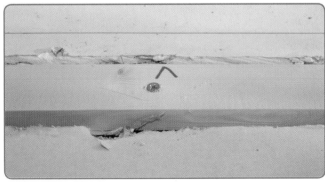

7 Now undo your single screw and remove the baton. Use the 8mm drill bit to make your holes bigger and deeper, and fit the wall plugs.

8 Refit the baton, securing it in place using all the screw holes you've made. You ought to use at least 3in, size 10 screws – you might want to add a bit of grab-adhesive to the back of the baton at this point, just to be doubly sure.

9 Redraw your lines showing the base line and hanging bracket positions.

In terms of looks and utility the countertop, or worktop, is probably the most important thing in your kitchen. You can completely change how your kitchen looks just by changing the countertop. Possibly because of that fact, they come in a huge range of colours and materials; some of which are fairly cheap, while others will have you hiding from your bank manager for months, if not years.

Many kitchens will have the kitchen sink and the cooker hob set into the countertop, and the material you opt for will directly affect what type of hob or sink is going to work in your kitchen and just how expensive and time-consuming the fitting will be.

What are the options?

This is an area where you really can get spoilt for choice, although how many options are truly available to you is dictated by the size of your budget, as the price range between different materials can get quite frightening.

LAMINATE

A laminate countertop is typically made from a thin layer of plastic melamine bonded to a base of compressed particleboard or MDF. Here in the UK this is the option most people go for, and for very good reason; they are easy to fit, come in a vast array of finishes and are fairly cheap. If you're planning on fitting your own countertop, this is the first place you should look.

While fairly cheap, there is still quite a wide range of prices. Usually, the colour and design is the primary reason for the price difference, but the edge shape and thickness of the countertop will also affect the price – the standard thickness is 38mm (1½in) but you can get thicknesses varying from 28–40mm (1⅛–1⅝in).

PROS
Because it's so popular, you can find pretty much any look you desire at a price that the vast majority of us would regard as affordable – some of the modern wood and granite-effect laminates are almost identical to the real thing, but come at a fraction of the price. Laminate is durable, resistant to most stains and requires almost no upkeep other than an occasional wipe down with mild detergent.

CONS
Laminate isn't heatproof, and a hot pan will melt and warp the surface. While colours aren't a problem for laminate, texture is, and they all tend to have the same fairly bland texture. You can

get high-gloss finishes, but they show up the slightest mark so a matt finish is a better long-term option.

While the laminate itself is waterproof, the base material it's bonded to isn't. As a result, if water gets under the laminate, either because the adhesive has failed and the laminate has started to peel away or because the countertop has been cut but not sealed afterwards, then the whole work surface will start to swell up and warp. For this reason, laminate isn't suitable for undermount sinks.

SOLID SURFACE – CORIAN

You'll hear people using the term 'solid-surface countertop' to describe a host of different things, but here we're talking about countertops where a relatively thick, decorative acrylic resin is bonded to MDF to create what is, in effect, laminate-plus. The most popular example of solid surface is 'Corian' by Du Pont, and in many areas of the world this is the name given to all solid-surface products.

The decorative surface is much thicker and harder than a standard laminate, and as a result they tend to be much better wearing. Of course, the downside of this is that they are much more expensive and fitting them tends to be beyond the remit of the DIY enthusiast, so you'll have to factor in the fitting cost.

PROS
This is a very flexible product that can be thermally shaped into pretty much any design. The main upside of this is that you can get a kitchen worktop that is completely seamless. They tend to be far more scratch- and heat-resistant than laminates and far less likely to get damaged if a heavy object is dropped on them. Like laminates, they are very stain-resistant.

CONS
Like laminates, the MDF the surface is bonded to isn't waterproof, so if it gets exposed to water or steam the surface will become warped and damaged.

COMPOSITE
The terms 'solid-surface' and 'composite' seem to be readily interchangeable these days. Yes, they are both made using resin,

but in solid-surface worktops this is just a relatively thin layer (5–8mm) that is then bonded to an MDF substrate. In composite countertops, the resin mix goes right through.

What you mix the resin with also tends to change the name. The most common mix is crushed stone (usually 80–90%) and the most common crushed stone is quartz, so you will often hear them called 'quartz countertops'.

If you buy a composite countertop it will usually be designed and fitted for you to create a seamless work surface. You can make them yourselves (see 'Epoxy resin countertops' on page 78), although the manufactured countertops usually use acrylic or polyester resin, which acts slightly differently to epoxy.

There are a number of companies who, rather than bonding the resin surface to a substrate and selling the result as a composite worktop, will fit a thin layer of the resin/stone mix over the top of your existing laminate worktop, effectively creating a composite worktop in situ. The resin-stone surface is about 7mm (²⁄₇in) thick, and the result is a thicker and more luxurious-looking worktop, although this extra thickness can create problems when fitting sinks and cooker hobs into the worktops afterwards.

PROS
Acrylic resin is a thermoplastic, which means that you can warm it up and do pretty much what you want with it. As a result, the designs available are close to limitless, although you'll pay for this imagination. It is a suitable work surface for undermount sinks.

These can give a very realistic stone look, on account of being composed mainly of stone, but they're usually very resistant to staining. They're not quite as scratch-resistant as granite countertops, but they don't lag far behind and, because the resin gives them more flexibility, they are unlikely to crack. Most are very heat resistant, but they can crack if subjected to very high temperatures. Unlike natural stone, most don't need to be sealed and the colours and effects are not limited by nature.

Usually the stone used is a waste product, so composite countertops can be considered 'green' and the stone content 'reclaimed', although the type and amount of resin used will have an impact on these credentials.

CONS
They can be very expensive, although they are usually cheaper than natural stone. Check when you buy, as some composite countertops will need regular sealing and oiling. Also, be wary of how some of these countertops are sold. Many companies will describe these as being 'granite' or 'stone' worktops, which isn't strictly wrong as the primary component is granite and stone, but isn't really true either as it's not actually a solid sheet of natural stone.

You can make these resin worktops from pretty much anything you like, but some of the 'bits' within the worktop might not be as hardwearing as others. For example, a lot of companies make wonderful-looking countertops from mixing stone and small fragments of shell into the resin. The stone is usually very hardwearing, but the shell can be dissolved away by repeat exposure to things like lemon juice, leaving the surface pitted after a few years. So find out in advance exactly what the resin mix is if you require a very hardwearing work surface.

SOLID WOOD
These seem to be very popular at the moment and I must confess that I'm not sure why. OK, they can look lovely, but they can be a right pain to maintain and they can get very pricey.

When buying, you should always check to see what wood is being used. You can get countertops made from exotic hardwoods, which may look great but come from unsustainable sources and can have an enormous negative impact on the environment. Good sustainable alternatives are maple and bamboo, and you can even get countertops made from reclaimed wood.

The type of wood and the way in which it's been put together will determine how hardwearing the worktop is going to be, but most aren't really suitable for hardworking areas – better to use them in serving areas rather than food preparation zones, for example.

PROS

They can look terrific, they are much quieter to work on and they can lend a richer, warmer feeling to your kitchen. Because it's a natural product, the look and colour will develop over time. If you have a fairly extensive knowledge of woodwork then you can fit, or even make these yourself.

While they are prone to scratches, these can be easily sanded out and, while they are vulnerable to many stains, citrus – which can stain stone – isn't a problem. Rumour has it that they tend to be more hygienic because the surface has natural anti-bacterial properties.

You can use a clear epoxy resin on the top of your wood. This still lets the natural look shine through but the surface is now protected, making it far easier to maintain and more useful in hardworking areas.

CONS

When they are first installed they require a quite elaborate oiling and sealing routine – once a day for a week, then one a week for a month, then once a month for a year, then every three months or so for the rest of its life is a fairly typical upkeep regimen. Just how much maintenance is going to be required depends on the type of wood you opt for, so always ask the supplier for the recommended maintenance process before you buy.

The surface is vulnerable to heat damage and scratching, although the damage can be sanded out quite easily and some woods are more resistant than others. Stains can be a problem, so you need to wipe things up fairly quickly.

Water damage can ruin them, so you need to be very thorough with your sealing procedures around sinks, or anywhere where steam might be an issue – dishwashers, tumble driers etc. You often see them used with undermount sinks but, if you go back a few years later, more often than not you'll see that the wood around the sink has become dull and cracked.

STONE

In terms of price, and often looks, solid stone is the Rolls-Royce of kitchen countertops. The most common stone used is granite because it's extremely hardwearing and looks good. Marble tends to look even better, but it's usually a bit softer and more likely to stain. Other stones such as soapstone, while good looking, are far more prone to scratches.

In terms of price, the main factors are the type and quality of the stone and its thickness. You'll also need to factor in the installation cost, because cutting and fitting a solid stone countertop is beyond the remit of anything but the most skilled – and expensively equipped – DIY enthusiast.

Thinner sheets of stone reduce both the weight and the cost. Some companies offer a solid stone surface set onto particleboard with a solid stone edge to give the illusion of a thicker stone countertop.

PROS

Granite, especially, is so hard that it can tolerate pretty much anything the average cook can throw at it. It's resistant to water, heat and scratches and, if you do manage to inflict a scratch, it's always possible to polish it out. How resistant to staining they are depends on the stone but if they've been sealed properly, most get by pretty well. Soapstone is particularly renowned for its stain resistance.

CONS

The most obvious downside of solid stone is the price, which varies between expensive and very expensive. They are also very heavy and brittle. To avoid cracking the worktop, your kitchen base units need to be solid with absolutely no movement in them. As a general rule, the fitters will test this when they measure up your kitchen but you need to get them to confirm in writing that they're happy with the units, as this will affect any product guarantees.

Most stone will stain to an extent – red wine and citric acid are the most popular culprits. To avoid this, the stone needs to be sealed when it's first installed and the seal should be reapplied every ten years or so – check the requirements before you buy. Even then, it still pays to wipe up any spills as soon as possible.

METAL

Stainless steel has long been the material of choice for commercial kitchens, mainly because it's durable and easy to keep clean. If shiny steel doesn't float your boat, you could opt for zinc or copper.

Zinc stains at the drop of a hat, but if you nurture rather than wipe away the stains you eventually get an interesting blue-grey patina that can look pretty good. Copper can look spectacular, but like zinc is a 'living' surface i.e. it will oxidise and change colour over time. You can get around this by sealing the surface with a resin.

While copper gives a rich colour to your kitchen, zinc and steel are very much an 'industrial' look, which people either love or hate.

PROS

Metal worktops are easy to keep clean with just soap and water and are very durable. Steel will scratch, but if you go for a brushed steel look you can just brush the scratches away or at least blend them in a bit. Steel is completely heat-resistant and hot pans can be put directly onto it.

All metals, especially zinc and copper, tend to be antimicrobial so it's a very hygienic surface to prep food on. It's also a relatively light work surface, therefore it's suitable for all kitchen units.

As a general rule, metal worktops are built and fitted to order. However, if you have any metal-working skills and tools I can't see that it would be too much of a challenge to make these yourself. They are, after all, just sheets of metal applied over an MDF template – or your old worktops – with nice edges.

CONS

Metal worktops can be very expensive. Steel is durable and hardwearing, but zinc and copper are not; both will easily dent and scratch and neither can really cope with a lot of heat. Steel will also dint, but you have to put far more effort into it.

Steel shows up scratches, drops and stains very readily, although they can be washed away easily, and brushed steel tends to be more forgiving for both stains and scratches. Copper and zinc can be high-maintenance surfaces unless they are sealed. They can be very noisy surfaces to work on and can also be very cold in winter.

© creoglass.co.uk

GLASS

You can use glass in lots of different ways and, as a result, the kitchen countertop design options are immense. That said, it's not that popular a material at the moment, so you might have to hunt around a bit. If you want something truly unique you can design your own countertop and use clear glass on top as the final finish – you can also use epoxy resin in the same way.

To make the most of their clear or semi-opaque characteristics you can fit LED lights into hardened (tempered) glass worktops. This can look amazing, especially if you're entertaining in the evening and have the rest of the lights turned down.

PROS

Easy to keep clean and, being non-porous, glass is a very hygienic work surface that can be made entirely from recycled material. Glass worktops are heat, water and stain resistant, although very hot pans might cause them to crack. Because it reflects light, glass can also make a kitchen look larger.

CONS

Glass shows up fingerprints and smudges very well and can scratch and break. Acids can permanently etch them. Textured glass looks good, but it can be a pain to work on and keep clean. Glass worktops are expensive and are generally made-to-measure and professionally fitted, which just adds to the bill.

DO-IT-YOURSELF

The only truly 'off-the-shelf' DIY countertop product is a laminated countertop, which we'll discuss shortly. In terms of fitting there's not much difference between laminate and solid wood. However, with solid wood, the cost of a mistake can be more than a little worrying, so you might want to consider leaving it to the professionals.

OTHER MATERIALS

If you're feeling truly adventurous, these options are worth a look at:

▪ Tiled countertops (see 'A tiled countertop' on page 72)
▪ Concrete (see 'A concrete countertop' on page 75)
▪ In-lay resin (see 'Epoxy resin countertops' on page 78)

Installing a laminate countertop

Most cabinets are about 600mm (24in) deep with the doors fitted. As such, most laminate worktops are designed with a width of between 605–615mm (24–24¼in). This means that they should just overhang the cabinets when the doors are fitted and closed. That said, always check this width before you buy, especially if you're buying cabinets from one supplier and worktops from another. Having to reduce this width to fit your units is a bit of a pain and, while a splashback does allow some room for manoeuvre with regards to the worktop depth, it doesn't offer much. A worktop that is too narrow just isn't going to work.

Fitting laminate countertops (worktops) is relatively straightforward, but like all DIY, practice makes perfect. As luck would have it, you can generally only buy laminated countertops in 3m (10ft) lengths, which means that you'll have excess worktop to practice on. It makes sense to plan where these offcuts will be and use them to practise cutting holes for sinks and corners etc. If you aren't going to have any sizable offcuts then I'd suggest buying a length of the cheapest laminate you can find and using

it to practise on. Before you start, find a friend. This isn't always a two-person job, but manhandling worktops is always easier when there are two of you.

Cutting worktops will always release a lot of fine wood dust, so make sure you don a dust mask and protective glasses before you start. You can buy tools that claim to extract the dust as they cut, but they rarely do this very well, so it pays to do your cutting outside.

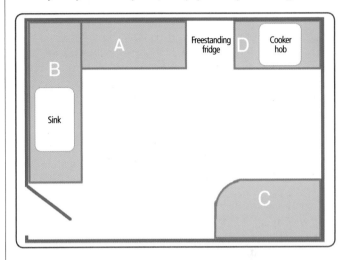

1 Start by fitting all the countertop lengths that don't require a corner. In our example shown above, it would make sense to fit worktops C and D first, as we just cut them to length.

2 For worktop D we need the worktop to finish flush with the side of the units, as we need to be able to push our full-height fridge into the 600mm (24in) gap between the units. Since we're tiling all the walls, we are going to have at least 5mm (⅛in) to

play with so, in this instance, we'd just measure the width of the units, between the gap and the side wall, and cut our worktop to this size.

If your worktop is just finishing over the top of a unit – as with the end closest to the door on worktop B – it's a good idea for the worktop to just overhang the cabinet beneath it. There's no set width for this overhang, but 10mm (⅜in) is about right.

3 Before you start cutting, take a good look at the worktop and check it out for any dints, scratches and blemishes, while you still have the opportunity to take it back to the store.

If all is well, have a look at the ends. You should notice that the ends – or at least one end – don't actually have any laminate on them. The manufacturer

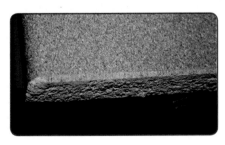

Tools
The tools you will need are as follows:

- Jigsaw with downward cutting laminate blade and a fine wood scroll blade for cutting the corners (the latter is optional but comes with most jigsaw blades sets)
- Bench or circular saw (optional)
- Electric screwdriver with a selection of bits
- Masking tape
- Pencil
- Woodworking square or combination square
- Set of woodwork chisels
- Level, at least 600mm (24in) long
- Sealant and sealant gun
- Router with worktop template (jig) (these can be hired)
- Two or more workbenches
- Dust mask and protective glasses.

has left these little bits of bare wood there to prevent the laminate snagging and getting damaged, but it also means that you can't use these as an exposed edge. In theory, you could use them on the edges that are hard up against the wall because they will eventually be hidden under tiles, but it's best to measure back about 50mm (2in) and make your own clean cut. Make your first cut on an edge that will eventually be hidden under a tiled wall or splashback, so if there are any 'issues' they can be hidden away out of sight.

4 To prevent damage and make your pencil marks easier to see, use some wide masking tape to tape off the area you're going to cut, about 50–75mm (2–3in) on either side of the cut line.

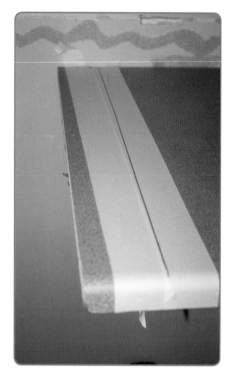

5 Use a tape measure to measure in 50mm (2in) from your current edge in two places and use the level and a pencil to join them up with a straight line right across the width of the worktop.

6 You can make the cut with a jigsaw and a downward cutting blade, but it's easier to get a straight line with a circular saw – an alternative is to cut the worktop roughly to length and use a bench saw to get a perfectly straight edge. Most circular saws come with a movable 'fence' that you can use to ensure a straight line off your existing edge.
Alternatively, you can clamp a straight edge to the worktop and use that as a fence –

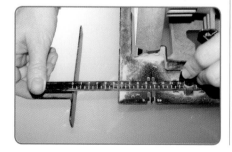

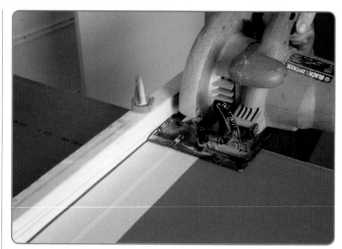

you'll need to measure the distance between the edge of the shoe and the blade to determine where to mount your fence.

Most circular saws also come with a maximum depth setting. It's not critical to set a maximum depth, but it's safer if you only cut through the worktop, plus a few millimetres, so for a 38mm (1½in) worktop you'd set the maximum depth to just over 40mm

Before you cut, make sure you have the right type of blade – it should say that it's suitable for wood laminate, it ought to have at least 40 teeth and it should be new. You also need to check which way the blade is going to turn on your circular saw.

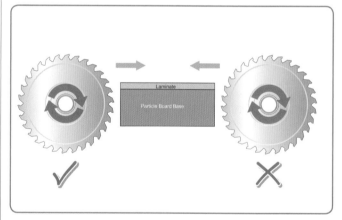

To prevent the laminate chipping or tearing as you cut it, the blade needs to cut through the laminate and then the wood underneath. Do it the other way around and the blade will come up through the wood and lift the laminate a little before it cuts through. At best, this will chip the laminate; at worst, it'll rip it completely. The direction of rotation is usually clearly shown on the circular saw. If you have an upward-cutting blade – and most are – you need to turn the worktop over before making your cut. You should always start cutting from the front edge of the worktop and apply masking tape over the cut line before you begin, to reduce the chances of the laminate chipping.

7 Whatever tool you use, you need to let the blade get up to speed before starting the cut. For the circular saw, the lower blade guard ought to move back of its own accord as you start the cut, but it sometimes needs a little encouragement from the lever. Don't rush the cut.

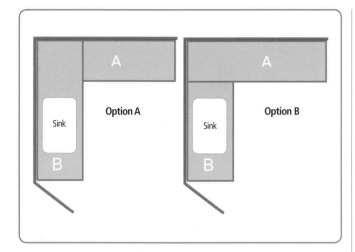

Option A — Sink — A — B

Option B — Sink — A — B

8 In our example we can roughly cut worktops A and B to size, which makes them easier to carry and manoeuvre if nothing else. However, it doesn't pay to cut them exactly to size yet as, if we make a mistake with our corner we can use the extra length to have another go. If you can, leave an overhang of about 300mm (12in), so you have enough room to make a mistake, possibly two, before you have to buy a completely new worktop.

Before you make any cuts to these two worktops, think about which way you want the corner to go. In the example above, we have two options: A and B. If possible, you should avoid having a joint near a sink or primary work area as the joint will always be more vulnerable to water damage than the rest of the worktop. It also makes sense to put any joints in as discrete an area as you can, which means as far away from windows as is feasible. With all those principles in mind, you ought to be able to see that option A works better in our example.

9 There are two main approaches to cutting corners. For the very easy way, have a look on page 150 at 'Fitting corner and edging strips' and, for the slightly more adventurous amongst us, see 'Mitred corners', 'Mitred straight connections' and 'Mitred rounded edges and curves'.

10 Once your worktops are cut to size and all your joints are completed, you're ready to secure the worktop into position. Before you do so, it's worthwhile checking that any holes you have to cut out for sinks and hobs etc. are going to be easy to cut once the worktops are secure. If you have any doubts, it's best to cut out these holes first while it's possible to move the worktop a little and then secure the worktop into position. Be aware, though, that once you've cut out these holes, the worktop in that area is going to be weakened and is far more liable to break when lifted. If you're going to move it, just slide it out enough to make your cutting easier and then slide it back into its final position afterwards – see 'Fitting the sink'(page 154 and 'Fitting the hob' (page 156).

Once any holes have been cut, securing the worktop is simply a matter of screwing up through the cabinets and into the worktop itself. On longer sections the weight of the worktop will keep it in position while you secure it to the cabinets, but for shorter sections you might want to clamp the worktop into position first. Ideally, you want two screws at the front and two at the back of each cabinet supporting the worktop. You'll want these to be fairly discrete so it's an idea to use a pilot drill to start your holes and

a countersink to ensure the screw heads are flush with the cabinet surface when you've finished.

If you have a long span of worktop that is not supported by cabinets, it's best to fit a 50 x 50mm (2 x 2in) baton of wood to the wall under the worktop to support it. The only danger here is with using screws that are too long and go right through your worktop or getting carried away with your pilot drill and drilling right

through. To avoid this, set a stop on your drill and aim for screws that go about midway into the worktop.

11 The exposed edges of your worktops can be finished off with either laminate or metal edging strips. The metal ones don't provide as good a colour match, but are more robust than laminate edges. They're essential if you are fitting a freestanding cooker between two close-fitting worktops, as they'll provide you with a non-combustible edge (see 'Fitting corner and edging strips' on page 150).

Below: A metal edging strip.

12 You now need to seal the back edge of your worktop. Not only does this make the worktop more secure by sticking it firmly to the wall, but it also ensures that water can't get behind the worktop and damage it. Use clear silicone sealant and make sure you completely seal all the back edges (see Chapter 2, 'Using silicone sealant').

With the sealant complete, you're ready to fit any splashback you like.

MITRED CORNERS

This is the best way to cut a kitchen worktop because it will give you an almost invisible join that won't collect dirt and grime and will last as long as the life of the worktop. You can buy everything you need for this task, but it's far cheaper to hire it all. Most hire shops will hire out the kitchen worktop template and router, complete with a few straight, worktop router bits, as a kit. If you want to buy your own, see the buying guide on page 42, 'Router and Template'.

Tools

The tools you need for this task are as follows:

- Worktop 'template' or 'jig'
- Plunge router with a 12mm (½in) collet and a 30mm (1¼in) guide bush
- 12.7mm (½in) diameter straight router bit (often called a 'worktop router bit')
- Combination square
- Set of worktop connector bolts (two or three for each joint) and a spanner – usually 10mm (⅜in)
- Tube of jointing compound matching the colour of your worktop and a tube of solvent, e.g. 'Colorfill', to remove excess
- Dust mask and eye protection

THE BASICS OF A ROUTER

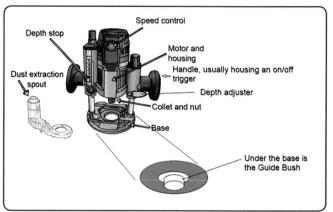

At first sight, a plunge router can look an intimidating piece of kit but it's actually not as bad as it looks. We'll have a walk through the basics here, but bear in mind that while virtually every router you buy/hire will have these features, they may not always be in the same place, so have a flick through the manual that came with the router and familiarise yourself with all the parts and how they work.

First off, you have the housing where the motor is. Attached to this is usually a switch that lets you adjust the speed (rpm) of the router bit – for precise, clean cuts the general rule is 'the faster, the better'.

At the bottom of the housing is the collet or spindle, where you attach the router bit you want to use – all kitchen worktop templates insist that this is a 12mm (½in) collet. Most work by loosening the collet with a spanner, fitting your bit and then tightening it back up again. To do this you have to lock the spindle in place to stop it rotating. Just where the spindle disappears into the housing there is usually a button or a bar that can be pressed to stop the spindle rotating. The more expensive routers tend to have 'quick-fit/release' collets.

For a mitred corner you'll need a straight router bit that's long enough to cut right through your worktop – 50–60mm (2–2½in) long,

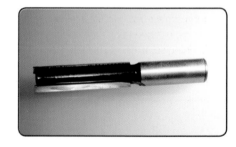

as a general rule, and often called 'worktop router bits'. If you hired a router it should have come with at least one of these. It's important to use a brand new router bit.

The main router housing is sat on two legs attached to a base plate. The legs are usually spring loaded, so you can push down on the router and the whole housing will 'plunge' down; you then let go and it springs back up.

On one leg you usually have a metal bar that acts as a depth stop, determining the maximum you can 'plunge' the legs and so setting the maximum depth of your cut. On the other leg there's usually a little lever that locks the legs into position. Loosen this and you can plunge the router down. Tighten it back up again and the router is now fixed at this depth.

If you rest the router on its side and look at the base you'll see the hole through which the router bit 'plunges'. The actual base

Above: Fitting the guide bush into place.

is usually made of smooth, shiny plastic that will slip over your template with ease but, in the middle, the hole is usually fitted with a round steel 'guide bush' that projects past the main base. It's this 'bush' that fits into the holes of your template and allows you to accurately and smoothly follow the template shape. Most templates stipulate that this guide bush should have a 30mm (1¼in) diameter. If you can't see this 30mm (1¼in) diameter metal ring in place then you need to fit one – they're usually attached to the base with two screws.

THE WORKTOP TEMPLATE (JIG)

Again, these usually aren't quite as complicated as they at first seem. The first thing you need to do is have a read of the documentation that came with your template, but we'll just walk through some of the basics here.

First off, the template should state what it requires from the router. Usually they'll specify a 12.7mm (½in) diameter, straight router bit and a 30mm (1¼in) guide bush. These aren't optional – if you don't have the correct sizes your cuts won't work.

Your template will have a number of 'stops'. These are usually metal pegs, designed to fit into the numerous holes in your jig and, in doing so, fix the jig into the correct position for the cut you require. Put the wrong stops in the wrong holes and you'll get the wrong cut, so it pays to go through the template manual until

you're clear how these work for the cuts you require. These holes are usually colour coded so, for example, to make a 'male joint', you put stops into all the red holes.

Be aware that many templates have an upside and a downside, and that different joints require you to turn the template over – the holes are usually only coloured on the side where they're to be used.

Some templates are just designed for use on worktops of a specific width – usually 615mm (24½in). A hired template is usually longer and designed to work with various worktop widths. To achieve this, they have a series of holes along their length, all cunningly marked with the depth of worktop they are designed for. So, the first thing you need to do is check the width of your worktops and then insert a 'stop' into the hole that corresponds to your worktop width.

There are often multiple shapes cut into a jig, but the only ones we're interested in are the long cut with a little 45° bend at the end and the crucifix-shaped cut. The first is the actual corner joint and its shape tends to only differ in that some jigs have a 45° bend just at one end and others have a bend at each end. The second shape is designed to cut the holes for our worktop connector bolts – these will be explained later. On some jigs these are crucifix shaped, on others they look more like a mushroom or broccoli. Some jigs will have a number of these holes in a row; others will just have one.

CUTTING A MITRED CORNER

1 Cutting a mitred corner is a surprisingly easy task, but it's one for which exact precision is required and where mistakes are costly. I'd strongly advise you to use some worktop offcuts to practise a few times until you're ready for the real thing – remember, you might need to fit a new router bit after all your practising. This task is also going to get messy as the router will kick up a lot of dust. It's best to do these cuts outside, or at least in a well-ventilated area, and to wear a dust mask and eye protection.

Above: It's easier to work outside but you may have an audience.

You need to have the worktops set up securely, at a comfortable height. The best way to achieve this is to rest the worktop onto two or more workbenches and have a friend around to help you carry the worktops in and out of the kitchen.

2 There are two parts to a corner joint – the 'male joint' and the 'female joint', and all corners are deemed to be either 'left hand' or 'right hand'. A rudimentary knowledge of biology should mean you can spot the difference between male and female joints. The left-hand, right-hand notion is a bit more complicated, but the diagram below should clarify the difference.

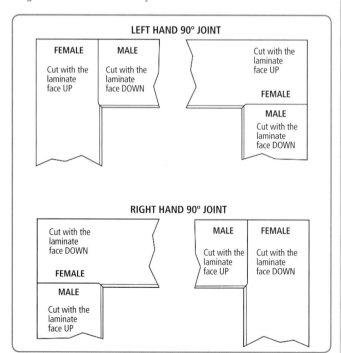

Note also that some joints require you to make the cut with the laminate facing UP and others with the laminate facing DOWN. It's very important you do this, as it's the difference between a nice clean cut and splintered and damaged laminate.

3 In our original example diagram (page 137) you can see that we only have one corner and that it's a left-hand joint with the female cut on worktop B and the male cut on worktop A. The female cuts are always cut into the side of the worktop and, as a general rule, it's easier to cut these first.

In our example we don't need to cut worktop B to the exact size, but in most kitchens at least one of your worktops will span two walls, in which case you'll need to carefully measure the distance between the walls at the front and back of the units. Here, we should play safe and cut worktop B with an excess of at least 300mm (12in) and then put it into place to check that the end is flush with the wall. If our corner isn't a right angle, we need to cut the worktop, as shown in the example diagram.

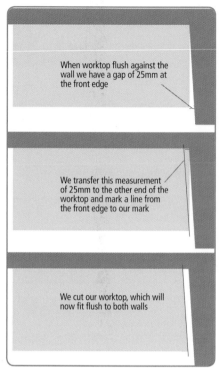

Use a jigsaw or circular saw to cut your worktop, remembering to use masking tape to protect the surface.

4 Measure the width of your worktop and set the template to the right width setting using the stops provided with the template. Note that some templates use a little bar to set the depth; this can be moved back and forth and then tightened up once it's at the right depth.

5 We're going to cut a left-hand female joint, so make sure the worktop is laminate side up and check the template documentation to see which side up the template should be and where the stops are to be placed.

6 If you haven't had to cut the corner edge of the worktop at all because the walls were a true right angle, jump to step 7. If you've cut your worktop at an angle then the width stop is going to be slightly out, so it pays to measure everything by hand just to be sure:

Let's say your worktop is 615mm wide. Measure this back from the edge where you're going to cut out your female joint and mark it on your worktop.

Draw a 45° angle from this mark about 100mm in length.

As we have already discussed, our guide bush is 30mm in diameter and our router bit is 12.7mm in diameter. This means that the gap between the edge of the bit and the guide is (30 − 12.7)/2 = 8.65mm. As a result, the router bit will always cut 8.65mm in from whatever template edge it is running up against. To account for this, you need to measure this distance back from our 45° line and draw this new line in – in reality 8.5mm or 9mm will suffice. Now put the template in place, pressing all the stops firmly up against

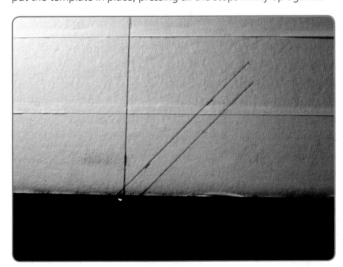

the worktop. If all is well you should see that the edge of your template is on the line you've just drawn. In our example, because we've had to cut the worktop at a slight angle, the width stop isn't measuring exactly 615mm from the front of the worktop and, as a result, the template is a few millimetres too deep.

Before using your marks rather than the stop, it pays to just double-check all your measurements and then remove the width stop, push the template up firm against the other stops and move it until the 45° angle is exactly on your line.

7 Clamp your template firmly in place using two G-clamps (or any heavy-duty clamps), making sure that they don't get in the way of your router and that the laminated surface of the worktop is protected.

When you cut the worktop with laminate side uppermost, the template protects the worktop from the clamps but when you make a cut with laminate side down you'll need to use wooden blocks between the laminate and the underside of the clamps to protect the laminated surface.

8 With the template fully secured in place, put the router into the template with the bit fully retracted. You don't want to make a cut at this stage, you just want to be sure that the clamps aren't in the way, that you can run the router smoothly right across the template and that the template doesn't move.

9 Before you start your cut remember, once again, that laminate will only cut cleanly if the blade cuts the laminate first and then passes into whatever substrate the laminate is bonded to. In this instance, it's the 'laminate up/laminate down' instruction that ensures you aren't going to damage the laminate on the front edge of your worktop. Providing that you follow that instruction and start your cut from where the template makes its little 45° bend at the front edge of the worktop, you can't go wrong.

10 The template will overhang the worktop, so you can place the router into it and get everything ready before you start your cut. Use the 'plunge' mechanism

to lower the router bit so that it cuts about 5–10mm into the worktop. For a nice clean cut it's very important to keep the blade turning at full speed; to achieve this, make a number of passes across your worktop taking about 5mm out of the worktop each time – about five passes should get you through a 38mm worktop. Once you have the depth right, lock it in at this depth.

11 Start up the router and let it get up to full speed. Once it sounds like it's running at maximum, gently push it along the template until it starts cutting into the worktop. Push gently against the cutting edge as you move along the template until you've finished the cut.

12 Now turn the router off. Wait until the router bit has stopped turning then go back to your start position. Brush all the sawdust out of your cut, drop the bit another 5mm or so and repeat step 11.

Before you make the final cut right through the worktop, double-check that you're not going to be cutting through anything below the worktop. To play safe, set the final cut so that the bit is only a few millimetres below the base of the worktop, so if you do cut into anything else you'll only just do so and it shouldn't slow the router down or dull the bit.

Rather than just letting the unused end of the worktop fall to the ground as you complete your cut it's best to have it fully supported, or at least have a friend hold it steady for you – this isn't really an issue for the female joints but is important for the male ones.

13 That's your first cut made, so take this worktop back into the kitchen and place it into its final position.

You now need to make the other side of the cut. It's highly unlikely that this worktop will meet your first one at exactly 90° so mark exactly where they will meet and set up your template on this line. The easiest way to do this is to lift the worktop you've just cut by putting an offcut of worktop under it.

14 You can now slide the next worktop underneath. For this cut, if you leave yourself with enough excess worktop you can always re-cut the joint if you make a mess of your first attempt. Where possible, don't cut this worktop to size until you're happy with your joint.

15 Check that both worktops are in position, tight up against the walls, and that the start of your first joint lines up exactly with the front edge of your new worktop.

The easiest way to do this is to use a combination or T-square. Hold it against the edge of your new worktop and tap that back towards the wall until it's perfectly lined up with the start of your earlier joint. Make sure when they're aligned there isn't too big a gap between the worktops and the walls. If there is you may have to cut your worktops back a fraction. If you can't get the two worktops aligned, then you have a problem and you might have to knock out some of the wall behind the worktop to get them to fit.

16 Now use a sharp pencil or fine whiteboard marker to draw a line where the new worktop disappears under the worktop you've just cut – cover the worktop area with masking tape first so your marks are easier to see.

17 If you have a look back at our example layout and the diagram showing the basic cuts, you'll see that we need to cut this worktop with the laminate side down. This means we need to take the line we have just drawn and replicate it on the other side of the worktop.

For the back edge we can just use a combination square, or anything else with a perfect 90° angle, and draw a line down the side to the underside of the worktop.

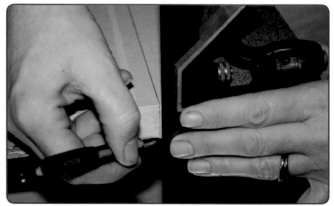

18 The front edge of the worktop is usually rounded and your line veers off at 45° at this end. As a result, it's usually easier to extend your line before it veers away and take it close to the front edge of the

Above: Extend your line to the front edge.

worktop. Now rest your combination square on the side edge of the worktop. Note down the distance from the side edge to your line as shown by the ruler on the combination square – it doesn't matter if this is the actual distance, we just want to make sure we use the same marker. Mark the top of the worktop at this side edge and then take this line down the side face as we did in step 17.

19 Turn the worktop over, and use the distance we noted down in step 18 to mark the underside of the worktop. You can now use a straight edge to redraw your line on the underside of the worktop.

Above: Note the distance from the side edge to your line.

20 You now need to use this line to set up your template. Remember, if you set the template up on the line you've just drawn, the router will actually cut into the worktop 8.65mm away from this line because of the bush guide. If you've yet to cut the worktop to size this is unlikely to be a problem, but otherwise

you'll need to ensure the cut is made exactly on the line you've just drawn.

To do this you need to measure back 8.5mm from your original line and draw a new line, onto which you'll set the template. If you don't do this it won't be a tragedy; you'll just end up with a worktop that is 9mm too long. This excess can always be removed from the other end.

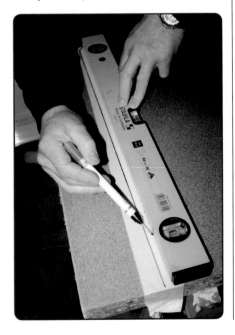

21 Follow the instructions that came with your template to set it up for your cut. Most templates will ask you to turn the template over for this cut and will have holes coloured only on one side for the 'stops' you'll need to insert. This is the critical stage, so go over the instructions until you're sure you have the template the right way around with the 'stops' in the right holes.

Note that if you're not making this cut at a perfect right angle – and you usually aren't – then when all the template 'stops' are hard up against your worktop you won't be following the line you've just drawn. In this instance, draw the template up against the stops and then, still pulling it a little so that at least one 'stop' is hard against the worktop, manoeuvre it until it's perfectly aligned with your line.

22 Because the laminate surface is upside down on this cut, you can actually screw the template into position – most templates come with screw holes for this. Before doing this it's still best to use clamps, with wooden blocks underneath to protect the

laminated surface from damage, to hold the template in the right position. Use 1in, size 6 screws to screw the template to the worktop – just double-check they won't go right through

your worktop and that the screws are countersunk so they won't interfere with the movement of the router across the template surface.

Now remove the clamps, as this generally makes it easier to move the router across the template. To ensure a clean cut, it's best if both sides of your cut line are supported. This becomes more important the larger the section that is being cut off, as the extra weight will ensure that it falls away earlier and damages the joint more as a result. If need be, get a friend to support the

section of worktop that is being cut off.

23 Start at the front edge of the worktop where the template curves around at a 45° angle, to ensure that you don't damage the laminate. Place the router here and repeat steps 10–12 to make your cut.

24 You should now have two joints that fit together perfectly.

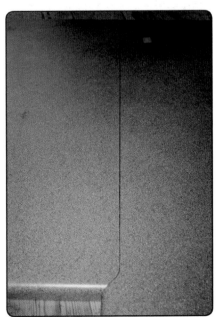

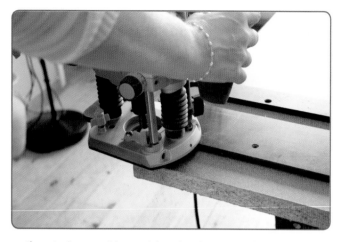

If you're happy with your joints, it's time to cut the worktops to size. You can use a jigsaw or a circular saw but, since you have your router out, there's no reason you can't use this. Use the outside straight edge of the template as your straight line, clamp the template in place and remember that your actual cut will be 9mm beyond this line, so adjust it accordingly. Always start the cut at the front of the worktop and move the router from left to right – note that if you had the worktop face down to make the original joint, you'll need it face up now and vice versa.

25 In order to draw your joint together you need to use your connector bolts to draw the two surfaces together. To use these you need to make holes in the underside of your worktop to accommodate the bolts.

Your template will have a shape in it specifically for these holes. They usually look like a small crucifix, but they can look more like a sprig of broccoli or an odd-shaped mushroom. To draw the surfaces together properly the depth of these bolts need to be as close to the centre of your worktop as you can manage. If you put a bolt up against the edge of your joint you can mark the top edge and then measure that distance. For 38mm worktops this is usually about 25mm.

26 Set the depth stop on your router to 25mm so that it can't be plunged down any deeper than this.

27 You need to mark where your bolts will go. For a 600mm wide worktop you can usually get away with two bolts set about 150mm from each edge. If you're going to use three bolts, set one in the centre of the joint and the other two roughly 100mm in from each edge.

Note that some templates actually have a number of holes for these bolts set at the right distances for 600–615mm worktops. If this is the case, just use these positions as it allows you to cut out all your holes without moving the template around.

Before you commit to making these holes, mark their positions on the underside of both worktops in pencil. Now fit the worktops back into position on top of your cabinets and check that your marks are lined up for both worktops, that they won't interfere with anything else and that you can actually get access to fit and tighten a bolt in these positions – you only need to get access to one end to tighten the bolt.

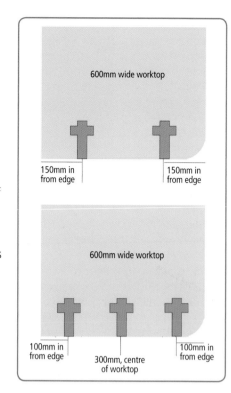

28 Now have a quick read of the documentation that came with your template and set the stops up for the bolt holes. Since these are all going on the underside of your worktop it's usually easier to screw the template into position with 1in, size 6 screws, rather than use clamps.

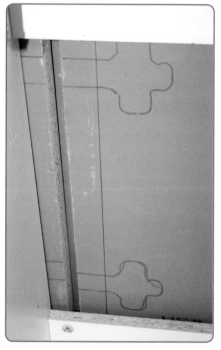

29 Place the router into position – the template should overhang the worktop a bit so the router can be put in place and allowed to get up to full speed before you start the cut. Fully press down the router and verify that it's stopping at roughly 25mm, as you set earlier.

If you're happy with the maximum depth you've set turn the router on, allow it to get up to full speed and then make a shallow cut (roughly 5mm) around the template hole – you usually have to wiggle it from side to side to cut out the centre of the hole. Now increase the depth a little and make another pass, continuing this until you reach your maximum depth of 25mm. Repeat for all bolt holes.

30 Place your worktops back into position and verify that the holes are lined up and accessible.

If they are lined up, move the joints apart and apply some jointing compound. If you can't get a colour match for your worktop, go for a clear jointing compound or clear sealant. Jointing compound is used to hide the joints, to help stick worktops together and to create a watertight seal. Run a wavy bead of the jointing compound across the face of both sides of the joint and a line just below the top edge of the joint.

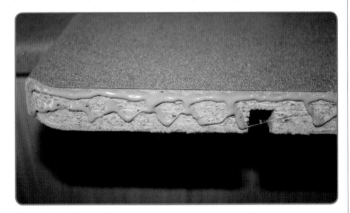

NOTE: *If you're following this guide to cut a solid wood worktop you can use clear sealant at this stage instead of jointing compound.*

31 Slide the two worktops together and push the joints together by hand. When you're sure they're in the right position, insert a bolt into each of your holes under the worktop and tighten them up using a spanner until they just hold in position but aren't fully tight.

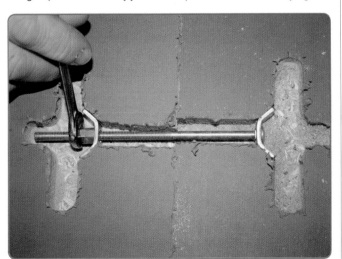

TIP *It's always best to fit the joint in situ, but this isn't always possible, usually because you just can't get to the bolt holes to draw the joint together. If this is the case,*

try sliding both worktops out a bit so that they are still supported by the cabinets with the joint now accessible – you'll probably have to use some workbenches, or cabinets that haven't yet been fitted to support the ends of the worktops to keep them stable and level.

32 At this stage it's usually easier to have one person tightening the bolts while another looks on to make sure the joint is being drawn together correctly. As a general rule, it's easy enough to get the two front edges of the joint to align perfectly, but often the worktops will not be at exactly the same height so you end up with a little ridge along the joint.

If this is the case, you can get the front edge level by putting an offcut of wood across the joint and then clamping this down. You can then place an offcut of worktop across the rest of the joint and use a hammer or rubber mallet to give it a good tap until the joint is level on both sides and you can't feel a ridge when you run the back of a fingernail across the joint.

33 When you're happy that the joint is lined up correctly, start tightening the bolts. Don't fully tighten one and then move on to the next. Instead give one a couple of turns, then do the same with the next before moving back to the first one to ensure the joint is tightened up evenly along its whole length at the same time.

34 You should now be able to see the jointing compound being squeezed out of your joint along the whole of its length. Remove this excess by just running a craft knife blade lightly along the length of your joint – it doesn't matter if it smears a little at this stage.

Keep an eye on how level the joint is as it's drawn together, using your hammer and offcut of wood to tap it firmly, as required.

35 Once all the bolts have been tightened, the joint should be almost invisible with jointing compound squeezed out along the entire length. These compounds dry pretty quickly so after a few moments you can use a craft knife blade to gently lift off most of

the excess. Once the excess has been removed use a piece of cloth or tissue and the solvent that came with the jointing compound to wipe off any smears.

36 If you completed the joint out of situ you can now slide the worktops back into their final position.

MITRED STRAIGHT CONNECTIONS

TIP *You only have to use this odd dogleg mitre joint if the front of the worktop has a rounded or decorative edge. If you have a worktop with a square face you can avoid*

the intimidating process of mitring the corner; instead, all you have to do is remove the laminate from the side of one worktop where the two worktops will meet (have a read of Chapter 3 'Renovating and adapting existing countertops' for how to remove the laminate) and then secure the two worktops together in much the same way as you'd secure two straight sections – see below.

If you have a very long run of worktop you might find you need to connect two worktops together. You can do this either by using a straight edging strip, as discussed later, or you can use your router to make an almost invisible mitred connection, as follows:

1 Have a read of the 'Mitred corners' section above, as we're going to use all the same principles. The only difference is the shape of the template – it's a straight line now.

2 Decide where you're going to make the join. This is always going to be an area of weakness, so it's best if it's not right over the middle of a cabinet where it will be unsupported, close to a sink or hob or in a heavy-usage area.

You'll be connecting the worktops using connector bolts, as per the mitred corner we discussed above. This means fitting the bolts and tightening them from underneath the worktop, so you need to ensure you'll be able to get at them.

Making the join right where two cabinets meet can be a good move, as the connection will be fully supported. Yes, it can be more awkward to fit the bolts, but it's not that difficult.

3 Put the first worktop in situ and mark where you want the cut line to be. Use a combination square or any good right angle to draw a line across the top of the worktop and then use a perfectly straight edge to continue this mark right across your worktop.

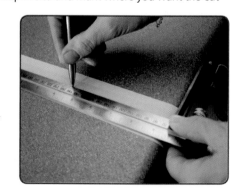

4 Your router will make its cut exactly 8.65mm in front of your mark, so you now need to draw a second line 8.5mm (9mm will do) back from your first line so that the cut will be exactly on your first line – you can use a circular saw with a very fine new blade, but a router is the better option.

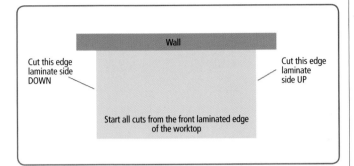

Wall

Cut this edge laminate side DOWN

Cut this edge laminate side UP

Start all cuts from the front laminated edge of the worktop

5 Consider how you're going to avoid damaging your laminate. The diagram above shows which side up the laminate needs to be. If it's laminate-side-down, you'll have to transfer your lines to the other side of the worktop (see 'Cutting a mitred corner', steps 17–19).

TIP *You can buy connector bolts that are closed using an Allen key. They are a little more expensive, but they are easier to use, especially if space is at a premium.*

6 Take your worktop to wherever you intend to do your cutting – a garage or the great outdoors is ideal. Now place a perfectly straight edge on top of this second line. It needs to be hard, smooth, raised about 10mm and perfectly straight – the back edge of a worktop jig template is ideal. Use two clamps to lock your straight edge into position, remembering to protect the laminate surface.

7 Follow steps 8–12 of 'Cutting a mitred corner' for the routing process. This time, push the router up against your straight edge a little firmer to ensure it remains in contact with the worktop throughout the cut.

8 That's the first cut made. So place this worktop into position and slide an offcut of worktop under it, near the back.

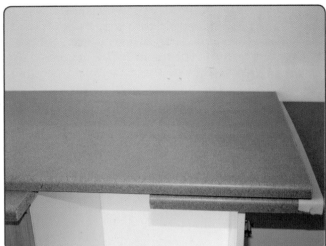

9 Now slide your next worktop under the first so that it's in exactly the right position.

10 Use a sharp pencil or marker pen to mark where the two worktops intersect.

11 Move your new worktop to where you're going to make your cut and once again redraw your line 8.5mm back from the original.

TIP

Whenever you have more than one line but only intend to use one of them there is always going to be room for error. To avoid this, always put a squiggle or a wavy line through the line you no longer want to use. Where you have more than one line, it pays to use different colours.

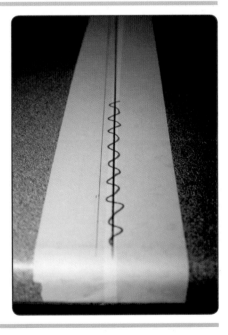

12 Decide if the worktop needs to be laminate up or down and, if down, transfer your line to the underside.

13 Secure your template in place and make your second cut as you did the first.

14 Follow Steps 25–36 of Cutting a mitred corner, to make the holes for your connector bolts and join the two sections of worktop together.

MITRED ROUNDED WORKTOP EDGES AND CURVES

From a DIY point of view, making your own curved edges is only possible if you've opted to fit a square-edged worktop. If your worktop has a curved or decorative edge, you really need to get in touch with a professional. The only difference here between a curve and a corner is the template you use and laminating the finished cut. With this in mind, have a read of the 'Mitred Corner' section starting on page 142.

Larger worktop templates, or jigs, usually come with the shapes needed for curves. If yours doesn't, you can always try making your own out of 12mm plywood, although this is a bit too advanced to cover here.

When you come to make your cut, you don't have to worry about damaging the laminate as you're going to have to replace it anyway. That said, make sure you have enough matching laminate to cover your new curve.

Once you've made your cut, use a craft knife and a combination square to carefully slice through the laminate edge about 50mm from the end of your cut. Carefully remove the laminate – warming it up with an iron can make this easier.

You should now have a nice clean section of worktop edge ready to be re-laminated – see 'Fitting laminate edging strips' opposite.

FITTING CORNER AND EDGING STRIPS

FITTING METAL CORNER STRIPS

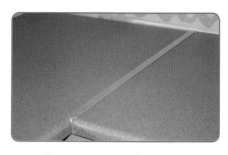

A simpler alternative to a mitred corner is to use a corner strip. These are usually metal and come in a variety of different colours. I'm not a big fan of them myself, but they're a lot less intimidating than making a mitred corner joint.

1 Using the example above, fit the edging strip to the edge of worktop B and then fit this worktop up hard against worktop A to create your joint.

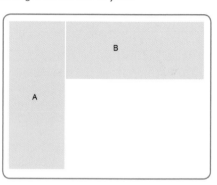

In an ideal world, your worktops will butt up to each other at a perfect 90° angle; however, it's OK if they're out by a few millimetres. If the gap is bigger than that you'll need to cut the edge of worktop B at a slight angle.

2 To determine this angle, fit worktop A into position and put an offcut of worktop underneath it to raise it up. Slide worktop B under it and push both worktops into position, hard up against the walls.

3 Use a sharp pencil to mark the angle of the join, using masking tape underneath so the pencil line is clearly visible.

4 You can use a steady hand and a jigsaw, although a circular saw or router will generally make a straighter cut. If you opt for a jigsaw, use a downward-cutting blade to avoid damaging the laminate. With a circular saw or router, always check the direction of the spinning blade to make sure you aren't going to damage the laminate – if in doubt, test it on an offcut.

5 The corner strips are usually a bit too long, so you'll need to cut them back using a junior hacksaw. If the worktops aren't yet fitted, the easiest way to do this is to put the strip into position so that its rounded front is perfectly flush with the front of your worktop. If the worktop has already been fitted, just place the front of the edging strip hard up against the wall and mark off the end of it against the front of your worktop.

6 Now mark your cut line on the back of the strip and use a hacksaw to cut the strip to size. A splashback will usually cover the back edge of the worktop, so it doesn't matter if your cut line is out by a few millimetres.

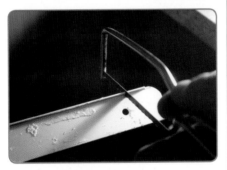

7 To ensure that moisture can't get into your joint, run a few beads of clear sealant across the exposed chipboard face of your worktop and use something to spread the sealant so that it completely covers the exposed wood – a bit of cardboard usually does the trick.

If you don't have any clear sealant to hand, use PVA glue or varnish to seal the wood and let it dry before fitting the corner strip – if you use sealant you can apply the strip straight away.

8 Place the strip into position and screw it into the worktop with 1in, size 6 countersunk screws. Make sure the top of the edging strip is firmly up against

the top of the worktop. Use a sealant spreader to remove any excess sealant, and wipe the worktop down with tissue afterwards.

9 Now slide your worktop, with its fitted strip, up against the other worktop to make your corner.

There are no special clamps or bolts for these joints; just secure the worktops in place, as discussed in 'Installing a laminate countertop', steps 10–12, page 139.

FITTING METAL JOINING STRIPS

The steps for fitting a metal joining strip are almost exactly the same as those for making a mitred straight connection, so have a read of that section, above. The only difference is that a metal edging strip gives us a lot more leeway, so often there's no cutting involved at all. If there is, rather than using a router you can get away with a jigsaw or circular saw.

As with the metal corner strips, seal all exposed wood – on either side of the joint this time – and then secure your joining strip to one of the worktops. Slide the two worktops together (see 'Fitting metal corner strips' opposite).

FITTING METAL EDGING STRIPS

Most laminated kitchen worktops have exposed wood at the end – usually chipboard or MDF. It's not something you'd ever want to see, so you can either cover it with a metal strip or stick laminate over the exposed wood. The advantage of using metal strips is that they are heatproof and protect your worktop from the day-to-day bangs and bashes of kitchen use. The downside is that it's difficult to get a good colour match, so they can be a bit too 'in-your-face'.

If you're planning on fitting a cooker inbetween two close-fitting worktops then you really do need to use metal strips, as it's never a good idea to have a cooker sandwiched neatly between two bits of combustible material. On a brighter note, getting metal strips to match your cooker top is usually a lot easier to achieve.

Fitting the strips is very similar to fitting the corner strips, so read 'Fitting metal corner strips', opposite. You're usually going to be able to see your screws, so it pays to shop around for ones that match the colour of your edging strip.

FITTING LAMINATE EDGING STRIPS

Your worktop will usually come with a few strips of extra laminate specifically for finishing the edges. Sometimes these will be 'iron-on' strips, but usually they'll just be bare laminate – the iron-on laminate tends to have a shiny side; the ones that you glue on tend to have a dull, slightly roughened side. If you have a shiny back to your laminate, jump down to the 'Iron-on strips' section.

The advantage of a laminate edge is that it will perfectly colour match your worktop and can be used to make a rounded edge on square-faced worktops. The downside is that, in busy areas especially, it can get dented and generally knocked about until eventually the laminate splits and comes away.

Glue-on strips

1 First off, you need a nice clean edge. I wouldn't recommend trying to get a clean cut using a jigsaw; you really ought to opt for either a router or a circular saw (read the start of 'Installing a laminate countertop' on page 137 if you're unsure).

2 Clean the edge to remove any sawdust and put masking tape along the top laminated edge to protect the worktop surface.

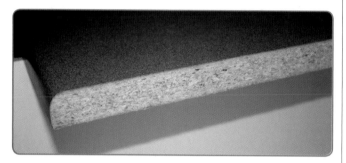

3 The strip supplied is always wider and longer than your worktop – sometimes dramatically so. If you're going to be able to get to the laminate easily once it's been stuck down, cut it to size afterwards, otherwise cut it to size beforehand. If you've opted for the latter, hold your strip up against the worktop edge with the top of the strip just a few millimetres higher than the finished worktop surface. Now use a pencil or a fine marker pen to draw around the front and base of the strip.

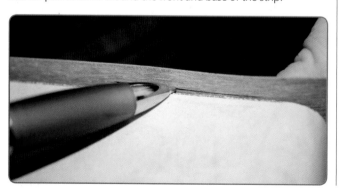

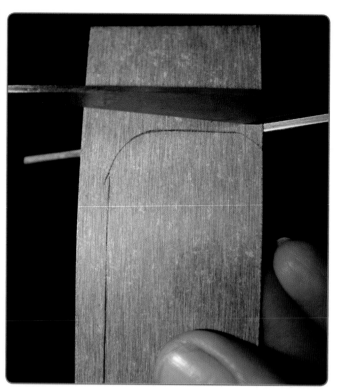

4 Use a pair of good quality kitchen scissors to cut around your pencil line. Don't go right to the line; leave yourself a bit of room to manoeuvre by cutting about 2mm back from your line.

5 Use a contact or impact adhesive, following the instructions that come with it.

6 Carefully apply the strip to the worktop edge so the front and top are a few millimetres proud of the finished work surface. Both contact and impact adhesives take no prisoners when it comes to applying the laminate strip to the worktop edge; if you get it wrong it's not going to let you have another chance. So hold the laminate close to the edge, make certain the front of the worktop edge will be covered and then gently apply the top edge before smoothing the rest of the strip into position.

Press the strip hard against the worktop and use a cloth to rub along the length to make sure it's completely smooth and in contact with the worktop edge. A small laminate or wallpaper roller is handy for this. Wait a few minutes for it to bond.

TIP *If you make a mistake positioning the laminate strip, you can slide the blade of a utility knife under the strip and lift it off. This will save the edge of the worktop but usually damages the strip itself, so you'll need to buy a replacement strip.*

7 There are umpteen ways of removing the excess laminate but the simplest way, in my opinion, is to use scissors to cut away the majority of the excess, the back of a sharp utility knife to remove most of the remainder and a flat file to finish it off.

When using the knife, angle the blade a little so that you don't touch the worktop surface with it, and don't press too hard or go too close to the edge as the blade can chip the laminate..

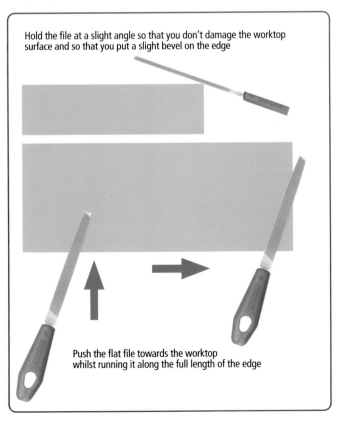

8 Once you've removed almost all of the excess, finish it off by using a flat file. Angle the file slightly and always push it forward towards the worktop, while letting it run left to right along the surface to get a smooth, slightly bevelled final edge. After every 'sweep' along the edge, use your finger to check for a ridge. If you can feel one, do another sweep and stop as soon as the edge is completely smooth.

Hold the file at a slight angle so that you don't damage the worktop surface and so that you put a slight bevel on the edge

Push the flat file towards the worktop whilst running it along the full length of the edge

9 Use a cloth and a little white spirit to remove any excess adhesive.

10 If there are any gaps or blemishes use a colour matching jointing compound to smooth them away and use the solvent that comes with the compound to remove any excess.

Iron-on strips

These have adhesive already applied to the back of the strips – you just need some heat to activate the glue.

1 Set your iron to the 'woollen' setting and let it get hot.

2 Put your strip into position – you might want to get a friend to hold it for you – and place a sheet of greaseproof paper over it. Heat up the back of the strip first so it adheres to the worktop and will stay in place on its own.

3 Keep the iron flat against the laminate strip and smooth it along the whole length, heating it up through the paper. Repeat until you're sure the laminate has glued right along its length.

4 Set the iron to a slight angle and run it along all the edges, heating it up through the paper.

5 Now put away the iron and finish off the strip as per the 'Glue-on strips' (see steps 7–10 above).

FITTING THE SINK

Cutting holes in your worktop weakens it considerably, so it's always best to fit the worktop and then cut the hole for the sink. You don't have to screw the worktop into position, but it should be cut to size and held in place with clamps. This way you can always move it out a bit if you really need to, but it's secure enough to work on.

If you insist on cutting the holes first and then moving the worktop into position, always try to carry it edge up and try to support it around the hole you've cut to reduce the chances of it breaking.

1 Most sinks will come with a template (often the box it arrives in IS the template). If you don't have one, don't worry, just turn the sink upside down and use the sink itself as a template.

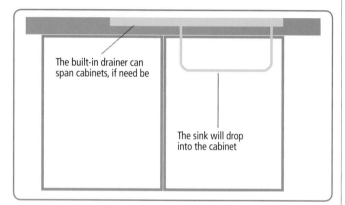

The built-in drainer can span cabinets, if need be

The sink will drop into the cabinet

2 Place your template/sink carefully into position. If your sink has a built-in draining board it's not a problem if this spans two cabinets, as the drainer will rest on top of the worktop. The same isn't true of the sink itself; you need to make sure that this will sit inside a single cabinet, if possible.

Check the distance from the front and back of the worktop. If you're too close to the front or back you'll end up cutting into the cabinet itself, which you want to avoid. As a general rule, 60–80mm is a good distance from the front edge of the worktop. You may still need to cut into the top of the cabinet at these depths, as most of them have a strengthening strut across the top of them, but you need to avoid the cabinet sides.

Most sinks are designed so the taps fit into the sink itself. However, if you have taps designed to fit directly into the worktop, you need to check their position at this stage – again, the hole for each tap needs to be over the inside of a cabinet and not over an edge or side. You'll need to be able to reach into the cabinet and attach the tap to your pipework, so make sure the tap base will be accessible. Also, check the distance from the tap to the sink; you need to make sure that the spout is actually over the sink.

3 Use masking tape to hold your template in position. If you're using your sink as a template, stick masking tape around the edges of the sink, then remove the sink and apply more masking

tape around the inside.

Now fit your sink back into position, check that it's aligned with the front of the worktop and use a sharp pencil or fine marker pen to trace the outside edge of the sink onto your masking tape.

4 Skip this step if you're using a template.

Remove the sink. You should now be able to see the edge of the sink marked out on your masking tape. We need to cut a hole about 10mm in from this edge, so carefully mark 10mm in and redraw your rectangle using a level, or any straight edge. This new, slightly smaller rectangle will be your cut line.

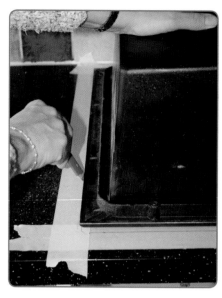

5 Use a 10mm or larger wood drill bit and drill holes at the four corners of your rectangle so that the outer edge of your hole touches your cut line.

6 Use a jigsaw with a fine wood cutting blade. You don't need a downward cutting blade here as any chipped laminate will be hidden under the sink and standard blades are far less likely to jump up and damage the worktop. Insert the jigsaw blade into one of the holes you've just drilled, get your weight over the top of the jigsaw to stop it kicking up, and start it up. Carefully cut along your cut line.

7 Get a friend to support the section of worktop you're cutting out so that it doesn't just drop away, as this can damage the worktop.

8 You now have a nice hole in your worktop. Carefully drop the sink into it and make sure it fits properly. If you're happy with your hole, remove the sink. If the hole is a little too small, carefully mark where it's too tight and use the jigsaw to enlarge it a bit.

9 Eventually, water will get under your sink – it always does. To prevent this causing damage to the worktop, you need to seal your cut edges. You can use PVA glue, marine varnish or silicone sealant for this task. Personally, I prefer the sealant option. Just run a wiggly line of sealant around the edge and then use a piece of cardboard to smear it over the exposed wood, making sure it's completely covered. I've used white sealant in the photo so that it shows up, but clear sealant is better for this task.

10 While your sealant dries, prepare the sink. We're not going to go into this in depth as this is covered in other Haynes manuals, but if the taps fit into the sink do this now and tighten them up fully.

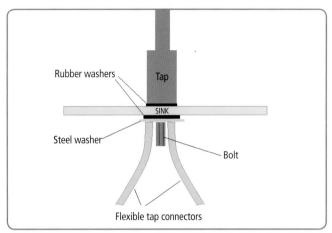

Rubber washers Tap

SINK

Steel washer

Bolt

Flexible tap connectors

▦ Most taps are connected with a rubber washer between the base of the tap and the top of the sink. Another rubber washer then fits under the sink, on top of this goes a metal washer and this is then tightened up with a bolt or two.

▦ Most taps now come with 'flexible tap connectors' – steel braided flexible pipework. If yours don't it's well worth buying these, as they make fitting the taps a lot easier – especially if you opt for push-fit connectors. This will change depending where you live but in the UK, the connector will need to be 15mm on the end that connects to your pipework and either 15mm, 12mm or 10mm where it connects to the taps. If in doubt, just take your taps with you to the store.

▦ Most sinks will come with a seal provided in a strip. Peel off the plastic backing and apply the seal around the edge of the sink.

▦ Steel sinks need to be drawn down onto the work surface with little clips. Attach these to the sink by pressing the plastic clip section over the holes on the edge of the underside of the sink – be careful, steel sinks can have razor-sharp edges.

■ Fit the waste and overflow to your sink. There is usually just one washer for the waste, which fits under the sink. It's good practice to apply a ring of clear sealant to the hole where the waste will go, just to ensure a watertight seal.

■ The overflow – if supplied – also has just one washer, which fits to the outside of the sink. The overflow is connected to the waste via a short section of flexible plastic tubing, which just pushes onto the main waste.

FITTING THE COOKER HOB

The act of cutting out the hole for the cooker hob is exactly the same as for the sink, so have a read of that section.

The hob is usually secured to the work surface by metal clips underneath it. These fit under the worktop and are then screwed to the base of the hob, drawing it down onto the worktop.

If you have a gas hob you'll need to leave the actual fitting of it to a gas engineer. Similarly, if it's an electric hob, leave it to a professional electrician.

FITTING A COUNTERSUNK CHOPPING BOARD

If you've managed to damage a section of laminated worktop, a good way of hiding this damage is to turn the area into a countersunk chopping board.

There are a number of ways of going about this task, some are easier than others, some are better than others. We'll start off with the easiest way and then talk about other approaches.

11 Apply a line of clear sealant around the edge of your hole and then carefully drop the sink into the hole.

12 If your sink came with securing clips you'll need to climb under the sink and fit these. Pull them down so the metal teeth fit under the worktop and then draw them tight by turning the centre screw. If your sink didn't come with any clips, the line of sealant you applied will hold it in position. To ensure a good fit, place some heavy objects onto your sink to push it down, especially at the edges. If you can get it plumbed in quick enough, you can fill it with water to act as a weight until the sealant has dried.

1 Find a chopping board you like that is thinner than your worktop. Place it over your damaged worktop and apply masking tape under and around it. Now use a marker pen or a pencil to draw around your chopping board, having first made sure the board is aligned properly so that it's an even distance from the front of the worktop.

2 In our example we're using a simple rectangular board so, having marked out the shape of it on our worktop we can now use a 10mm wood drill bit to make a hole in each corner.

3 Now use a jigsaw with a downward cutting blade to carefully cut out the shape of the chopping board. We're going to cut right the way through the worktop so check that all is clear underneath. Fit the jigsaw blade into one of the holes we've just cut and let it get up to speed before starting the cut. Remember, downward cutting blades will kick upwards given half a chance so keep your weight over the jigsaw as you make your cut.

4 Having cut out our section just make sure the chopping board fits it. If it doesn't, check where it's catching and use the jigsaw, a rasp or a hand wood plane to adjust the hole.

5 Once we're happy with our hole, cut out a section of 6mm plywood about 100mm wider and longer than our hole. Now use a few screws to hold it in place, making sure the screws are not going to go right through our worktop.

6 We want our chopping board to be flush with our worktop. The easier way to do this is to place the section of worktop we've just cut out next to our chopping board and then put various sheets of plywood under the chopping board until the top of the board is flush with the worktop.

7 Use the section of damaged worktop we cut out as the template for our plywood. Just draw around it and then use a jigsaw to cut out our plywood. Cut just inside the line you've drawn so as to make sure the plywood will fit in our hole.

8 Loose fit all your sections of ply and fit the chopping board in place. Once you're sure it fits well and is the right depth, unscrew the base we fitted in step 5 and carefully lower out the plywood and chopping board. Now refit the base as in step 5 but use screws and grab adhesive now. Refit the rest of the plywood – you can apply a small amount of grab adhesive between sheets if you think you need to raise your chopping board a fraction more. When you have fitted the final sheet of plywood, paint it with varnish and run sealant around the edge to create a water tight base.

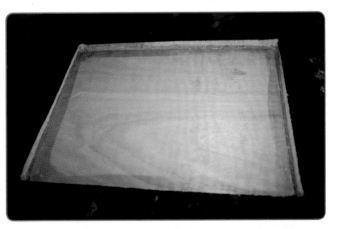

9 When the varnish and sealant are dry, apply a zigzag bead of colour-matching worktop compound around the exposed edges of our hole and use a piece of cardboard to smear this over the surface until it's completely covered.

10 Now drop your chopping board into the hole and run more colour fill around the edge of the hole to fill any gaps. Let it dry a little then remove the excess with a sharp blade and then rub the area down with the solvent supplied with the colour-matching compound.

The problem with using a jigsaw to make the initial hole through the worktop is that it's very difficult to get a perfect cut. With that in mind you might want to use a router to make this hole. A hand router or trimmer is easier to use but you can use a standard plunge router – just make sure any guide bush has been removed and use a 'top-bearing flush-trim' straight router bit to make the cut – this is often called a profiler router bit.

TIP *If you use a router with a simple, single edged, template you'll need to ensure that the router bit follows the template and doesn't try to pull away from it. Most router bits will rotate clockwise in the router, which means that pushing it from left to right will ensure the bit hugs your template.*

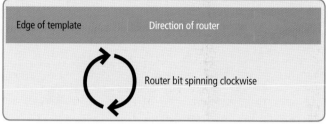

Edge of template	Direction of router
	Router bit spinning clockwise

You'll need to make up a template for your router. If you are using a simple rectangular chopping board you can make one by just placing your chopping board on a flat surface and fitting batons of wood around the board. Once you have the batons cut to size, use a mitre-bond glue to stick them together and a few screws to keep everything secure. When you make your template remember that you'll need to clamp it into place on your worktop, so have a few 'legs' of the template long enough to reach the ends of your worktop.

If you want to be really clever, use the router depth settings to create a ledge for your chopping board. It only needs to be about an inch wide and you can then use a jigsaw to cut out the middle section.

Installing a solid wood countertop

Installing a solid wood countertop is pretty much the same as fitting a laminate one. The only difference is that you don't have to worry so much about chipping the top surface and the cost of a mistake is invariably much greater. With the latter point in mind, you might want to think about buying a cheap laminate worktop and practising a bit on that first.

If you're going to fit an undermount sink, you're better off cutting out the worktop hole using a router rather than a jigsaw. Use plywood to make the template and a top bearing flush trim bit to cut the hole.

Repairing damaged countertops

We discussed how to replace sections of damaged laminate and how to repair granite worktops on page 79, 'Renovating and adapting existing countertops', so have a read of that section.

The easiest way to hide small damaged areas and scratches is to use a colour-matched jointing compound. Just work it into the scratch, remove the excess using anything with a hard straight edge and clean it up using the solvent provided with the jointing compound.

8 SPLASHBACKS

The splashback – lower versions are usually called upstands – are designed to provide an 'easy-clean' area at the back of the worktops that will catch any splashes from your food preparation and cooking. It's not essential to have a splashback but it does let you keep the kitchen area clean, especially in the area behind the cooker hob and, done well, it acts as a nice decorative effect.

Any splashback behind the cooker hob should be non-combustible, which, combined with the 'easy-clean' requirement, is why tiles are the splashback material of choice for most people. Other materials that work well for splashbacks are metal, usually steel; glass, which can be combined with lighting to great effect; stone; and where they won't be close to a heat source, laminate, designed to match your worktop; and stone.

How high you make your splashback is up to you, but to be effective and to create a uniform look, it's usual for them to cover the wall area from the worktop to the base of any wall cabinets and, behind the cooker, for them to run from the top of the hob to the base of the extractor, or even right to the ceiling. A high splashback can be a bit awkward, as you'll need to cut holes for all your plug sockets. With this in mind, it's well worth considering a lower splashback that finishes below the height of your sockets. Not only is a high splashback difficult to fit in stone/steel/glass, but it can also be prohibitively expensive, so it's not unusual to see a small section of the more expensive materials used as a low 'upstand' with contrasting tiles above to make a full height splashback.

If you opt for steel, glass or stone it's probably best to get them installed professionally, not because it's difficult, but because the tools to cut them are expensive and a mistake is going to be very costly. With that in mind, we'll content ourselves with covering laminate and tiled splashbacks here.

Tiled splashbacks

Here are a few buying tips:

- There's a lot of cutting involved when fitting tiles in a kitchen. As a result, it's usually easier to fit fairly small tiles.
- Avoid porcelain tiles. They're much harder to fit because of their strength.
- Measure the square metreage. You'll then need to add about 20%.
- Cheaper tiles are usually cheap because they are end-of-line. This means you'll struggle to ever find replacements, so it pays to have at least one box left over that you can hide away in the house to cover yourself for future damage.
- Have a think about how you want to arrange your tiles. You can fit bigger tiles sideways, and a brick pattern can look effective.

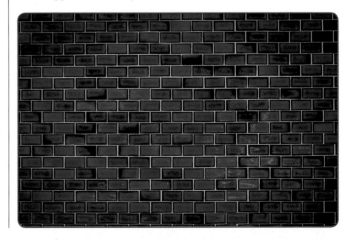

There are lots of books about tiling so we're not going to go into the process in immense detail but we'll cover enough to get you started. The golden rules are: plan in advance, don't rush, don't apply too much adhesive or grout at once and stop regularly to clean everything up with a damp sponge.

Tools

If you're going to tile yourself, you'll need the following equipment:

■ **Tile cutter**

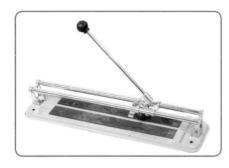

These work by etching the surface of the tile and then breaking the tile along this mark. They're great for cutting straight lines, but if you want to cut out an edge you'll need a tile saw. If you use porcelain tiles you'll struggle to break them using a cutter and will probably need to use a tile saw for every cut, which takes a lot more time. If you're going to use large tiles you'll need a big enough tile cutter to cope with them.

■ **Tile saw** You'll need one of these for cutting out corners, etc. Never use them without wearing eye protection. They come with a water reservoir to wet the wheel and keep the dust down, but they still make a right old mess so it's an idea to do your cutting outside.

■ **Tile nipper/ nibbler** For taking out small bits of tile, usually if you've measured a cut incorrectly.

■ **Jigsaw tile blade/tile hole cutter** The tile saw is fine for most cuts, but you'll need a hole cutter to cut out holes in the middle of tiles. The jigsaw tile blades are fine for ceramic wall

tiles, but struggle with harder tiles and are close to useless with floor tiles. See 'Using a tile hole cutter' on page 165 for more details.

■ **Adhesive trowel/ spreader**

You can get small adhesive trowels, usually called adhesive combs. However, I've always found it easier to use a floor tile trowel, as they spread the adhesive a little thicker (handy if the wall isn't completely flat) and you can cover a large area more quickly. For smaller areas you might want a smaller spreader.

■ **Grout/tiling sponge** Grout sponges are denser than most sponges and have rounded edges so they don't dig into your grout.

■ **Tile spacers**

The grout you use will have a huge impact on how your tiles will look. How thick the grout line is will be determined by how thick your spacers are.

■ **Grout spreader**

These have a soft rubber edge. They are used to work the grout inbetween the tiles and then smooth it down and remove the excess.

■ **Good-quality pre-mixed wall tile adhesive** For floor tiles, opt for a flexible adhesive that you mix with water before use. The pre-mixed adhesive is quicker and easier to use for wall tiles.

■ **Bag of grout** I'd advise against using pre-mixed grout or adhesives that double up as a grout – these are usually either not a very good adhesive or not a very good grout. Opt for the powdered form and mix as much of it as you need in a bucket.

When mixing, add the water to the bucket first and then add the grout powder and mix. You have the right consistency when the mix can hang from the edge of your grout spreader and only drop off very slowly.

You can get grout in many different colours. White is most popular, but it does show stains readily. Ivory is a nice compromise.

■ Edging strips

These come in different thicknesses, so make sure you get the right ones for your tiles. You can colour match them to your grout or go for something more striking and use chrome edging strips, for example. You'll need a mitre block and a mitre saw for cutting these to size.

■ Buckets You'll need a bucket to mix your grout and a bucket of water to keep everything clean.

FITTING A TILED SPLASHBACK

1 Before starting, make sure the walls are flat and clean and the whole kitchen area is free from dust. If you're tiling directly onto plasterboard give the boards a wash with PVA glue and water, mixed roughly 1:4. This will stop the adhesive drying out too quickly, which leads to very poor adhesion.

2 You need to work out where you're going to start:

■ Make sure you're not going to finish a row or column of tiles with a tiny sliver. If this might be the case, then start the row or column with a tile cut in half.

■ Walls are rarely straight, so it's not a good idea to start in the corner of a wall with a full tile. You'll either have a column of tiles that isn't truly vertical, as it follows the angle of the wall, or an ever-widening gap between the tiles and the corner of the wall.

■ Have a look at the position of things like plug sockets. You're going to have to cut around these, but this is going to be far more complicated if the hole is right in the middle of a tile. If this might be the case, then cut back the tiles at the start of your rows and columns so that the cuts you need to make are simpler.

3 If you've decided to cut the first row of tiles, it makes sense to cut them all to the right height at this stage. You ought to have a perfectly level worktop that you can work off. If this isn't the case, draw a perfectly horizontal line across the wall at the height you want the tiles to be.

Hold your tile up to this line with the back facing you and use a pencil to mark the back of the tile where it crosses your line. Now transfer these marks to the front of your tile and cut along this mark. If you fit the tile with the cut edge down, it should be perfectly level with your line.

To use a tile cutter, just place the tile in position and draw the tile wheel over the surface with enough pressure to etch a straight line right across it. Now press down firmly to break the tile on this line. Different tile cutters achieve these goals slightly differently from each other, so always read the manual first.

4 With just a modicum of planning you should know where you're going to have to cut a hole in a tile. Work up to this point, then stop. It's best not to have adhesive on the wall yet while you position the tile and mark where the hole is going to be. Once you're sure you have the hole right (see 'Using a tile hole cutter' on page 165), apply your adhesive.

5 Having decided where you're going to start, apply tile adhesive with a trowel or spreader. You want to get a perfectly level spread of adhesive on the wall. Don't put too much adhesive on the trowel all at once, as it will just drop off and get everywhere. Don't try to cover too much wall in one go; otherwise the adhesive will start to dry out before you're reached it with your tiles.

Above: Spreading the adhesive horizontally helps stop the tiles slipping down

---

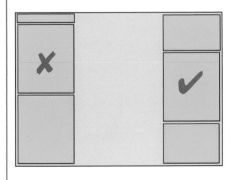

Starting off the first row with cut tiles avoids ending with small, unsightly slivers of tile

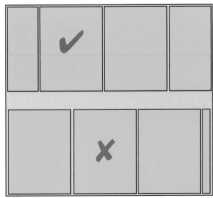

Avoid starting in a corner with a full tile as walls are rarely straight. You also want to avoid ending with a thin sliver of tile

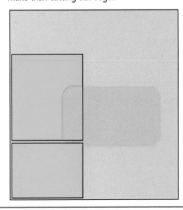

Think about how you are going to cut around the likes of plug sockets. Straight cuts are much easier to make than cutting out edges

6 Press your tile firmly into place. Use a spacer underneath to raise the tile off the work surface – you need a small gap between the tiles and the worktop to get a good seal with your silicone sealant.

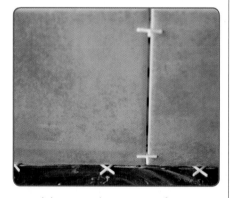

7 Apply the next tile, making sure the face of the tile is level with the first, and then fit your tile spacers in place at the top and bottom.

8 Complete the first row and then start the next one. If you have your tile spacers in place you shouldn't have to worry about keeping the tiles perfectly vertical.

9 Use a damp sponge to clean the tiles as you go. If the gap between the tiles is filled with adhesive it's best to scrape this excess out with a small flat-headed screwdriver and then clean the area with your sponge – your tile spacers should keep the tiles firmly in place while you do this.

10 The easiest way to cut around plug sockets is to unscrew the socket cover and cut the tiles so they just fit around the back plate. Once you've finished you can then screw your sockets over the top of your tiles – you occasionally need to buy longer screws for this.

If your sockets are live, be very careful not to touch any wires – turn the electricity off for the sockets if you can.

11 To fit edging strips, use a mitre block and saw to cut the strips at a 45° angle. Once you've cut them to size, slide them behind your tiles.

For areas such as the windowsill, tile up to the bottom

edge of the sill and fit the tile edging strip on top of the tile, then tile to this edging strip inside the sill.

12 Check that the gaps between all the tiles are free of adhesive. You don't need to get rid of all the adhesive but you don't want any

on the front edge, as this will show up when you come to grout the tiles. Leave the tiles to dry overnight.

13 Give the tiles a good clean and remove any spacers that are projecting past the tile face.

14 Don't make up too much grout, as it'll just go dry before you're ready to use it. Apply it with the grout spreader, getting it into the tile gaps and then smoothing away the excess by sweeping the spreader diagonally across the face of the tile.

If you find you're getting grout everywhere then you've either made your mix too wet – it should only just drip off the grout spreader when held up – or you're putting too much grout on your spreader. If it's the former, you can still add a bit of grout powder to your mix at this stage.

15 Leave the grout for about ten minutes to start to harden. You want it to still be damp but not wet.

16 Dampen down a clean grout sponge and gently start to clean the excess grout off the face of the tiles using a diagonal sweeping action. Now gently sweep down and across the grout line to smooth the grout between the tiles. Make sure the sponge is damp and don't press down too hard, as you'll lift too much grout out from between the tiles.

17 Leave the grout to harden overnight. The next morning you can clean off any residue with an old dry towel.

Below: Golden rule of tiling: clean as you go.

USING A TILE HOLE CUTTER

For small holes you can use a tile drill, but for larger holes you're better off using a diamond-tipped hole cutter.

METHOD 1
For those with an adventurous, devil-may-care temperament – who also have a ready supply of replacement tiles – you might want to try letting the drill, which is NOT on hammer action, get up to top speed and then very carefully apply one edge of the drill bit to the tile. Once the tile has been scored you can slowly bring the drill to the vertical.

This method works fine with softer tiles but it's difficult to get a very accurate cut and there is always the risk of the bit just running away and ruining the tile. With this in mind, I'd always recommend method 2.

METHOD 2
1 Get a small offcut of 6–9mm (¼–⅜in) plywood.

2 Use method 1 to drill a clean hole through the plywood.

3 With this achieved, use the hole in the plywood as a guide. Just hold it in place with one hand – use your knee if you're drilling into floor tiles – and start cutting your hole.

It's possible to buy core bits that come with a guide that you stick into place. There's nothing wrong with these, but plywood is cheaper and seems to work just as well – although there is a slightly higher risk of the plywood slipping if you're not careful.

Above: Laminate upstands are common but you can get a complete splashback.

Laminate splashbacks

You can buy these to match your worktop, or go for a contrasting colour and design. The upside of laminate is that it's an easy surface to keep clean; on the downside it's not really suitable for behind cookers and hobs and it's more prone to scratching than a tiled splashback.

When you buy your splashback make sure you buy the edging strips to go over the exposed edges and to cover internal and external corners – this is essential if you're going to use the laminate to cut into a windowsill. Before fitting the laminate yourself, try to figure out how expensive any mistakes are going to be and decide if it's worth the risk.

If you're fitting very expensive laminate you might want to consider making a template out of 6mm (¼in) plywood first – just follow the steps below to cut the plywood to fit and, once you're sure all your cuts are in the right place, clamp your plywood template over your laminate and use it to make all your cuts.

Tools

To fit laminate yourself you will need:

■ Jigsaw with a new, standard and downward cutting blade
■ Drill and a 10mm wood drill bit
■ Combination square, or any other true 90° angle
■ Grab adhesive (Evo-stik is very good)
■ Masking tape
■ Level, or any long straight edge
■ Edging strips to fit your laminate, with a mitre block and saw to cut them to size

FITTING A LAMINATE SPLASHBACK

1 Decide how high you want the splashback to go. Having a high splashback that reaches up to the base of your wall cabinets can look great, but it will mean cutting out holes for plug sockets and shaping the laminate to fit around the wall units. On the other hand, if you cut the laminate so that it just fits under all your plug sockets when any edging strips are fitted, you're going to have a much easier time of things.

2 As with tiles, it's easier to fit the splashback if you first remove all your plug sockets so that all that remains is the back plate and the wires. Don't even think of doing this until you've turned off the electricity.

3 You'll need to mark out all your cuts in order to fit your laminate. The easiest way to do this is to put the sheet up against the corner of the wall and just check that it fits flush with the wall. If your wall is way off vertical you'll have to cut this edge to fit the laminate flush.

Right: You'll need to cut this edge to fit it flush with the wall.

4 With the laminate cut so that it fits the wall properly, lay it face down on the worktop surface and mark the edges of your plug sockets etc. by drawing a vertical line down from the obstruction and marking the laminate – it's easier to mark if you apply masking tape over the area first.

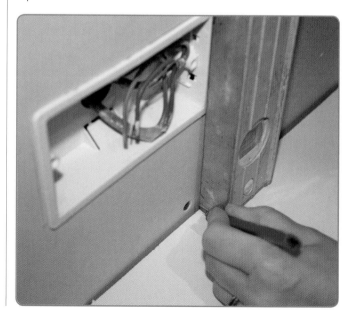

5 Use your combination square and a level to draw your marks right across the back of the laminate.

6 Measure the height of your sockets from the top of the worktop, etc. and transfer those heights to the back of your laminate. You should now be able to draw up the holes and angles you need to cut out.

TIP *If your kitchen is longer than the sheet of laminate you can use 'joining strips' to connect two sheets together. However, these can look a bit ugly, so you might want to shop around a bit and buy laminate that comes with a jointed edge, allowing you to connect the sheets together almost invisibly.*

Above: An ugly joint?

7 Double-check all your measurements and then start cutting. For the holes, use your drill bit to make a hole at each corner and then use the jigsaw with a standard blade to cut the hole.

8 With a modicum of luck your laminate sheet should now fit into place. To keep it there, use a sealant gun to apply umpteen dabs of grab adhesive across the back of your laminate. Now lift the laminate up and press it hard against the wall.

9 Fit any edging strips you need using a mitre block and a fine-toothed saw to cut the strips to size.

10 Use caulk to fill any gaps between the laminate and the wall at the top and sides of the laminate. Use silicone sealant to seal the edge between the laminate and the worktop.

9 THE FLOOR

The colours and materials you use here will have a huge impact on the look and feel of your kitchen. The way our vision works means that changing the colour of the floor can actually change the way we see the cabinets, worktops and walls and vice versa, so this isn't an area to rush into just because you've found a load of cheap tiles. Online planners are useful tools for seeing which various floor colour schemes will work, but there are other things we need to consider besides colour.

What makes a good kitchen floor?

COPING WITH IMPACTS

A kitchen is, first and foremost, a work area and sooner or later something heavy will be dropped on to your floor. How great a disaster will unfold will be dictated by how well your floor handles the impact.

Tiles are a popular kitchen floor material but they do need to be designed specifically for floors and, ideally, be porcelain. Ordinary wall tiles are ceramic, which are fairly soft and, if used on the floor, will be damaged before the week is out. Porcelain tiles are a pain to work with because they are so hard, but this is exactly what we need in a kitchen. You can get hard ceramic tiles specifically designed for floors, which are a good compromise.

If you drop something on a solid wooden floor, the odds are you'll be left with a dint. You can either sand this out or embrace the dint and call it 'character'. There are lots of very hard varnishes around these days that can improve the robustness of your wooden floor, but the biggest factor will be the type of wood used. Pine, while cheaper, is usually too soft for kitchen flooring and you're better off going for something harder, like maple or oak. Bamboo is a good compromise, as it's usually not too expensive, is pretty hard and can look lovely.

You can reduce the price by buying wooden laminate floors. Cheap laminates are easy to fit, but the decorative surface is usually only about 1mm thick and as a result they can get damaged very readily.

COPING WITH WATER

Spills are a day-to-day consequence of cooking, or at least they are in my house. As a result, whatever flooring you go for needs to be able to cope with the wet. This doesn't just mean being able to withstand dampness, it also means still being safe when wet.

The latter point is particularly relevant for floor tiles. You want to avoid buying a tile that takes on the properties of an ice-rink the moment it gets the least bit damp.

COMFORT

While comfort shouldn't dictate your choice, it is important to consider. Tiles can get very cold to the touch during the winter months. You can get around this by fitting underfloor heating – either wet or electric – but that can be an expensive option. A cheaper alternative is to fit 'tile-effect' laminate flooring. This is far warmer to walk on, although you'll need to ensure that the laminate is deemed suitable for kitchens – water resistant and heavy duty.

Tiling a floor

When selecting tiles, you need to consider how they will look when grouted. White grout lines look lovely when first installed, but the grout will quickly discolour. It's a better long-term option to select a light grey or darker-coloured grout from the start. Read about the basics of tiling in Chapter 8, 'Tiled splashbacks'.

1 It's pointless tiling on a floor that moves. A concrete floor just needs to be cleaned thoroughly, but if you have a wooden floor you'll need to make sure it's secure enough to support the tiles without them moving and cracking. As a general rule, it's best to overlay a wooden floor with 6mm (¼in) concrete backer board before you start tiling. If you're tiling onto a wooden floor it's also best to use 'flexible' tile adhesive and grout.

2 Your floor needs to be clean and level. For concrete floors it's best to apply 5mm of latex self-levelling-compound over the floor first. To do this you need to ensure there are no holes for the compound to run away through – sealant can be used to fill any holes. If you have to apply more, apply it 5mm deep at a time and let it dry in between. Use a float to 'encourage' the compound to get into all the corners.

3 Consider how much of the floor you want to tile. If you've installed a fitted kitchen the odds are that the layout will remain static for decades. As such, you can save yourself time and money by just tiling up to the kitchen cabinets rather than tiling wall-to-wall.

If you opt to tile up to the cabinets then you'll need a kickboard (plinth) to hide the untiled space under the cabinets and the idea is to just tile up to the cabinet legs.

4 Work out the amount of tiles you'll need by calculating the square metreage. If you have a fairly complex shape then separate it out into a number of rectangles and add them up together afterwards.

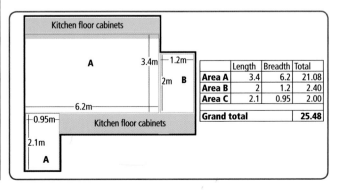

	Length	Breadth	Total
Area A	3.4	6.2	21.08
Area B	2	1.2	2.40
Area C	2.1	0.95	2.00
Grand total			**25.48**

If you look at our example at the foot of the previous page, you can see that we've separated the shape out into three rectangles. We work out the square metreage by measuring the length and breadth and recording that measurement in metres (if you're buying tiles sold as 'per square foot' then record all your measurements in feet).

So, in our example we have added up our three simple rectangles and got a total square metreage of 25.48m², which we'll round up to 25.5m².

It's always a good idea to add 20% to this value to cover breakages and tile cuts. To get 20% just divide your total by five and add it to the original. In our example this is (25.5/5) + 25.5 = 30.6m², which we'll round up to 31m².

In an ideal world, if you break a tile in a few years' time, you'll be able to wander off to the store and buy replacements. Alas, modern tiles seem to have a life expectancy akin to that of an asthmatic mayfly and after a few months you'll be hard pushed to buy replacement tiles anywhere. With this in mind it's a good idea to buy at least one extra box of tiles just in case you do decide to change your kitchen layout at some time and to cover you for the inevitable damage that will occur over the years.

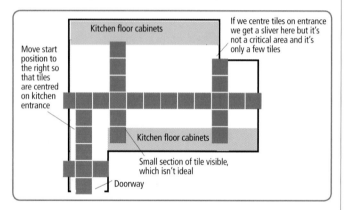

Move start position to the right so that tiles are centred on kitchen entrance

Kitchen floor cabinets

If we centre tiles on entrance we get a sliver here but it's not a critical area and it's only a few tiles

Kitchen floor cabinets

Small section of tile visible, which isn't ideal

Doorway

5 To work out where you're going to start tiling, place a tile roughly in the centre of your room and then, using the tile spacers you intend to use, lay out tiles to all of the walls from this position.

TIP *If wall tiles are slightly uneven it's no big deal. If floor tiles aren't exactly level it can be a real issue. With this in mind, you might want to consider spending a bit more money on tile spacers designed to ensure your tiles are perfectly level with each other. Raimondi, shown here, do a tile levelling system, but I suspect there are a number of other companies selling similar products.*

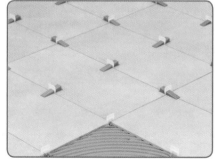

© raimondispa.com

There are invariably compromises to make at this stage. If you look at our example, you can see that the green tile, while not perfect, is a pretty good place to start. Yes, we might only have a small bit of tile showing under the bottom kitchen floor units but

we have an almost full tile at the doorway into the kitchen, which is more important as this is the main thoroughfare. We can also see that the tiles we see on entering the kitchen are not centred on this pathway, so we'd usually move our green tile slightly to the right as this will create a more aesthetically pleasing layout, even if it does mean a tile sliver on the top right wall.

6 It's easier to keep all your tiles level with each other if they're fitted at the same time. As such I prefer to lay out all the tiles using the spacers I'm going to use without using any adhesive at this stage. I make all my tile cuts and fit these tiles into place. Once I'm happy with everything I carefully mark my starting position, stack my tiles carefully together, one row at a time, and start mixing up the tile adhesive ready to fix the tiles into place.

7 Where you start tiling depends on your layout – you don't want to end up stuck in the corner of your kitchen unable to get out without standing on your freshly lain tiles. In our example, we'd start at the top of the diagram and work down, finishing at the doorway into the kitchen.

8 Invest in a good-quality floor tile adhesive. These invariably come as a dry powder and need to be mixed with water on-site.

Check how long it's going to take for your tile adhesive to go hard. There are lots of quick-setting adhesives that can save time, but can also mean you have to rush to get your tiles down before the adhesive sets. I'd steer clear of the quick-setting stuff unless you're an experienced tiler.

You'll need a big bucket, a drill – not on hammer action – and a stirrer to make up your mix. As a general rule, add the adhesive powder to your water rather than the other way around. When you lift the stirrer out of the mix and the adhesive stays as it is, only sinking back very, very slowly, then you have the right consistency.

9 Start laying out your tiles and fitting your spacers (see 'Tiled splashbacks', Chapter 8). It's very important to keep everything clean so make sure you have a bucket of water and a sponge to hand and clean the adhesive out from between the tiles as you go.

If you're planning on just going under the kitchen cabinets rather than to the kitchen walls bear in mind that it's easier to screw the kitchen cabinet legs up a bit so that you can lay a full tile underneath them. The wall brackets should keep the cabinets in place and, once the tiles are dry, you can reset the cabinet legs.

10 Once your tiles can be walked upon you can grout them (see Chapter 8).

11 Once you have the floor tiled you can fit kickboards and any skirting board.

Fitting laminate flooring

Before you start, verify that your laminate is going to be suitable for kitchens.

NOTE: *There are two basic types of laminate – ones that require glue and ones that don't. As you might have guessed, the glue-free solution is much easier to fit.*

Always check the instructions that come with the laminate you're planning on buying, but the following guide should be fine for most products.

Tools

You'll need the following tools:

- ▦ Suitable underlay (usually a thin layer of plastic sponge)
- ▦ Set of flooring clamps (strap clamps)
- ▦ Rubber mallet
- ▦ Saw – a table saw (bench saw) is best, but a jigsaw will do the job
- ▦ Knee pads
- ▦ Expansion spacers or shims
- ▦ A friend who is willing to help – although you can now buy 'one-man' fitting systems.

1 Calculate the square metreage (see 'Tiling a floor' on page 169). For standard laminate there is almost no wastage, as sections you cut off one board can usually be used in the next row. The same isn't true if the laminate has a pattern, for example, tile-effect laminate usually results in far more wastage. You need to bear this in mind when buying.

2 Work out your layout in much the same way as you did for the floor tiles. If you have a look at the example diagram you can see many of the things you need to get right and what to avoid.

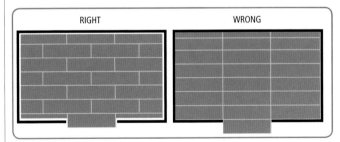

- ▦ Avoid slivers at the edge of the room
- ▦ It's better to have an almost full sheet of laminate in the doorway, even if this mean more cutting along the rest of the wall
- ▦ You need to leave a 5mm (¼in) gap around the room to give the flooring space for expansion
- ▦ Aim to lay the flooring brick-fashion to avoid single points where four boards join together. You don't have to have the boards exactly halfway between each other but the bigger the distance between joins the better, and try to keep the gap consistent.

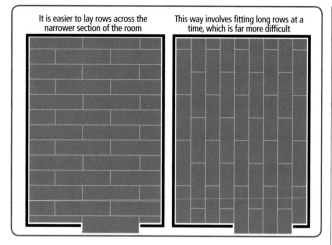

It is easier to lay rows across the narrower section of the room

This way involves fitting long rows at a time, which is far more difficult

■ It's easier to fit shorter rows. So, if you have a rectangular room, lay the rows of boards across the narrow side of the room.

3 Lay out your underlay. It can get scuffed and damaged as you go, so rather than lay it out all at once it's often best to lay it out in front of you as you go along – fibre-boards are often a lot easier to use and provide a more stable underlay.

4 Most laminates use a 'click' system – also called 'angle-to-angle' or 'drop-lock'. The easiest way to use this is to lay out an entire row. To do this make all your cuts for one row, remembering to fit your spacers to leave a gap near the walls for expansion. Connect all the boards in that row together and then, with a friend to help, 'click' this entire row into the previous row. This is easier if you have the smaller 'top' edge

at the front of the row so that you lift the next row up, click it into place and then drop it down to lock it into position.

5 After you've laid about four rows use the floor clamps to draw the rows together and squeeze out any small gaps. Fit offcuts into place and put the clamps on these to avoid damaging the boards. The edge up against the wall is going to be covered by skirting board or an edging strip, so it's not too much of an issue if this edge gets a little damaged.

To use the clamps: pull the cord out, fit the clamping plate to the laminate edge that is up against the wall and ask a friend to stand on it. Fit the lever clamp to an offcut of flooring and pull the cord tight. Now use the handle mechanism to tighten the cord up. You just want to remove any small gaps, so don't overtighten or you'll just damage the laminate boards.

TIP *If you have a small gap between the side edges of the boards, you can either use the floor clamp or try taking a step back and then jumping forward to hit the board with both feet together. If you get it right, your shoes will make a squeak as they slide briefly on the board and the gap will close.*

6 To get the cut right for the end of your rows and for the last row in the room, put a board exactly over the top of the last board in the row you've just fitted. Place another board on top of this but push it hard up against the wall. Bring this board back from the

wall a little to create an expansion gap and then mark the board underneath. Now cut the board you've just marked.

7 To cut around radiator pipework, etc. use a holesaw to make the hole then use a jigsaw to cut out a triangular section so that the board can be put into place.

Use wood glue to stick the triangular section into position and a colour-fill product to hide your cut lines.

The hole can be hidden by fitting pipe covers over the top.

8 Once you've lain the floor you'll need to either fit skirting board or an edging strip to cover the expansion gap between the laminate and the wall.

Alternative flooring

In Chapter 3 we discussed some of the alternative materials you can use to build a kitchen countertop. Most of these can also be used to create unique flooring. For example, coloured concrete and epoxy resin can create some amazing effects. There's a lot of trial and error involved in using these materials so you really should undertake a series of small-scale experiments before tackling a floor. If you use epoxy resin for flooring you need to be aware of the following issue.

An epoxy floor needs to be installed over a concrete base, as it will just crack if fitted on anything vaguely flexible. Sadly, concrete floors also aren't waterproof; moisture will pass through them if they don't have a vapour barrier fitted beneath them. Because epoxy flooring is impermeable to water, the moisture will just build up underneath and the floor will eventually 'lift'.

You test for this issue by placing a plastic sheet over the concrete floor – a 500mm (20in) square sheet will do. Tape this sheet down so the edges are all sealed to the floor. Set the room temperature to about 20°C (68°F). Close the curtains to the room to keep the temperature fairly steady and leave well alone for a day. The next day, peel the plastic back. If there is moisture on the inside of the plastic sheet or the concrete has turned dark with moisture there's too much water coming up through the floor and you'll need to contact a professional before continuing.

10 LIGHTING